Praise for *Matchmakers*

"David Evans and Richard Schmalensee are masters at combining strategic analysis and economic theory. *Matchmakers* is a journey through the strategies of platform businesses, which are central to our economies. Full of stories, fun to read, stimulating, and rigorous, this terrific book is required reading, from the economics and MBA student to the entrepreneur looking at building a platform to any reader curious about how our economy evolves."

> —**JEAN TIROLE,** Chairman, Toulouse School of Economics; Winner, 2014 Nobel Prize in Economic Sciences

"*Matchmakers* will be mandatory for anyone building or investing in multisided platforms—in the cloud or on the ground. It's not only full of great stories like the rise of M-PESA, it's also a practical guide to getting your platform business off the ground. If the people behind Apple Pay had this book to read, maybe they would have started differently."

> —**BOB SOLOMON,** former Senior Vice President, Network and Financial Solutions, Ariba, Inc.

"This book provided me, as a cofounder of the International Securities Exchange, with a different lens through which to view my business and industry. This framework would have been a valuable addition to my playbook as my colleagues and I grappled with questions of pricing and building critical mass when we were planning the launch, eighteen years ago, of the first all-electronic options exchange in the United States."

> —**GARY KATZ,** President and CEO, International Securities Exchange

"The 'matchmaker' is one of the oldest business models, but it's ever more important in today's interconnected, networked world. This deep dive into today's multisided businesses provides a clear, compelling, and entertaining road map for how net platform businesses can blast off and ignite. Bravo!"

> —**CATHY BARON TAMRAZ,** Chairman and CEO, Business Wire

Praise for *Catalyst Code*

". . . an important book for anyone interested in understanding how breakthrough businesses can be built in today's economy."

—BILL GATES

"*Catalyst Code* shows that in the Internet Age, the greatest business successes will be based on creating communities in which buyers and sellers are brought together efficiently, rather than making a new product or providing a new service."

—PATRICK MCGOVERN, founder and former Chairman, International Data Group

"Evans and Schmalensee reveal the inner workings of what is rapidly becoming a new model for businesses."

—PETER S. LYNCH, Vice Chairman, Fidelity Management & Research Company

Matchmakers

David S. Evans and
Richard Schmalensee

Matchmakers

The New
Economics of
Multisided
Platforms

HARVARD BUSINESS REVIEW PRESS

Boston, Massachusetts

Printed in the United States of America

10 9 8 7

The web addresses referenced in this book were live and correct at the time of the book's publication but may be subject to change.

Library of Congress Cataloging-in-Publication Data
Names: Evans, David S. (David Sparks), 1954- author. | Schmalensee, Richard, author.
Title: Matchmakers : the new economics of platform businesses : how one of the oldest business models on earth powers the most incredible companies in the world / David S. Evans and Richard Schmalensee.
Description: Boston, Massachusetts : Harvard Business Review Press, [2016]
Identifiers: LCCN 2015046357 | ISBN 9781633691728 (alk. paper)
Subjects: LCSH: Multi-sided platform businesses.
Classification: LCC HD9999.M782 E93 2016 | DDC 338.7–dc23 LC record available at http://lccn.loc.gov/2015046357

The paper used in this publication meets the requirements of the American National Standard for Permanence of Paper for Publications and Documents in Libraries and Archives Z39.48-1992.

ISBN: 9781633691728
eISBN: 9781633691735

*To all the pioneers
who tried to cross the critical mass frontier.*

Contents

Part III

Creation, Destruction, and Transformation

Introduction

MANY OF THE BIGGEST COMPANIES IN THE WORLD, INCLUD-
ing Alibaba, Apple, Facebook, Google, Microsoft, News
Corp., Rakuten, Tencent, and Visa, are *matchmakers*. So
are many of the most exciting and valuable start-ups, such as Airbnb,
BlaBlaCar, Didi Kuaidi, Flipkart, Lending Club, Pinterest, Spotify,
and Uber. What these businesses have in common is that they all
connect members of one group, like people looking for a ride, with
another group, like drivers looking for passengers.

Matchmakers are very different from the businesses that have
been the staple of college economics classrooms and MBA lectures
for decades. They operate under a different set of economic rules.
Traditional manufacturing businesses, for instance, buy raw materials, make stuff, and sell that stuff to customers. But matchmakers'
raw materials are the different groups of customers that they help
bring together, not anything that they buy at all. And part of the stuff
they sell to members of each group is access to members of the other
groups. All of them operate physical or virtual places where members
of these different groups get together. For this reason, they are often
called *multisided platforms*. They're places where all of these different groups can meet.

If you've ever taken an economics course, you have heard a lecture on how traditional firms manage their production and set their

prices to maximize profits. When it comes to matchmakers, that lecture was dead wrong, in critically important ways. That's because the classic economic models don't account for the fact that the demand by each group of customers served by a matchmaker depends on the demand by other groups of customers it also serves. For instance, the American Express card connects consumers and merchants; consumer demand for the card depends on how many merchants have decided to accept it, and merchants' demand in turn depends on how many consumers have decided to use the card. Let's be clear: ignoring the interdependence of matchmakers' demands was a big mistake. Economic textbooks and business school courses made claims that just didn't apply to a large and growing part of the economy and, if followed, would have led matchmakers into bankruptcy if they were able to even get off the ground in the first place.

Economists, including the two of us, have been doing a lot of work to understand how matchmaker businesses work. We've made immense progress since 2000, when the difference between traditional and matchmaker businesses was first discovered. Once you understand the economics behind them, many of the seemingly counterintuitive strategies that matchmakers use—like actually paying customers to participate—make perfect sense. It's those insights that we share with you in this book.

Discovering the error in applying the economics of traditional firms to matchmakers was timely and perhaps inevitable. The use of this business model exploded around the time economists made this breakthrough. The mash-up of technologies—from software to the web to mobile broadband—made it cheaper to start matchmakers and vastly increased the power and reach of this business model.

But we think that to really understand the matchmakers—and we'd argue that you must, because you're increasingly surrounded by them, participating in them, or competing against them—you need to grasp the basic types of multisided platforms that have been around for a long time. What's so fascinating to us is how all the "new" business models that receive so much hype today have striking similarities to businesses in the past—from the lending exchange in Athens around 300 BCE to newspaper classified ads around 1750 CE to credit cards in Manhattan in 1950 CE. We can learn a lot simply by understanding the fundamentals that have endured over thousands of years and that are now being powered by technology and other innovations that make matchmaker businesses more vibrant and much more scalable.

We're going to share with you a lot that we have learned since 2000, when we first started working on the new economics of multisided platforms. Over the last fifteen years, we've written three other books on this subject and, together or separately, many widely cited articles that report our research. Most importantly, we've had the opportunity to work closely with many of the most significant multisided platform businesses in the world—including Ariba, American Express, Google, Microsoft, PayPal, Tencent, and Visa.[1] We've also served as advisers to many start-ups and have even started one that is doing quite nicely.

This book uses case studies to help you understand a kind of business that you will almost certainly interact with as a customer, investor, executive, entrepreneur, or regulator, and that you might even want to start yourself some day. We're going to explain the new economics of multisided platforms, how it differs from traditional economics, and how it explains what many successful and important businesses do. And help readers who have taken courses on business economics unlearn much of what they've been taught. We're also going to show you how matchmakers are transforming economies worldwide and how they are killing some established industries, creating some new ones, and forcing the reinvention of others. And that these powerful engines of commerce are making life easier and better for billions of people.

Matchmakers has three parts. Part I (chapters 1–3) presents an overview of the new economics of multisided platforms and shows how this business model with ancient roots has been turbocharged by modern technologies. Part II (chapters 4–10) provides a deep dive into key concepts that matchmakers must deal with in building, igniting, and operating their businesses. Finally, part III (chapters 11–13) describes how turbocharged, multisided platforms are creating new industries, destroying old ones, and forcing existing businesses to reinvent themselves to survive. A glossary at the back of the book provides definitions for the key concepts surrounding multisided platforms.

To understand the perils and promise of multisided platforms we begin by describing the arduous journey, and near-death experiences, of a matchmaker we often use.

Part One

Economics and Technologies

Chapter 1

A Table for Four at Eight

How a Matchmaker Took the Friction
out of Restaurant Reservations

T'S SATURDAY MORNING IN THE SUMMER OF 1998. JULIE TEMPLE-
ton's mom and dad are coming into town the next weekend. She
and her husband, Chuck, want to treat them to a gala restaurant
weekend in San Francisco, with dinners out Friday, Saturday, and
Sunday nights.

Julie starts dialing for reservations. No answer. She leaves a message. She keeps calling, restaurant after restaurant. Some don't have
anything on the evenings she wants. One she wants to go to on Sunday isn't open. Almost four hours later, after a lot of calling and juggling, she's got the weekend planned.[1]

Back then, making dinner reservations was hard. Taking them
was, also. Most restaurants still took reservations over the phone.
Someone wrote them down with a pencil, on paper, in a notebook.
Often, tables went empty if the phone didn't ring enough. Restaurants
had no way to let people know when they had tables available.

Julie Templeton's persistence paid off. Most people, though, just
aren't willing to work that hard to get a restaurant reservation. As a
result, in 1998, on a typical Saturday night in San Francisco, there

were unhappy couples sitting at home, perhaps having takeout pizza, who had given up trying to get a table for their date night, and unhappy restaurant owners with tables sitting empty, not making ends meet in a tough business.

The market for matching up diners with tables at restaurants wasn't working very well. Restaurants and diners spent a lot of resources—time and effort—getting together, and even so tables went empty and diners stayed home. That's the sort of problem that an important, but until recently overlooked, type of business sets out to solve by helping parties who have something valuable to exchange find each other, get together, and do a deal.

Multisided Platforms

In 1998, this important type of business didn't have a name. That's surprising, in retrospect. Many businesses had been built to reduce these sorts of market frictions, which economists tend to call transaction costs. Their basic business model had been around for thousands of years. But business schools didn't teach classes on how to start or run businesses that help different parties get together to exchange value. Economists didn't have a clue how these businesses worked. In fact, the companies that reduced these market frictions charged prices and adopted other strategies that economic textbooks insisted no sensible business would do.

Now we call these businesses *multisided platforms.*[2] Don't let the economists' unsexy name fool you.[3] Multisided platforms are anything but boring. Some even facilitate mating. Multisided platforms can create great value for society and fortunes for their entrepreneurs and investors. Three of the five most valuable companies in the world in 2015—Apple, Google, and Microsoft—use this business model.[4] So do seven of the ten start-ups with the highest market values—including Uber and Airbnb.[5]

Let's get one thing clear, though, before you invest more time in learning about multisided platforms from us. This isn't a gee-whiz "use the [fill in the buzzword] strategy and you'll make a billion, impress your boyfriend or your mom, and retire by the age of thirty-five" book. We aren't going to tell you that the matchmaker strategy, which did make Bill Gates the richest person on earth, will work for you. It probably won't.

Many entrepreneurs—and many otherwise highly successful businesses—have tried this "simple" strategy and failed. Everything they and their investors put into their multisided platform ventures went up in smoke.

A multisided platform is one of the toughest business models to get right. The entrepreneur has to solve a tough puzzle and use counterintuitive strategies to make a go of it. Just ask Julie Templeton's husband, a former Army Ranger. He found out exactly how hard it was to fight the frictions in the restaurant-reservation business. And he's one of the rare success stories.

OpenTable's Quest for Critical Mass

After his wife's frustrating morning, Chuck Templeton figured there had to be a better way to get people and restaurants together. In October 1998, at age twenty-nine, two months after getting married, he quit his job to do just that.

Like many others that year in Silicon Valley, he started a dot-com and quickly got funded. OpenTable was ready to rock.[6] Droves of consumers were coming online. Chuck thought at first that he just needed a website to which they could connect. The rest would be easy.

Except, as he soon discovered, most restaurants didn't even have a computer, much less Internet connectivity at the host stand, where they managed reservations. Three years after the commercial Internet got kicking and two decades after Apple introduced the first mass-market personal computer, restaurants were still doing things the old-fashioned way. There was no way to connect to restaurants online, much less to make a reservation online.

Templeton realized he needed to get restaurants to ditch their reservation notebooks for a computer-based table management system. And to get that hooked up to the Internet at the host stand. So his company first built a table management system. With it, restaurants could type reservations into a database, monitor table availability, record cancellations, keep track of their best customers, and, in principle at least, take reservations online.

Finding that restaurants were reluctant to make large investments to purchase table management systems, OpenTable decided to charge a small installation fee and a monthly rental for its new system instead of requiring purchase. It then went knocking on the doors of restaurants in San Francisco to get them to lease the new software.[7] Even without the promise of new reservations, this was good enough for some of the better restaurants that needed more help with managing their tables and tracking their best customers than with filling seats. One by one, restaurants signed on. By early 1999, the company had about ten.

OpenTable also built a consumer website where people could make reservations. That opened in March 1999. People didn't have to pay to use it. In fact, the company offered to give people points for making reservations. If they got enough points, they could redeem them to get a discount on their next meal. Restaurants, though, had to pay $1 for every person who sat at one of their tables as a result of a reservation made through the OpenTable site.

Even with the subsidies for making reservations, however, the website wasn't attractive to customers at first. There just weren't that many restaurants to choose from. The odds were slim to none of making a reservation at a restaurant in San Francisco where a diner wanted to go at a time when he or she wanted to go. Hardly anyone used the website. That made it difficult to recruit more restaurants beyond the early adopters who were content with just the table management software.

With limited time and resources, OpenTable had to strike the right balance between getting consumers and restaurants on board. Money wasn't a problem. Chuck raised $36 million in venture capital financing between 1998 and early 2000.[8] He also helped recruit an experienced CEO who joined the company in May 2000.[9]

OpenTable, with a flush bank account and a new CEO, decided to focus on signing up as many restaurants as it could. By the summer of 2001, the company had restaurants in fifty cities. But, more than two years after its launch, and a year after its new CEO pursued aggressive growth, OpenTable had a serious problem.

While it had some restaurants in many cities, it didn't have a lot of restaurants in any city. If you want to go out to dinner on Saturday night in San Francisco, a table for four in Seattle doesn't do you much good. In fact, OpenTable found that diners wanted to have at least a dozen choices of restaurants for the time, cuisine, and part of town where they wanted to go.[10] To give diners that many options in any city, OpenTable had to sign up many restaurants there. Because it offered few choices in every city, consumers weren't using its website much to make reservations in any city.

OpenTable was floundering. It was burning through $1.1 million a month. The investors considered cutting their losses and shutting it down. They decided, however, to double down but with yet another CEO and strategy. A board member and investor, Thomas Layton, took the helm in the fall of 2001.

The company shifted its focus to recruiting restaurants in just four cities: San Francisco, Chicago, New York, and Washington, DC. The idea was that once OpenTable had signed up enough restaurants in a city, its website would become attractive to consumers in that city. As consumers began making online reservations, it would persuade more restaurants to sign up, which in turn would lead even more consumers to use the website.

That worked. OpenTable got enough restaurants in San Francisco to get many consumers to come to its website and make reservations. And as more people used its website, it became easier to recruit more restaurants in San Francisco. Restaurants, particularly new ones, realized the value of filling up empty seats. Since most of the cost of running a restaurant is fixed in the short run, a restaurant can make a significant profit on every additional seat it fills.

By 2004, around the time Chuck Templeton left the start-up to pursue other endeavors, OpenTable had *ignited*. It was growing rapidly in its four target cities as diners attracted more restaurants, which attracted more diners, and the process continued. It then adopted the same approach in other cities. It had learned that it should initially focus on recruiting the most popular restaurants in every town. Its salespeople just went down the lists provided by Zagat.[11] OpenTable went public in 2009 with a market cap on its first trading day of $626 million.[12] It was sold to Priceline for $2.6 billion in 2014.

In 2015, seventeen years after Templeton's insight that technology could be used to reduce the friction that kept diners and restaurants apart, thirty-two thousand restaurants, mainly fine-dining establishments with tablecloths, use OpenTable's table management software. Sixteen million people use its website to make reservations every month. Since its inception, acting as the matchmaker between restaurants and diners, it has put more than 830 million diners in seats at restaurants in the United States, Canada, Germany, Japan, Mexico, and the United Kingdom.[13]

OpenTable still has the same business model that Chuck Templeton proposed to investors back in 1999. Let people make reservations for free and even give them a little reward. Charge restaurants a buck for every seat the reservation website fills and a monthly fee for the software. Secure a *critical mass* of restaurants and diners in each city, and they will ignite growth by attracting still more restaurants and diners.

Ancient Roots, Weird Economics, and a Puzzle

OpenTable used software and Internet technology to match restaurants and diners. It made it easier for consumers to make reservations and gave them more choices than they had in the dialing-for-a-table days. It made restaurants money by filling empty tables and thus generating extra margin. OpenTable employed a multisided platform strategy that companies like Didi Kuaidi are using to reduce frictions in transportation, Airbnb in lodging, and Instacart in grocery shopping.

In 1998, however, Chuck Templeton probably didn't know that entrepreneurs had been using this strategy for a long time with more primitive technologies than he had available. The *Book of Songs*, compiled by Confucius in the eleventh century BCE, says, "How does one find a wife? Without a matchmaker one does not."

In China, the *meiren* would help find suitable marriage partners. She would keep track of the eligible men and women in the various villages. Then she would put candidates forward who would be good matches. And she'd broker the deal for a fee. OpenTable, and other multisided platforms, are all matchmakers in one way or another.

Chuck Templeton also didn't know, we suspect, that there were other important businesses that had faced the same kind of challenges he did and that had adopted similar strategies to get off the ground.

In 1950, Frank McNamara started Diners Club.[14] It was the first credit card that people could use to pay many different merchants.[15] Diners Club gave the credit card to selected wealthy people on the Upper East Side of New York City. This made it relatively easy to persuade fourteen upscale restaurants in Manhattan to take the card for payment. The restaurants agreed to pay Diners Club a commission of 10 percent for the same reason they were willing to pay OpenTable $1 per person. They thought the cards would drive additional people to their restaurants and they'd make some additional margin from filling up the tables. The cardholders didn't have to pay anything at first.[16]

Diners Club ignited quickly. More restaurants signed on, more people got the card, and even more restaurants signed on. Like OpenTable, Diners Club went city by city and created a critical mass of restaurants and diners in each.

Even though it has been around for a long time, the matchmaker business model is much more complicated than it appears. On a closer look, in fact, it is more than a little strange.

If you think about it, it seems crazy that OpenTable doesn't charge diners anything for using it and, in fact, gives them rewards. Julie Templeton could have saved almost four hours with a phone attached to her ear if there had been a company like OpenTable to find places to eat. Surely, she'd have paid something—a lot perhaps—for that service, as would others. If OpenTable had taken advantage of this demand and had charged diners for reservations, one might think it could have made more money. But it didn't, and it hasn't. "Free" wasn't some temporary promotional gimmick. OpenTable hasn't ever charged diners a penny.

On the other hand, if diners are so valuable that OpenTable finds it optimal to pay them (via rewards) to use its service, why does it refuse to deal with some of them? If a diner fails four times in a year to show up for a reservation that she has not canceled at least thirty minutes in advance, her account is terminated, even if she's kept many reservations that made OpenTable money.[17]

Then there's the fact that OpenTable, which met obvious needs of both diners and restaurants, barely survived. Chuck Templeton had a great idea. And developing a website and table management software was hardly rocket science, even back then. Yet the company almost died three years after its birth because it couldn't solve the *chicken-and-egg* problem. Just as you can't have chickens without eggs, but you need chickens to get eggs, a matchmaker can't attract diners without restaurants, but no hungry consumer would use a reservation system that had no restaurants available. OpenTable eventually solved this puzzle. Most matchmaker start-ups don't.

As a consumer, you probably use many matchmakers over the course of a day. More than a few of them also make some of their services available for free or pay "customers" to use them. Almost all had difficult childhoods. Many barely made it out of the crib.

Now economists know why multisided platforms can create immense value, and how they do it, and also why most matchmaker start-ups sputter and die.

The Discovery of Multisided Businesses

In 2000, our colleagues Jean-Charles Rochet and Jean Tirole, working at the University of Toulouse in the southwest of France, made a discovery that is still reverberating through economics departments and business schools. Over the previous five years, they had conducted research on telecommunications networks, payment card businesses, and computer operating systems. Like all other economists, they thought these businesses had little in common.

Then they had the insight that these businesses, and many others that look very different on the surface, have the same underlying business model. They all facilitate direct interactions between different types of customers. And they must use nontraditional, counterintuitive strategies to make money and survive.

After working out a pioneering economic model, they wrote a paper, "Platform Competition in Two-Sided Markets," which began circulating among economists in 2000.[18] Economists now call these businesses *multi*sided platforms because some of them actually facilitate interactions between more than two types of customers, as we will soon see. Jean Tirole received the Nobel Memorial Prize in Economic Sciences in 2014 for a number of important accomplishments, including his pioneering contributions to the new economics of multisided platforms.

In the intervening years, economists, including ourselves, have written hundreds of papers on multisided platforms that have deepened our understanding of how these businesses work and how they differ from traditional firms. Economists now know that many of the formulas we've derived over the last century for traditional firms are wrong for multisided ones. The right formulas must account for the fact that the demand by the customers on the different sides of the platform—such as diners and restaurants—are interdependent.

The old formulas—including many of the ones we have taught generations of undergraduates in Econ 1—do not give the right answers for multisided platforms. The math is simply wrong. Traditional economics holds, for example, that it's never profitable to sell products at less than cost. The new multisided economics shows that even paying some customers rather than charging them anything can be profitable in theory and often is in practice.

The differences between single-sided businesses and multisided platforms are stark. Ordinary businesses buy inputs of various sorts from suppliers, sometimes transform them into finished products, and sell goods or services to customers. Their main focus is on attracting customers and selling to them on profitable terms. Multisided platforms, in contrast, need to attract two or more types of customers by enabling them to interact *with each other* on attractive terms. Their most important inputs are generally their customers.

A traditional grocery store like Whole Foods is *single-sided*. It buys goods and resells them to its customers. Whole Foods buys the granola. The customer pays Whole Foods for the granola. The customer and the granola supplier don't interact directly. A restaurant-reservation business like OpenTable is *two-sided* because it brings diners and restaurants together to interact directly. It takes no part in transactions between them.

Matchmakers are called multisided *platforms* because they usually operate a physical or virtual place that helps the different types of customers get together. Nightclubs have physical places where men and women go, hoping to find someone they like. In contrast, online dating services have virtual places that serve the same purpose. Men and women connect to servers in the Cloud, over the Internet, where a software program helps them find matches.

The basic idea of a two-sided platform is seen in a simple diagram. Two different types of customers, let's call them Customer A's and Customer B's, join a platform and form its two sides (see figure 1-1). These platform participants all have the option of using the platform to seek partners but don't necessarily do that all the time. As shown, some Customer A's and Customer B's that belong to the platform decide to look for matches: they are the ones shown on the platform where customers can make connections and decide whether to enter into a trade. A few of them have found partners for engaging in mutually advantageous exchange: the ones with the arrows connecting them.

This depiction is obviously abstract and one can quibble about whether the details fit particular multisided platforms. To see how it applies in practice, consider OpenTable. The Customer A's are restaurants and the Customer B's are diners. A number of restaurants and diners have joined this reservation platform. At any time, some of the diners are looking for reservations and some of the restaurants have tables available. They are using the reservation system to seek matches. Some of those find what they are looking for, and they make matches. The platform consists of the software and databases that OpenTable has for matching restaurants and diners and the software that restaurants and diners use to make reservations.

FIGURE 1-1

A simple two-sided platform

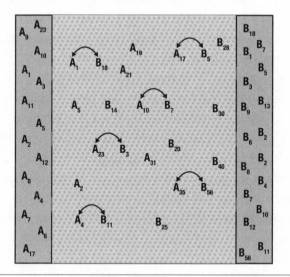

For a nightclub, the Customer A's are men and the Customer B's are women. Men and women go to the nightclub. Assuming they get in, they go to the dance floor or the bar—that's the physical platform—to interact with each other and look for partners. There's no sophisticated matching technology. But the design of the space, the dance music, strobe lighting, and cocktails do the trick to help men and women connect on their own.

No one knew how common these multisided platforms were, or what an important role they played in the economy, before Rochet and Tirole pointed this out.

Matchmakers in Our Midst

Most of us, in most countries, go to shopping malls. Few of us think they are anything special. Their business model may seem pretty simple. Developers build them and then rent space to retail stores. Construction and rental are well-known, straight forward businesses.

If you look at shopping malls more closely, though, you'll see they are multisided platforms that connect shoppers and retailers. There's more to shopping-mall matchmaking than meets the eye. Mall developers match particular kinds of shoppers and retailers by deciding where to locate their malls and what kind of stores to recruit for them. They build upscale malls in well-off areas and recruit high-end stores for them, for instance. They then design the mall layout to balance increasing the amount of foot traffic that passes by the retail stores against annoying shoppers by making them walk more.

Computer operating systems are often multisided platforms. They have the same economic code as shopping malls and a different code than automobile manufacturers. Microsoft Windows is an intermediary between app developers and end users. Microsoft provides Intuit with access to code in its platform, so Intuit can write apps like QuickBooks, an accounting software package for small businesses. A small business owner can then install QuickBooks on her personal computer running Windows. Microsoft licenses Windows to computer manufacturers, which is how it makes all of its money on Windows, and it gives developers like Intuit pretty much free access to its platform.

Magazines are matchmakers as well. *Vogue* is a multisided platform for getting women with an interest in fashion together with companies selling upscale clothes and accessories. Condé Nast, its owner, prints a thick, glossy, full-color magazine, replete with articles on fashion and many attractive ads. It sells the magazine to consumers at a price that might not even cover printing and distribution, and it sells advertising space, which is where it really makes its money, to the companies that want to reach women who buy fashion.

Websites that help people list, find, and rent lodging are some of the newest matchmakers. Airbnb is a multisided platform for connecting people who have spare rooms, or houses, with people looking for a place to stay. It charges a service fee to people who book a place to stay (that's where it makes most of its money) and a modest commission to the host (which just covers the cost of processing payments).

To identify whether a business has the economic code of a multisided platform, you need to examine, as we did in all these cases, whether it is providing value by connecting two or more types of customers. This is not always obvious at first blush, since when one group of "customers" is getting something for free, we tend not even to think of them as customers.

In fact, a pretty good clue that a business is a matchmaker is that it isn't charging some important group (shoppers at malls) or seems to be giving them a deal that's almost too good to be true (cheap, thick, glossy magazines).[19]

Turbocharged Matchmakers

If Julie Templeton had gone on her long quest for a dinner reservation a few years earlier, it would have been much harder for Chuck to have found a way to improve the reservation process. The telephone, after all, was a great innovation in its day. Then the Internet, together with the spread of personal computers, made it feasible for an entrepreneur to reduce friction in restaurant reservations dramatically. It provided a way for restaurants and people to connect almost in real time. Neither had to use a phone.

The Internet has provided the foundation for many other multisided platforms by making it possible to connect potential trading partners residing almost anywhere in the world. Rapid advances in the Internet's coverage, speed, and reliability have made those connections easier over time. Then smartphones and advances in the speed and reliability of wireless networks have put connected computing devices into the hands of almost two billion people around the world.[20] More countries are getting wireless networks that can support Internet-connected devices, so that number will increase considerably in the coming years.

The birth of the commercial Internet in the mid-1990s and mobile broadband in the early 2000s, combined with the earlier invention of personal computers and programming languages, has sent forth armies of multisided platforms working to reduce transaction costs of all sorts in most countries on the planet. Some stay within their own national borders. Others use the power of global connectivity to try to conquer the world. The pace has been frenetic for the last two decades and is quickening. The Internet and smartphones have turbocharged the ancient matchmaker business model.

Whether turbocharged or not, the same economic principles for building, starting, and operating a multisided platform apply. Before you can understand the new economics that makes these matchmakers tick, you have to clear your heads of the old concepts about traditional businesses.

Chapter 2

The "Grab All the Eyeballs" Fallacy

How One-Sided Analysis Led
Many Dot-Coms Astray

W HEN CHUCK TEMPLETON STARTED OUT, HIS INVESTORS told him, "grab all the eyeballs you can and figure out how to monetize them later."[1] For OpenTable, that meant signing up as many restaurants as possible anywhere there was interest without worrying about how that would translate into revenue; after all, isn't that what venture money is for? Chuck's first successor as CEO took that advice to heart. It almost destroyed the company.

Other dot-coms that followed this advice weren't so lucky. Most didn't see the other end of 2001. The new economics of multisided platforms has revealed why that, and a lot of other business advice, is often wrong when it comes to most businesses that have what economists call network effects, in which adding customers attracts other customers.[2]

The Great Network Effects Mistake

Economists started the serious study of network effects in the early 1970s. That work gained momentum in the 1980s. By the time entrepreneurs were starting dot-coms in the mid-1990s, there was an extensive academic literature. Business writers had latched onto the concept. Simple versions of network effects seeped into popular writings along with simplistic strategic advice. Unfortunately, right around the time dot-commers in Silicon Valley were being told they should build market share as quickly as possible, Rochet and Tirole in Toulouse were realizing that network effects were much more complicated, and different in practice, than many economists had thought.

The early work by economists on network effects nevertheless laid the foundations for the later research on multisided platforms.[3] So it is worth spending some time describing the older research before we explain what went wrong when people started applying a simple theory with just one kind of customer to a complex multisided world with several different kinds of customers.

A pioneering paper by Jeffrey Rohlfs dealt with the early days of landline telephone service, which was introduced in the United States following the 1876 invention of the telephone.[4] A telephone was useless if nobody else had one. Even Bell and Watson started with two. A telephone was more valuable if a user could reach more people.

Economists call this phenomenon a *direct network effect*. The more people connected to a network, the more valuable that network is to each person who is part of it. Economists also refer to this as a *positive direct network externality*. When one person joins the network, she directly benefits other people who might want to reach her. Economists call this an *externality* because one person is having an impact on another. It is *positive* because the effect benefits that other person.

Telephone companies tried to persuade households to pay to subscribe to this new communication service. If enough did, they could make a lot of money from this business, which had significant scale economies. Rohlfs concluded that if a new telephone system acquired a critical mass of subscribers, it would become attractive enough that others would want to sign up. If it had fewer, however, current subscribers would be inclined to leave, reducing its attractiveness still further. Business success or failure depended on building up a critical mass of subscribers.

Economists initially applied these new concepts to traditional network industries such as telephones and railroads. Then, in the 1980s, economists started looking at "high tech," and this resulted in an outpouring of research papers. During that decade, fax machines, personal computers, video games, videocassette recorders, and other electronics-based businesses were booming. Some of these industries involved the adoption of technology standards so that products from different manufacturers could work together.

Several economists wrote influential papers on the most visible high-tech battle of the time: over the standard for videocassette recorders (VCRs). This revolutionary technology allowed people, for the first time, to rent or buy prerecorded movies, to record television shows, and to watch this content whenever they chose. Until these devices, people could watch movies and other shows on television only at the precise time when a station broadcast them. Sony was behind the Betamax standard, and a consortium of other Japanese companies was behind the VHS standard. They duked it out.

Economists argued that if two standards were roughly comparable in cost and performance, consumers would find the video-recording standard used by more people more attractive. That's because content providers, such as movie studios, would release more shows that consumers could watch on the VCRs based on the more popular standard. Because of this network effect, they theorized that the standard that got a head start, for whatever reason, and no matter how small, would ultimately win the race.

The idea was that if a VCR standard had a slight lead, it would make more sales, then it would become even more attractive, then it would get even more sales, and so on. Indeed, if the poorer technology got into the lead—because it was first, for example—it could win, just because of the power of these network effects. The VHS standard took an early lead. The Betamax, which some claim was the better technology, was left in the dustbin of history.

Many writers on business strategy took this apparent lesson to heart and emphasized the importance of *first-mover advantages* in industries with network effects.[5] They drew two conclusions. The first was that network effects meant that one firm, or standard, would control the market, since bigger was always better in the eyes of consumers. These were, therefore, winner-take-all markets. The second was that, if you wanted to be the winner who took all, you had better start first and keep your lead. Since direct network effects would magnify the effects of even the slightest of leads, there's always a first-mover advantage.

One can see the influence of this work from a Google Ngram that shows the frequency of these phrases in books published after 1950. There was a surge in the term *network effects* in the early 1970s following the publication of Rohlfs's paper, references died down, and then grew explosively after 1995 (see figure 2-1).[6] References to the *first-mover advantage* started increasing rapidly in the early 1990s and then grew explosively after 1995 as well. By the mid-1990s, when the dot-coms flooded the market, supported by plentiful venture capital funding, the view that entrepreneurs should build share quickly and worry about money later was the accepted wisdom.

It turns out there was a fundamental problem with this view. Economists had developed a one-sided theory involving just one

FIGURE 2-1

Mentions of "network effect(s)" and "first-mover advantage," 1950–2008

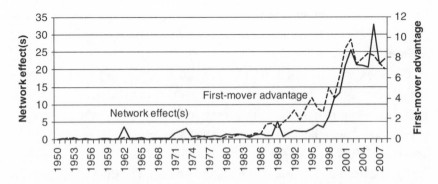

Note: Both Ngrams are case-insensitive. The Ngram for "network effect(s)" includes both the singular and plural. The Ngram for "first-mover advantage" includes both the hyphenated and unhyphenated forms. The units for both axes are per 10 million, e.g., a value of 32 for "network effect(s)" indicates that 32 bigrams per 10 million bigrams (two-word phrases) in the Google Book database were "network effects."

type of customer, but were applying it to multisided businesses that, in fact, served two or more distinct kinds of customers. As Rochet and Tirole realized in their pioneering paper,"[M]any, if not most markets with network externalities are characterized by the presence of two distinct sides whose ultimate benefit stems from interacting through a common platform."[7] The French economists pointed to the general significance of *indirect network effects.* A network effect is *indirect* when the value of a matchmaker to one group of customers depends on how many members of a *different* group participate.

The importance of indirect network effects is obvious, at least in retrospect, when a business has two distinct types of customers who desire to interact with each other. The value of OpenTable to us, as restaurant-goers in Boston, for example, has increased over time as more and more fine-dining establishments in Boston have signed on to the platform, increasing the odds that we can find just the right place, at just the right time, for just the right number of people.

The importance of indirect network effects is less obvious when everyone who uses the network looks the same. Consider YouTube, which we will discuss in detail in chapter 5. At least in its early years, ordinary people used it both to upload videos and to watch videos. A mom might upload a video of her child's first birthday party and then watch a crazy cat video that someone else put up.

The key fact is that those ordinary people played different roles at different times. One role involved making and uploading videos, and the other involved viewing videos. People who viewed videos benefited when more people uploaded videos, and people who uploaded videos benefited when more people watched those videos. Since some people are more likely to upload videos, and others are more likely to watch videos, YouTube had to court both types of people to make the network successful. It couldn't count on the fact that many people did both. Early on, it really needed the sort of people who liked to make and upload videos to get more content to attract more viewers.

We suspect the same was true for the early telephone networks. Some households and businesses are more likely to make telephone calls, and others are more likely to receive calls. Some people are just more gregarious and talkative than others, and different businesses use the telephone differently. The willingness of households and businesses to sign up for the telephone network likely depended on how much the phone company was charging for making versus receiving calls and the extent to which they were more likely to make calls than to receive them. People who tended to make calls benefited when they could reach more people, and people who tended to receive calls benefited when more people could call them.

Let's return now to the VCR standards war that was the inspiration for the "build share first and fast" mantra. On reflection, it is obvious that the standards wars for VCRs were between competing two-sided platforms. Betamax and VHS were both technology platforms that connected consumers, who bought VCRs for their televisions, and content providers, who released shows on videotape that people could buy or rent and watch on those VCRs.

The economists who concluded that VHS won because it had gotten more consumers had done a one-sided analysis of a two-sided platform. They just assumed that content providers would respond automatically to the number of VCRs using the Betamax or VHS standard. But the business didn't work in this mechanical way. In fact, the promoters of the VHS and Betamax standards worked actively to attract content providers and consumers, just as OpenTable worked actively to attract restaurants and diners. VHS won because it was more successful in getting both consumers and content providers to use its standard. Consumers bought more VHS-based VCRs, and content providers provided more VHS-based cassettes. These reinforcing, indirect network effects drove VHS to victory and drove Betamax out of the market.

It didn't have to work out that way. Betamax could have invested more in persuading content providers to create cassettes for its standard. The important role that platform vendors play in getting both sides on board became apparent with the standards war involving high-definition DVD players, which began in 2005.[8] The Blu-ray platform—backed by Sony, Apple, and others—was pitted against the HD-DVD platform, backed by Toshiba, Microsoft, and others. Both standards had advantages, but neither standard was broadly superior to the other.

The dynamics of competition played out differently in the DVD war than in the VHS war. The HD-DVD camp sold more stand-alone DVD players to consumers than the Blu-ray consortium. It won the battle to get more consumers on board.[9] A one-sided analysis would conclude that, because of that lead, it should have won a winner-take-all war easily. In fact, it lost. The HD-DVD camp conceded defeat after Warner Brothers abandoned the HD-DVD format in January 2008. By then, Blu-ray had attracted more content providers that made more movies and other content available only in its format.

The Blu-ray victory and HD-DVD loss plainly didn't happen by accident. Sony's own studio produced only Blu-ray DVDs. There were press reports, unconfirmed, that Sony made large cash payments to Warner Brothers and to Fox Searchlight Pictures, which were reportedly thinking of abandoning Blu-ray.[10] It appears that the Blu-ray group used price and other contractual terms more effectively to get both the consumer and content provider sides on board than the HD-DVD group. A better two-sided strategy made the difference.

Mastering Multifaceted Network Effects

It turns out that networks effects are far more pervasive and complex than economists and business strategists thought they were before 2000. Rochet and Tirole's deep insight that year was that businesses in a diverse range of industries faced indirect network effects. The way they built their businesses, designed their products, ran their operations, and priced their offerings were heavily influenced by these network effects. These businesses operated multisided platforms.

Economists, including ourselves, then started studying how these firms and industries worked in fact. It soon became apparent that much of the received wisdom about network effects was wrong. The first-mover advantage and winner-take-all theories, for example, were shaky at best. In the United States, for example, there are four major payment card networks, several major shopping mall developers, many magazine publishers, and several major stock and options exchanges. The largest credit card network, Visa, expanded nationally sixteen years after the first national card network. We can't think of many multisided platform industries where the first mover won it all. In fact, for most industries with indirect network effects, the first movers mostly died and few remember them.

There are some important industries where "winner takes most" may apply. But even there, victory is likely to be more transient than economists and pundits once thought. In social networking, Friendster lost to MySpace, which lost to Facebook, and, while Facebook seems entrenched, there are many other social networks nipping at its heels. There were several first movers in social networking in the late 1990s, such as sixdegrees.com, that few, other than Internet historians, remember today.

Economists missed the fact that matchmakers, just like any other businesses, can differentiate themselves. Facebook focused on recruiting college students and providing a nicer environment in which people could interact than MySpace provided. Platforms can thereby win over participants—on two or more sides—even if they are initially smaller or enter later.

Participants can, and often do, use several platforms—a practice that the old network effects literature dismissed. The new economics of multisided platforms calls this *multihoming*. Most people use and most merchants accept several different brands of payment cards, for instance. That's what enabled Discover to squeeze its way into the US credit card business in the mid-1980s. It was able to persuade consumers to carry an additional card and merchants to accept an additional card brand. Sometimes participants do use only one platform of a single type or "single-home," of course. For example, most people use only one desktop computer operating system.

Economists also recognize now that the extent to which indirect network effects could be reversed varies across industries. They had focused on businesses in which people had to make a significant financial commitment to a new technology such as a fax machine or a video game console. Once a network business of that sort got someone on board using its standard, it didn't have to worry much about losing that person. For many matchmaker businesses, however, participants can easily decide to switch. People commonly stop going to a mall and retailers commonly decide not to renew their leases there. Even when it seems hard to switch from a platform, it often turns out not to be. Many people moved from Friendster to MySpace, and then from MySpace to Facebook.

The new economics of multisided platforms has also led economists, including us, to study the role of network effects more closely. Once you examine businesses that have multiple groups of participants, the direct and indirect network effects are much more complex than the simple landline telephone story.

Direct network effects, for example, can be negative as well as positive, and this can have tremendous implications for how platforms operate. Consider the classic singles bar where people go to a physical location to meet those of the opposite sex. For a particular side, direct network effects are likely negative at some point. Men would prefer less competition for the women and the women less competition for the men. The same story holds for many other platforms where the members of each side are competing with each other for matches with members of the other side. These platforms have incentives to limit participation, since that will make them more valuable to members on each side.

Indirect network effects can be negative as well. We know that people dislike radio and television advertisements because they spend money to avoid having to watch or listen to them. Pandora, HBO, and Netflix can charge a premium to users looking to avoid ads. People also pay for recording technologies like TiVo that allow them to skip the ads. Radio and television businesses must contend with the fact that their customers dislike ads. One way they do so is to provide content that is so good that people are willing to endure the advertisements that come with it. The other way is to limit the amount of advertisements. Radio stations in the United States, for example, compete in part by bragging about how few commercial interruptions they have.

Economists also learned that indirect effects aren't just a numbers game.[11] Multisided platforms have to make sure there are enough participants on each side who could benefit from getting together with participants on the other side. They need to make the market "thick."[12] But they can't do that do that by just getting more participants on each side. They have to make sure they are getting more participants on each side with whom participants on the other side want to interact.

We saw this with OpenTable. A restaurant reservation platform needs to have enough of the right restaurants, in the right city, at the right time. It can't make up for this deficit by having many restaurants that aren't relevant to the people making the reservations. OpenTable's "go narrow/go deep" strategy worked because it ultimately secured critical mass in cities where it had signed up enough popular restaurants and engaged enough diners that the positive indirect network effects between these two kinds of customers ignited further growth on both sides.

Lyft, Yelp, Instacart, and other businesses that provide local services have followed similar strategies. But the point also applies to multisided platforms that are trying to differentiate their offerings. If a mall developer decides to create a high-end shopping mall, it must get high-end stores to lease space at the mall, and it must persuade well-off shoppers to go to the mall. Packing the mall with people who aren't able to shop at expensive stores won't help it persuade high-end stores to lease space, and renting space to downscale stores won't attract high-end shoppers.

Once Rochet and Tirole had uncovered the complex role of network effects in these businesses, they started investigating the pricing strategies these firms should adopt to maximize profits. They made a breakthrough.

Pricing for a Profitable Balance

In a traditional business, pricing strategy is mainly determined by a trade-off between volume and margin. Higher prices reduce volume but increase margin; lower prices do the reverse. If demand is relatively insensitive to price, a higher price is more likely to lead to higher profits, while price-sensitive demand tends to dictate lower prices and lower margins, compensated by notably higher volume.

If a business sells more than one product, it sometimes needs to take into account how the price of each product affects the sales of its other offerings. Mercedes-Benz needs to keep the prices of its entry-level cars relatively high, for instance, so as not to divert customers who would otherwise have purchased its larger and more profitable vehicles. In some situations, it is worthwhile to think about selling the same product or similar products to different customer groups at substantially different prices or to offer discounts for volume purchasing.

It hardly ever makes sense, however, for traditional businesses to consider setting prices at or below the cost of providing an additional unit of output. A price below that incremental cost implies not only that selling more of that product doesn't help cover the firm's overhead, but also that selling more actually reduces profit. It is rarely sensible for a traditional business to put itself in a position where selling more of anything means earning less profit.

Of course, there are a few exceptions. Retailers use loss leaders designed to build retail traffic, for instance. But there are usually explicit or implicit limits on per-customer purchases of loss leaders. Milk is a good loss leader for grocery stores. Most families with children buy it, but there is an implicit limit on per-family purchases at any time because milk can't be stored for long. Traditional businesses sometimes have introductory prices so customers can try out a new product. But then they increase the price so that it covers costs and generates a margin.

These sorts of exceptions aside, it simply doesn't makes sense for a traditional business to sell anything for a unit price that doesn't cover the cost of supplying an additional unit. As we saw in the last chapter, however, it turns out that this cardinal rule doesn't apply to multisided platforms.

Matchmakers face much more complex pricing problems than traditional businesses because they must *balance the interests of all sides* in order to get all sides on board the platform, and keep them on board, and to get members of each group to interact with members of the other groups. Like traditional businesses, multi-sided firms also need to consider trade-offs between volume and margins. But with a twist caused by indirect network effects, which makes the demand of each group interdependent with the demands of the other groups.

A physical newspaper, such as the *Financial Times*, is a good example. It spends money on journalists to generate content, and it incurs costs to produce and distribute the newspaper. It can make money from charging readers and from charging for advertisements. If it increases the newsstand price or subscription price to readers, fewer people will read the newspaper. With fewer readers, advertisers wouldn't be willing to spend as much money. If, instead, it increases the price to advertisers, it has two things to consider. It will sell less advertising, which readers might actually like. But it might also earn less revenue and therefore be able to pay for less content, which readers won't like.

The important point is that, in considering the prices to charge, the *Financial Times* and other multisided platforms must recognize that the demands by the different types of participants depend on each other. The demand for advertising in the *Financial Times* depends on how many readers it has, and the demand for buying the *Financial Times* depends, in an even more complicated way, on the amount of advertising.

This interdependency of demands results from indirect network effects. It is what distinguishes multisided platforms from single-sided firms. Traditional economics, including what is still taught in most economic textbooks and in most MBA courses, completely ignores indirect network effects and the consequences of interdependent demand. When economists account for indirect network effects in our theoretical models, the profit-maximizing price to the participants on one side could be less than the cost of providing an additional unit; it could be zero or, in other words, free; or it could be less than zero in the sense that the business actually pays the participant something when he or she uses the product.

This theoretical result could have been just a curious possibility that we could use to try to keep students awake. But it turns out that pricing below incremental cost is not rare at all. Once economists had identified multisided platforms, we started looking at how they priced. In fact, many of them charge the participants on one side of the platform prices that do not cover cost, charge nothing, or provide rewards for using the product. That side is called the *subsidy side* of the platform. Platforms make up subsidy-side losses by charging prices that more than cover costs to the participants on the other side. That's called the *money side* of the platform. For OpenTable, as we saw, the diners were the subsidy side, and the restaurants were the money side.

For a selection of multisided platform industries, see table 2-1. The fact that the subsidy sides of all these businesses are charged less than cost, some are charged nothing (such as mall shoppers), and some are charged negative prices (such as some credit card customers who get rewards) means that these *really* are not traditional businesses.

Those who are new to the economics of multisided platforms often make a simple mistake. They think that free and negative prices are a gimmick that platforms use to get a critical mass of participants. In fact, matchmakers commonly charge free and negative prices permanently in order to maximize profits. All of the industries listed in table 2-1 have been around for a long time. Like OpenTable, they have chosen to make the low, zero, or negative prices a permanent feature for participants on their subsidy sides.

Despite these numerous examples, however, the new economic theory of multisided platforms doesn't say that it is *always* profitable for matchmakers to have a subsidy side. Only that it may be. In fact, many multisided platforms charge users on all sides. The *Wall Street Journal* charges for online access to its content, even though the cost of providing access to an additional reader must be very close to zero, and it then charges advertisers for reaching those readers. And while women may get a break sometimes, nightclubs in the United States typically charge both men and women for admittance and drinks, and online matchmakers generally charge men and women the same.

TABLE 2-1

Money and subsidy sides for common multisided platform industries

Multisided platform	Money side	Subsidy side	Typical price on subsidy side
Video game consoles	Game publishers pay royalties.	Consumers pay marginal cost or less for console.	Below cost
PC operating systems	Computer users pay directly or indirectly through computer maker.	Developers do not pay access fees for operating system APIs and only pay a nominal amount for a software development kit.	Free
Physical newspapers	Advertisers pay.	Readers usually pay less than the marginal cost of printing and distribution and sometimes pay nothing.	Below cost
US broadcast TV	Advertisers pay.	Consumers do not pay.	Free
Credit cards	Merchants pay for transactions.	Consumers do not pay for transactions and sometimes get rewards.	Negative
Enclosed shopping malls	Retail stores pay.	Shoppers do not pay, get free parking at suburban malls, and often get free entertainment.	Free to negative
US real estate brokers	Sellers pay commission.	Buyers do not pay.	Free
Equity exchanges	Liquidity takers pay commission.	Liquidity providers often receive subsidies.	Negative
Online marketplaces	Sellers often pay commission.	Buyers usually do not pay.	Free
Job recruiters and online job boards	Employers pay for postings or recruitment.	Job seekers do not pay.	Free
Yellow pages	Businesses pay for listings.	Consumers do not pay.	Free
Search engines	Businesses pay for advertisements.	Searchers do not pay.	Free
Nightclubs	Men pay.	Women sometimes get in for free or get below-cost drinks.	Below cost or free

Building, Igniting, and Designing
a Multisided Platform

Multisided platforms often must perform the business equivalent of walking a tightrope while juggling. These platforms are selling connections. They must *balance* their treatment of all customer groups to ensure that they have enough of the right members of all groups on the platform. Pricing is a key element of this balancing act. But many other decisions that multisided platforms make—from how they design their platforms, products, and services to how they govern interactions on their platform—are critical as well, for the same reasons.[13]

In some settings, the entrepreneur may have to decide whether he should design his new venture as a matchmaker at all. It isn't necessarily the best way to build a successful business. Some online retailers have opted to operate traditional one-sided businesses, while others have adopted the multisided platform model. Zappos, for example, began as a two-sided platform, linking consumers with shoe manufacturers. It found that it could offer a more consistent experience for buyers by becoming a traditional retailer and taking full control of the buyer experience.

Some businesses are natural multisided platforms. It wouldn't make sense to run a payment card system any other way, for instance. But even such businesses may have discretion on how many different sides to have. They may find that it is better to supply some things themselves than relying on platform participants to do this.

In the personal computer world, for instance, both Apple and Microsoft have mainly relied on independent software developers to write and sell apps to run on their operating systems. Except for one brief period, Apple has always produced its own hardware. It operates a two-sided platform linking app developers with consumers. Microsoft, in contrast, has operated a three-sided platform, with personal computer manufacturers being the third side.

Some design decisions involve trade-offs between the interests of different groups, and these decisions must be made with an eye to maintaining the balanced participation that a matchmaker needs to survive. A newspaper could make more advertising available by devoting fewer of its pages to content and more to ads. But then it would risk losing readers who don't like seeing many ads interspersed in what they are reading. Advertisers will value ads in the newspaper less if they reach fewer readers. The newspaper has to weigh the costs and benefits of the balance between ads and content in designing its newspaper.

The core of this book in part II uses case studies of multisided platforms to provide a deeper understanding of the concepts that we've presented in this chapter. We focus on six critical issues that multisided platforms must address.

The opportunity for a multisided platform ordinarily arises when frictions *keep market participants from dealing with each other easily and directly.* Entrepreneurs can identify opportunities for starting a matchmaker by looking for significant transaction costs that keep willing buyers and sellers apart and that a well-designed matchmaker can reduce.

Multisided platforms have to secure critical mass in order to ignite. They have to solve the chicken-and-egg problem of getting both sides on board, in adequate numbers, to create value. If they don't, they will implode. If they do, indirect network effects will generally fuel sustainable growth. This problem is so hard to solve that entrepreneurs need to make sure that the frictions they are trying to solve are substantial enough to persuade participants to join and to enable the matchmaker, possibly, to fund subsidies to one group of participants.

Getting the pricing structure *right is critical both for getting a new matchmaker off the ground and for making sure it is profitable in the long run.* The platform has to balance the interdependent demands of the multiple groups of participants.

Multisided platforms are usually situated within broader ecosystems of firms, governments, regulation, and other institutions. A platform has to make sure that it can play well with everyone else and it may have to cause changes in its environment to do so. It also has to decide how many customer groups it wants to connect and therefore how many sides to have.

Multisided platforms operate physical or virtual places where the participants get together. They have to make sure they *design* these places with a view toward enhancing the value of the direct and indirect network effects between participants.

Finally, matchmakers have to worry about how participants interact with each other. What is unusual about these businesses is that many of them have adopted *governance systems*, complete with "laws," "enforcers," and "penalties." The right rules can promote positive network externalities, both direct and indirect, and deter negative ones.

All these issues are harder for a *pioneering platform* than for an entrant into a relatively mature industry. OpenTable had no models to follow, for instance; it and its mostly forgotten competitors had to work things out from first principles and by trial and error. In contrast, the problems facing a new online or offline magazine are relatively well understood though rarely simple. It is important to note, however, that comfortable multisided platforms in mature industries can find themselves in uncharted waters when new competitive matchmakers appear, as print newspapers have learned to their sorrow.

Before we turn to these issues, we need to explain why multisided platforms have suddenly become much more prominent in the global economy, with preteens emerging as corporate giants and infants securing massive market values.

Chapter 3

Turbocharging

The Technologies Behind the Explosive

Growth of Matchmakers

E VANS WAS STANDING AT THE CORNER OF THE RUE DE LA LOI and Rue Royale in Brussels, late for his next meeting, in early June 2015. He had the address on his itinerary, somewhere in his e-mail inbox, but it was easier just to Google the firm's address on his iPhone. It was only twenty minutes away by car according to the search results, but there were no taxis in sight. So he tapped on his Uber app and found a driver. Marc picked him up in about ten minutes and delivered him to his destination, nearly on time.

All of the services Evans used for this trip—Google search, the Apple iPhone, and Uber—are provided by multisided platforms.

Those matchmakers are global. Evans could have, and often has, used those same platforms for the same purposes in many other cities around the world. Only deep poverty, and sometimes regulation, keep these companies out of any city on the planet.[1]

Multisided platforms have been an important part of the economic fabric of many countries for centuries. Several Western European countries had national stock exchanges, often called bourses, by the eighteenth century. Some matchmakers, such as payment card networks, obtained global scale by the late 1970s. None of these compared to today's matchmakers.[2]

As we were finishing this book on November 20, 2015, Apple had the highest market cap of any company in the world, at $672 billion, and Google the second highest, at $515 billion.[3] Uber was the most valuable of the "unicorns"—venture-capital-backed companies that are still private and are valued at $1 billion or more—at $51 billion.[4] Matchmakers are likely to be even more important in the future. Seven of the ten most valuable unicorns were matchmakers.[5]

The platform age is upon us because of the development of powerful information and communications technologies that have lowered the cost and increased the reach of connecting platform sides. It cost Uber virtually nothing to connect Evans and his driver in Brussels and to charge Evans and pay the driver, even though both of them were about fifty-five hundred miles from Uber's San Francisco headquarters.

Those technologies have also resulted in the creation of *foundational multisided platforms* on which other matchmakers can build. These "platforms-for-platforms" include fixed and mobile Internet service providers, which connect users and content providers, and computer operating systems, which, working on top of fixed and mobile computing devices, connect users and app developers.

These information technologies and the foundational platforms they power have turbocharged the ancient matchmaker model.

The Six Turbocharging Technologies

Six new and rapidly improving technologies have driven matchmaker innovation by reducing the cost, increasing the speed, and expanding the scope of connections between platform sides.[6]

More Powerful Chips

It required a lot of computer power for Evans to use his phone to ask Uber for a ride, for Uber almost instantly to figure out how to match up all the drivers and passengers who were looking for rides around the same time in Brussels, and to point Marc, the driver, to Evans, the passenger.

Since the mid-1950s, computer processing has been based on transistors, which have become much smaller over time. That has made it possible to pack more transistors closer together on a single chip, which in turn has increased the speed at which chips can execute instructions. By the late 1970s, these more powerful chips enabled the first personal computers. The chip for the first IBM PC, introduced in 1981, had twenty-nine thousand transistors on it; the chip for the iPhone 6, introduced in 2014, had two billion transistors. The iPhone chip is about three hundred times faster than the IBM PC chip was.[7]

In 2008, more than a billion personal computers were in use, but sales began to flatten in 2010 as PCs gave way to devices small enough to fit in a purse or pocket. Continued progress in miniaturization has made it possible to produce the fast and powerful computers that power the iPhone and devices based on the Android operating system. In 2014 alone, more than 1.2 billion of these smartphones were sold worldwide, along with more than 200 million tablet computers.[8]

The Internet

When Evans was looking for his destination and a ride to get there, and Marc was looking for a passenger and directions to the destination, they both used mobile devices connected to the Internet to communicate with Uber and Google.

The Internet refers to physical networks that wind through the countryside, traverse the oceans, and ultimately connect computing devices all around the world, using the same protocols to communicate. The development of standards and technologies, starting in the 1960s, enabled computers to communicate with each other over physical networks and for each of those physical networks to communicate with each other. The US government originally operated this network of networks, which was fully opened to worldwide commercial traffic in 1993.[9]

As companies emerged to provide transit services between networks within countries and between countries, capacity was added, and Internet traffic exploded. On November 22, 2015, at 12:00 p.m. in Boston, one source reported that more than 3.25 billion people worldwide had Internet access over fixed or mobile devices.[10] That was 44 percent of the 7.38 billion people in the world.

The World Wide Web

When Evans googled his destination in Brussels, he used the Chrome browser on his iPhone to access the Google search engine on the web. Google had indexed all the websites for its search engine, and it was able to find Evans's destination almost instantly in its database.

The web consists of all of the sources of content, written and transmitted in a standard way, that are available over the Internet and can be accessed by a browser. The software technologies behind the web, such as HTML, have improved drastically since they were introduced in 1990. Meanwhile, the Internet's capacity has expanded many times to handle the enormous growth in web traffic.

Globally, in November 2015, there were 173 million active websites connected to the Internet.[11] They included opentable.com, as well as sites that attract far more traffic, such as facebook.com, and a vast number of sites that attract much less, such as eckerts.com. Many websites are in the business of providing content and services. They are often referred to as "edge providers" or "Internet content providers." Many of these edge providers are matchmakers.

Broadband Communications

Mobile broadband connections made it possible for Evans to reach Google and Uber's servers and for Marc to reach Uber's servers from their mobile phones, and to do so nearly instantly and at negligible cost.

The speed and capacity of the Internet has improved enormously over the last two decades. Fixed-location connections have improved as a result of the introduction and improvements in broadband, which permits very rapid transmission of information along a coaxial cable, fiber-optic line, or even a copper wire. By the end of 2014, there were more than 750 million fixed broadband subscriptions around the world.[12] In 2014, the average connection speed, across 199 countries served by Akamai, which operates a global content delivery network, was 4.5 megabits per second (Mbps).[13] This speed is three times faster than it was in 2008, and fast enough to stream—or play—a movie sent from a server in real time.

Mobile connections have also improved. Before 2000, cellular networks could not handle significant amounts of data, since the average download speed of GSM networks was only 9.6 kilobits per second (kbps). Innovations by companies like Qualcomm and others made it possible to increase the speed and capacity of wireless transmission and led mobile network operators to introduce third-generation (3G) networks beginning around 2001 and then fourth-generation (4G) networks beginning around 2011. In July 2015, Verizon advertised that its 4G LTE network provided download speeds of five to ten Mbps. The number of mobile broadband subscriptions per one hundred people reached thirty-two globally, eighty-four in developed countries, and twenty-one in developing countries. Globally, mobile broadband penetration in 2014 was almost four times as high as it was in 2009.[14]

Programming Languages and Operating Systems

Computers are useless unless people can tell them what to do, and they are nearly useless without a convenient language that can be used to give them complex instructions clearly and correctly. The first useful programming languages were developed in the 1950s. Since then, many new and more powerful and flexible languages have been developed. Many of the modern languages descend from C, which was developed at Bell Laboratories in the early 1970s.[15] In the early 1990s, a team of engineers at Sun Microsystems developed Java, which has become one of the most popular languages for web-based and mobile-phone apps.

With these languages, developers could write programs that could run on server computers connected to the Internet and, potentially, could make their services available to everyone connected to the

Internet. They could write apps that would run locally on individual computers, as well as apps that would straddle the two. One survey identified more than 11 million professional software developers in ninety countries in 2014.[16]

As we discuss further later, these programming languages also made it possible to write complex "operating systems" that provide valuable services to apps and give detailed instructions to the underlying computer hardware. The development of operating systems, and the division of labor between operating systems and apps, has unleashed the power of the microchip.

The Cloud

There are now 5.5 million server computers connected to the Internet. Companies own or lease servers, on which they store the content that they make available to their customers and others.[17] Together, these servers, which sit on the edge of the physical network of networks, are called the "Cloud." They provide the computational resources and data for what people do on their personal computers and smartphones.

The Cloud, however, is more than a label for a collection of computers. As Internet speeds have increased, there is little difference between working with a computer on your desk and one on another continent. Companies, including giants such as Amazon, are in the business of providing storage and computation as a service to other businesses. This means a new Internet-based matchmaker doesn't need to buy and manage servers and write all its own software to create a web presence. It can instead pay to rent storage space and to use software made available by a Cloud provider. If its business grows rapidly, it can simply rent more resources from the Cloud. And it can make powerful software, with access to enormous databases, available to anyone with a mobile device or personal computer, with an Internet connection.

Developments in these six technologies continue, with no significant slowdown in sight. Programming languages and operating systems are becoming more useful, computers are getting faster, Internet access is spreading within and across countries, the amount of content on the web is growing, more people are getting faster connection speeds for fixed and mobile devices, and storage and computation is moving to the Cloud.

These six technologies have enabled the development of two foundational multisided platforms that support other multisided platforms: Internet service providers and operating systems.

Two-Sided Platforms for People and Content Providers

The companies that link users to the Internet and, thus, to online content providers are two-sided platforms known as "Internet service providers" (ISPs). Until recently, these ISPs charged users for access to edge providers (Internet content providers), but did not charge edge providers for access to users.[18]

"Fixed ISPs," such as Time Warner Cable in Manhattan, Free in Paris, or CNC in Beijing, provide a connection at a defined physical location. They are typically cable television or telephone companies that had been wiring homes and businesses long before people started browsing online. Fixed ISPs also enable people and businesses to operate wireless networks at fixed locations such as at home or at a café. Increasingly, people are able to access the Internet over fixed wireless networks operated by businesses or public agencies.

When people want to access an edge provider—to post on their Facebook page (which involves an upload from their computer to Facebook's computer) or stream a movie from Netflix (requiring a download from Netflix's computers to their device), they make a request on their computer. The fixed ISP takes that request and transmits it, generally using other physical networks to which it is connected, to the edge provider.[19] The edge provider sends bits back over the Internet, they arrive at the ISP, and the ISP passes the bits across its local network to the requesting device. Until a few years ago, fixed ISPs were the only way most people could access the web.

"Mobile ISPs" provide an Internet connection to mobile devices, so that users can access the Internet wherever they can get a wireless

signal. Mobile ISPs are mobile network operators that also offer telephone calls and SMS messages over cellular networks. Many of these
operators were building cellular networks well before it was possible
to use mobile technology to transit large amounts of data. They built
cell towers throughout the countries they served.

Mobile ISPs connect edge providers and mobile device users. An
edge provider gets to the front door of a mobile network operator over
the physical Internet. But instead of connecting to the end user with a
wire or cable, like fixed ISPs, a mobile ISP connects to the end user's
mobile device via radio waves, no matter where that device is located,
as long as there is a cell tower close enough.

Fixed and mobile ISPs have helped usher in the platform age by
making it possible for edge providers to connect with billions of people
around the globe at very little cost. All edge providers need is a connection to the Internet that is fast enough and has enough capacity to
carry their traffic to a transit provider, which ultimately connects to
ISPs worldwide through the network of networks.

It is impossible to overstate the importance of ISPs. By giving matchmakers access to most everyone in the world at low cost, these ISPs make
it possible for them to obtain enormous positive indirect network effects
without much investment. When Uber decided to expand from San Francisco to Brussels, it didn't have to build a physical distribution facility or
even hire a stable of dispatchers to handle calls and direct drivers. It just
needed to recruit drivers and hire lawyers to fight regulatory battles.

Users still have to get access to these foundational multisided platforms. The cost of obtaining a connection and the cost of uploading
and downloading data has declined dramatically, however, making it
possible for 44 percent of people on earth to have access to the Internet.[20] A considerable portion of the remaining 56 percent will obtain
access in the next few years as cellular networks expand and as costs
come down further. Global multisided platforms such as Facebook and
Google, which benefit from getting more people on board, are investing in satellite and other technologies for spreading the Internet to
the poorest parts of the world.

Thus, multisided platforms, powered by fixed and mobile ISPs,
themselves multisided platforms, can connect billions of people and

millions of companies around the globe. They have the prospect of reaching many more in the years to come.

There's a limit to how many people can go to a nightclub or participate in a speed-dating event to meet people of the opposite sex. As a result of these foundational platforms, however, Tinder, the dating app, which started in September 2012, can connect billions, if that many men and women want to participate. According to a September 2014 article, it is available in twenty-four languages and has 10 million active daily users.[21]

Two-Sided Platforms for App Users and Developers

A multisided platform that most of us never see, and few of us can really imagine, is the *invisible engine* that powers almost everything we do with personal computers and, most importantly, with mobile devices such as smartphones, tablets, and smart watches.[22] It is the operating system that lives, as bits, in the memory of these microchip-based devices. Before it was turned into bits, it was written in one of the programming languages we discussed earlier. It generally involves millions of lines of instructions—what's known as code—in that language.[23]

Some computer operating systems are multisided platforms. The Windows and Mac OS operating systems provided a standard environment connecting personal computer users and app developers. Application developers rely on these operating systems to provide services such as performing calculations or drawing things on the screen. People then use these operating systems to get access to those apps as well as to the computer power from the device. The flood of high-powered apps for these operating systems helped drive the massive adoption of personal computers around the world.

More recently, Apple's iOS and Google's Android operating systems for mobile devices have put the power of computers in the hands of billions of people and have enabled millions of developers worldwide to create apps for them. Their impact on spawning matchmakers has been enormous.

When Uber started, for example, it consisted of a few people with a vision. They hired developers to write an app, first for the iOS operating system platform on the iPhone, and then for the Android operating system.[24] They then put those apps in app stores that made them available to people who used these mobile platforms.

For a small fee, Uber obtained access to software development tools for building its apps and for access to all of the services provided by these software platforms—from the keyboard for typing in addresses to the geo-location services on the handsets. All the people who used Uber 140 million times in 2014, and all of those who used it in the more than three hundred and fifty cities in sixty-seven countries where it was available in November 2015, had downloaded the Uber app onto their smartphones.[25]

Mobile operating systems, particularly iOS and Android, are foundational multisided platforms that power other important platforms. They are critical components of ride-hailing apps such as Uber and its Chinese competitor Didi Kuaidi and important for music apps such as Spotify. Mobile operating systems are also important for "old" Internet-based matchmakers. Google earned 20 percent of its advertising revenue from the use of its apps on smart mobile devices in 2014, and Facebook earned 73 percent of its ad revenue that way in the first quarter of 2015.[26]

These mobile operating systems, combined with smart mobile devices, have begun to tear down the walls between the online and the offline worlds.

There's Just One World Now

People started making the distinction between the online and offline worlds in the early 1990s, as the commercial Internet took shape and the creation of interlinked HTML documents spawned the World Wide Web.[27] The online world was where we connected with our computers to do things, and the offline world was where we did everything else.

Now these worlds are being folded into one, and the distinction between online and offline is mattering less and less. When Evans was looking for a ride in Brussels, and Marc was looking for a passenger, both were living in the physical world of cars, city traffic, fumes, and buildings. But they found each other and navigated their way around the city by using their mobile devices to link to the Cloud.

We are moving rapidly to one world, where physical space is densely populated with connections to the Cloud. In developed countries, people are already connecting to one another with smart mobile devices, including phones, tablets, and watches. Businesses are using connected computing devices with sophisticated payment apps and small wireless devices, called beacons, to connect to consumers in the store. These smart mobile devices, with their invisible engines, connected by mobile broadband and fixed wireless networks to the Cloud, provide a foundation for new multisided platforms to solve more frictions, reduce more transaction costs, and make more mutually valuable connections in ways we can't yet envision.

Creative Destruction

Each of the six technologies we have described in this chapter reinforces the others. As they have advanced over time, they have compounded each other, resulting in a rapidly accelerating increase in the power they provide matchmakers. Even without these technologies, matchmakers have indirect network effects that can produce rapid growth for anyone who can solve the ignition problem. With them, matchmakers have an ever-increasing source of dynamism.

In 1942, the economist Joseph A. Schumpeter described the results of innovation in market economies:[28]

> [The] process of industrial mutation . . . incessantly revolutionizes the economic structure from within, incessantly destroying the old one, incessantly creating a new one . . . [This process] must be seen in its role in the perennial gale of creative destruction.

These turbocharged matchmakers are the forces behind a gale of "creative destruction" that is revolutionizing economies worldwide.

There is plainly more to come, but new turbocharged matchmakers have already roiled existing industries. In some cases, they have created value by reducing frictions without threatening existing firms. OpenTable, for example, helps white-tablecloth restaurants work more efficiently by reducing the amount of labor they need for taking reservations and reducing the number of empty tables. Perhaps some reservation takers lost their jobs, and restaurants bought fewer pencils and notebooks, but OpenTable didn't destroy businesses.

Looking over the last decade, however, it is clear that turbocharged multisided platforms have developed better ways of doing things that are devastating traditional businesses. Pioneering turbocharged matchmakers have even displaced traditional matchmakers.

Ad-supported web-based businesses such as Yahoo wiped out a significant chunk of the market value of newspaper businesses. As readers shifted their attention to online media, advertisers reduced spending because newspapers had fewer readers. Newspapers had made a significant amount of profit from classified advertisements. Two-sided platforms such as Craigslist, which connects buyers and sellers without needing to spend on content, and Monster, which connects companies looking for workers with people looking for jobs, took a large portion of those advertisers. Total advertising revenue for physical newspapers in the United States declined from $47.4 billion in 2005 to $20.2 billion in 2013, a 57 percent drop in less than a decade.[29]

With less advertising revenue, newspapers couldn't spend as much on content. And, as we discuss in chapter 6, they increased their reliance on reader revenue. As a consequence of reduced content and higher prices, they lost more readers, which made them even less attractive to advertisers. A death spiral set in for many. The average circulation of daily newspapers in the United States declined by 31 percent between 1995 and 2014: from 58.2 million in 1995 to 40.4 million in 2014.[30] Between 1990 and 2014, the number of daily newspapers in the United States fell by 280, 17 percent of the total.[31] Many of the survivors are shadows of their former selves: total newsroom employment fell by 42 percent over this period.[32]

Travel agents are another example. They used to act as intermediaries between people looking to travel and travel-related businesses such as airlines and hotels. Two-sided matchmakers operating from the Cloud, such as Expedia, offer more efficient and cheaper alternatives. According to the US Bureau of Labor Statistics, there were forty-four travel agents for every hundred thousand people in the United States in 2000. That had declined by 55 percent, to only twenty per hundred thousand people in 2014.[33]

Uber, along with similar companies such as Lyft and Didi Kuaidi, has created a great deal of value for consumers and drivers. But the traditional taxicab business is threatened as a result. Taxi drivers worldwide are protesting and trying to stop these new matchmakers. If they don't, the traditional taxi business will likely go into terminal decline. This may already have begun. The prices of taxi medallions— which provide a permanent right to drive a taxicab in some cities— are falling.[34] Medallion prices declined 23 percent in New York City between 2013 and 2015.[35]

In part III of this book, we present case studies of two major examples of creative destruction. In 2007, a multisided platform that uses mobile phones to move money between people started in an impoverished country in Africa. It grew explosively. As a result, it leapfrogged the traditional banking industry as well as payment cards. Meanwhile, in the United States, creative destruction has swept through one of the largest sectors of the economy—retail trade. It has completely destroyed some categories, such as video-rental stores, forced existing players to reinvent their businesses, and resulted in an accelerating wave of innovation in how people shop and buy.

Although the turbocharged platforms are more powerful than earlier ones, they follow the same economic principles as their older siblings. To better understand how matchmakers create value and, in some cases, destroy firms that aren't as efficient, in part II we look in detail at how matchmakers deal with frictions, ignition, pricing, ecosystems, design, and governance.

Part Two

Building, Igniting, and Operating Matchmakers

Chapter 4

Friction Fighters

How Multisided Platforms Create Value by
Finding and Reducing Transaction Costs

T IS 1998. ZHANG WEI OPERATES A SMALL MANUFACTURING PLANT IN
Foshan, about twenty miles outside of Guangzhou in southeast
China.[1] He makes plastic sheets, which he sells to other companies that use them to make other products. Twenty years before, in
1978, the Chinese Communist Party had started down the path of
economic reform. After it "let some people . . . get rich first," many
small businesses started throughout China.[2]

Wei was one of those. After working in a state-owned manufacturing business, he started his business, Foshan Plastic Sheets, in 1986.
By 1998, he had five employees, sales of 500,000 renminbi (RMB)
(roughly $60,000), and great ambitions. But it wasn't easy expanding
a business in China, which in 1998 was a poor country. Average GDP
per capita per year was a paltry $826, significantly limiting Wei's
market.[3]

The fundamental facilities and institutions that make market economies work were woefully underdeveloped in China. There were about
seven landline phones per one hundred people, compared to forty-four
in neighboring South Korea and slightly fewer than Ecuador, which

had eight per one hundred.[4] Hardly anyone had a mobile phone—about two subscriptions per one hundred people.[5] In addition, making calls was expensive.

The road system was dreadful, and the railroad system was also underdeveloped.[6] That made it difficult to move goods between the hundreds of cities in China and the vast rural areas. Businesses also couldn't depend on the slow-moving legal system, staffed by judges and lawyers with little or no knowledge of, or experience with, private business, to enforce contracts or property rights. Businesses couldn't trust people they didn't know.

Small and medium-sized enterprises (SMEs), like Wei's plastic factory, were penned into local markets. They depended on personal relationships with partners. When they bought raw materials or sold their products, they used cash. Doing business outside China was virtually impossible. Wei, for example, sold most of his annual production of plastic sheets to other companies near his factory. He knew the other owners he was doing business with. When he got a new customer, he usually insisted they pay him with cash when he delivered, and they inspected, the plastic sheets.

Despite these challenges, economic reforms had enabled Chinese entrepreneurs to create more than 154,000 SMEs in China by 1998.[7] Together with the elimination of most price controls and the privatization or closure of many state-owned businesses, the reforms spurred the economy. Between 1989 and 1998, average GDP grew at more than 10.2 percent a year.[8] A middle class was emerging that would drive the demand for the products of SMEs, including Wei's plastic sheets.

The huge frictions that SMEs in China faced presented an opportunity. Creating an online business-to-business (B2B) site to reduce the transaction costs separating business buyers and sellers was an obvious solution. China was connected to the commercial Internet that had taken off in the United States several years earlier. Many Chinese entrepreneurs, with an eye toward the US dot-com boom, had tried to start online businesses.

Friction is key to understanding whether an entrepreneur even has a hope of starting a viable multisided platform business. The reduction of substantial friction is a necessary condition, but not a sufficient condition, for a multisided platform to succeed.

The Value Pie

A regular business has to make sure that its customers are getting good value—that what they get is worth more than what they pay. And it has to ensure that it is making a profit—that the revenue it gets covers its costs and delivers a good rate of return for the business and its investors. It has to divide the value pie between itself and its customers so both it and its customers are happy.

A multisided business has a far more difficult problem. It has to make sure that not only do members of each of its customer groups get enough value to want to participate, but that enough of them participate to make members of each of the other customer groups want to participate as well—to generate the positive network or feedback effects that matchmakers need to survive and grow. Sometimes doing that requires giving such a large slice of the total value to one group that the platform doesn't make money from them. Recall that OpenTable didn't charge diners anything for making reservations and even gave them rewards for using its valuable service.

A multisided platform has to make sure that the value pie is big enough to give every group a large enough slice to convince them to stay, and to leave itself enough to cover its costs and provide a good rate of return. All else equal, the bigger the pie, the more likely there are large enough slices to make everyone happy.

Fundamentally, multisided platforms create value by reducing frictions. They are more valuable in total to all parties the more important the frictions they address are, and the greater their success at reducing them. Before OpenTable, people had to spend a significant amount of time making reservations at good restaurants for busy nights, and restaurants had to spend significant resources managing those reservations. Solving those frictions created a big enough pie to make all the stakeholders, the diners, the restaurants, and OpenTable significantly better off.

Some frictions aren't significant enough to sustain a multisided platform; reducing them wouldn't create much value. Americans can pay with plastic debit or credit cards at stores in a few seconds. It is hard to get them excited about paying with a mobile phone instead just to shave maybe a second off that process.[9] Several highly publicized attempts, by well-financed companies, to ignite mobile payments have failed. Indeed, as we discuss in chapter 10, even Apple has struggled to get its mobile payments solution, Apple Pay, widely used in the United States.

The smaller the value pie, the harder it is to slice it up in a way that gets all customer groups on board and leaves enough money for the platform. That's especially true when the platform must provide subsidies to a group that it needs to get onto the platform to attract the other groups it needs to generate profits.

An entrepreneur considering whether to start a multisided platform must consider what friction that platform would address, how much of the friction it could eliminate, how much value doing so would create, and whether that is enough to ignite a sustainable and profitable business. Anyone, from investors to suppliers to customers, who is taking a risk with a multisided start-up, should analyze these same issues to predict whether the platform could succeed.

Communication and Trust

In February 1999, Ma Yun brought seventeen colleagues together in his apartment in Lakeside Garden, in Hangzhou, to develop an e-commerce business focused on Chinese SMEs.[10] Known in the West as Jack, Ma was already an Internet veteran. Four years earlier, he had started China Yellow Pages, which provided listings of companies online for a fee, but he lost control of the venture to Hangzhou Telecom after their partnership deal turned sour. He then headed a company that set up trade websites for a government ministry. (It owned 70 percent; he had 30 percent.[11]) He quit that in frustration with government bureaucracy. His team left with him. They headed back to Hangzhou for their next adventure, with a lot of knowledge about working with small businesses in China and of the opportunities provided by the Internet.[12]

The team went to work, huddled together in Ma's apartment, to develop two related B2B online marketplaces. In March 1999, they launched alibaba.com, in English, to connect global buyers to primarily Chinese sellers. Ma chose "Alibaba" because the name and the tale were known around the world and had positive, magical associations. Later that year, they also opened alibaba.com.cn, in Chinese, to connect Chinese buyers and sellers.

Ma was clear about the friction he sought to reduce when he unveiled the business to the world. According to Reuters, Alibaba's view was that "poor telecommunications in Asia, particularly in China, make the Internet a fast and cost-effective tool for ensuring the flow of business information."[13] The site was designed simply as a communication platform to reduce the transaction costs of connecting sellers within China to buyers inside and outside China.

At first, there were no fees. Everything was free, as Alibaba worked aggressively to build a critical mass of buyers and sellers to do business with and attract each other.[14] Companies were given tools to create their own web pages on the new sites. That way, buyers and sellers could check each other out. By October 1999, more than forty-one thousand "subscribers" had set up free pages. About 55 percent were from China and the rest from around the world.[15]

Subscribers could also post offers to buy and sell. The websites organized products and services by categories, such as "industrial supplies" and subcategories such as "bearings." According to an archived snapshot of alibaba.com on a day in February 2000, there were 21,976 buy offers posted, along with 52,863 sell offers, and 275,879 responses between buyers and sellers.[16]

The Hengii Bearing Factory of Shandong China posted, for example, "my factory supplying the various type of bearings at low price, and supplying the various type carbon steel bearings at very inexpensive price." In the same section, Mantech International, based in Pakistan, posted that it was looking for a quote on particular kind of bearing.

Alibaba also provided an e-mail service called "BizMail," which enabled buyers and sellers to communicate directly with each other, as well as community chat rooms called "Biz Club." These efforts to enable buyers and sellers to communicate with each other and to do business online reduced a significant friction and helped ignite the new B2B marketplace.

By December 2001, Alibaba had more than 1 million "members."[17] According to one account, the number of members was increasing by one or two thousand a day. There were more than seven hundred types of products. The markets had become thick. One source observed that someone who wanted to buy a thousand badminton rackets "could find at least a dozen Chinese suppliers on Alibaba."[18]

The ability to communicate by e-mail, to interact in chat rooms, and to review company profiles helped reduce another major problem in doing business with distant, and previously unknown, buyers and sellers: whether they could trust each other. Nevertheless, trust was still a problem, particularly given the state of the legal system in China and the difficulty that any business has in dealing with problems with a distant buyer or seller when transportation and communications are poor. According to an Alibaba survey, "90% of businesspeople conducting business online cite 'Trust' as the most important factor in finding trading partners online, ahead of 'Quality' and 'Price.'"[19]

Starting in 2001, Alibaba set out to reduce this source of friction by creating International TrustPass, which was launched in August of that year. It launched TrustPass for its domestic site the next year. Alibaba provided authentication and documentation services for businesses in China and would even "use third-party corroboration to give objective evaluations of members."[20] According to Alibaba, "TrustPass's most innovative feature is the use of an open Feedback Forum, a live online platform in which members with TrustPass can view and post comments on the quality and service levels of other members."[21]

Over the next several years, Alibaba built more features into its two B2B websites to make it easier for buyers and sellers to find each other, to communicate, to consummate transactions, and to measure their trust in their trading partners. As Alibaba summarized the state of the sites in its 2007 prospectus, "Through active listings, inquiry exchanges, instant messaging, discussion forums and other easy-to-use community features provided by us, suppliers and buyers have formed large interactive online communities on our market places."[22]

During June 2007, TradeManager, its instant messaging tool, had a peak of 540,000 online users. There were over 200 online forums with more than 4.2 million registered users. By becoming "an efficient, trusted platform," it had gotten more than 20.9 million businesses on its Chinese community and 3.6 million on its international community, and it had grown into the largest B2B marketplace in the world.[23]

Alibaba succeeded by identifying and reducing key frictions that limited markets for Chinese SMEs. It believed SMEs in China confronted five challenges: "(1) limited geographic presence which restricts their ability to develop customer and supplier relationships beyond their local markets; (2) fragmentation of suppliers and buyers which makes it difficult to find and communicate with suitable trading partners; (3) limited communication channels and information sources to market and promote their products and services to find new markets or suppliers; (4) relatively small scale of operations which limits their resources for sales and market; and (5) absence of efficient mechanisms for evaluating the trustworthiness of trading partners."[24]

Consumers and retail businesses faced many of these same challenges. But there were other frictions that needed solutions as well.

Retail Frictions

By the early 2000s, China was booming. The average real GDP growth rate ranged from a low of 7.6 percent to a high of 11.0 percent between 1995 and 2004.[25] Retail spending was increasing rapidly as Chinese consumers, particularly urban ones, got higher-paying jobs and accrued wealth from investments in real estate and stocks. They wanted to shop.

Conventional retail businesses had trouble keeping up with consumer demand. China had few shopping malls outside of large cities and little retail space overall. The economic reforms had enabled markets and unleashed growth, but they hadn't reined in the local officials who stood in the way of anyone seeking to build brick-and-mortar stores. Getting a permit to build a store on the main street or build a shopping center could take a long time. Consumers couldn't find shops because retailers couldn't find space. That's a problem that continues to this day, especially outside of large cities.

Online merchants might have been able to fill the gap, but trust was the big problem there. Between the online retailer and the shipping company, consumers didn't have a lot of confidence that they would get what they ordered. It might never show up, it might be damaged, or it might not be what they had expected to get. They didn't know whom to blame. And even if they did know, they had little recourse. It wasn't like the United States, where consumers could pay with a credit card and get their card company to reverse the charge if they weren't happy.

Because of these frictions, Alibaba saw an opportunity to expand into consumer marketplaces. In the first half of 2003, it launched an online website called taobao.com. Small merchants and individuals could open up online stores where they could sell directly to consumers. Taobao entered into a highly publicized competition with eBay, which had bought a Chinese site, and succeeded in pushing eBay out of the market. Unlike eBay, Alibaba kept transaction fees at zero as it focused on building up scale, and its online stores offered fixed prices rather than auctions.

The next year, Alibaba introduced an escrow account to solve one of the major trust-related frictions in this marketplace. Using a new payment service, Alipay, a consumer would pay for goods when she purchased them and the payment would be deducted from her bank account.[26] But Alipay wouldn't release the funds to the merchant until the consumer verified that she had gotten the goods and was satisfied with them, or a certain period of time had elapsed without hearing from the consumer.

According to one online retailer, who used several e-commerce platforms at the time, Taobao had a much better system for monitoring buyers and sellers than its competitors did.[27] Before Alipay, a shopper had to go to a bank or post office to send the merchant a money order. After the merchant cashed the money order at a bank or post office, she would ship the merchandise. It usually took between fifteen and twenty days from the time she got the order until she shipped it.

Over the next few years, Alibaba also developed a highly sophisticated fulfillment operation. It partnered with companies in China that did the actual transportation, but Alibaba managed the process and maintained quality control. Once this system was in place, along with the escrow account and a rating system for sellers, consumers began to feel confident about ordering goods from merchants online.

The Alibaba Multisided Platform

By the late 2000s, Alibaba had evolved into a series of interconnected platforms with several sides in common (see figure 4-1).

FIGURE 4-1

The different sides of Alibaba's platforms

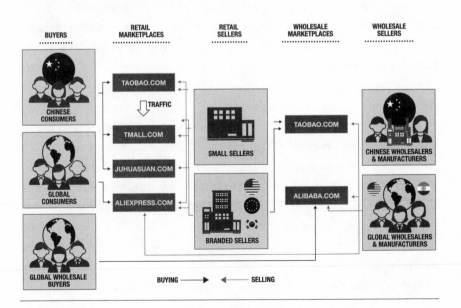

Today, there are the two wholesale buyer-and-seller B2B market-places, 1688.com for Chinese buyers and suppliers, and alibaba.com for international buyers and suppliers. Alibaba.com.cn was renamed 1688.com in March 2010. In spoken Chinese, "1688" sounds similar to Alibaba and to an expression for being on the road to prosperity, and is also easier for many Chinese to remember than a series of Roman letters.[28] Many of the Chinese buyers and suppliers also participate on the international platform.

There are two business-to-consumer (B2C) platforms—Tmall, started in 2008, specializes in branded goods and more upscale products, and Taobao for small merchants. Many of the retailers on Taobao and Tmall are also buyers on the B2B platform.

Alibaba also has other companies that provide services to these interconnected B2B2C marketplaces. They include its logistics part-ners, companies that provide various value-added services, and re-lated companies such as Alipay, which provides payment services, and Alimama, which provides marketing services.

During 2015, Alibaba had more than 367 million active buyers on its B2B platforms and more than 350 million storefronts on its B2C platforms.[29] Taobao alone had an average of 100 million unique daily visitors in March 2015.[30] For all its marketplaces combined, its gross merchandise value was $370 billion during 2014.[31] In September 2014, Alibaba had the largest initial public offering (IPO) ever on the New York Stock Exchange, and as of late November 2015, its market capitalization, exclusive of Alipay and some other affiliated compa-nies, was just under $198 billion.

The Western media and academics sometimes refer to Alibaba as the Amazon, or eBay, of China. It isn't. There isn't anything like it outside of China. In part, that is because it is the only major Internet property that has integrated marketplaces for B2B and B2C. Some of the difference is just cultural. But much of it involves features that are highly customized to solving problems—such as trust and com-munication—that have been more acute in China than in the United States or other developed countries.

Indeed, just because those frictions in China were large and pro-vided a value pie that enabled Alibaba to secure explosive growth and make enormous amounts of money, the same would not necessarily be true anywhere else. In fact, around the same time Jack Ma and his team were building their highly successful B2B business, hundreds of online B2B marketplaces in the United States were collapsing.

The Mass Extinction

By 2001, there were more than sixteen hundred B2B exchanges in the United States.[32] Most specialized in a particular commodity or group of commodities, such as the chemicals used in pharmaceutical manufacturing. They were among the market darlings of the Internet boom. A book published around this time was titled *B2B Exchanges: The Killer Application in the Business-to-Business Internet Revolution.*[33] Jupiter Communications estimated in 2000 that online exchanges would handle $6.3 trillion of B2B transactions, 42 percent of the total, by 2005.[34] Goldman Sachs was a bit less optimistic with an estimate of $4.5 trillion by 2005. In fact, by that year, virtually all of the B2B exchanges were dead.

Most of them went down soon after the 2001 dot-com bust.[35] It is hard to overstate the deafening silence that followed their collapse. Economists and business school professors had extolled the future of online B2B exchanges for more than half a decade, from 1995 to 2001. Analysts debated how big the B2B exchange business would be, and how quickly it would get there, not whether it would succeed at all. Venture capital money poured into the hundreds of start-ups that sought their fortunes in this new area. There were few doubters. Then, as simple search reveals, after 2001 hardly anyone talked about B2B exchanges anymore. There weren't even eulogies or postmortems.

Figuring out the cause of the B2B extinction is much simpler than that of the dinosaurs. In the United States, at least, there just wasn't a serious problem for which most B2B exchanges were the solution. Most business buyers and sellers didn't suffer from the problems that plagued their Chinese counterparts. They could telephone or fax each other for a pittance, and by the late 1990s, e-mail was in widespread use. The more sophisticated businesses could use electronic data interchanges to manage buying and selling. Large buyers, like Walmart, had set up portals to help handle suppliers.

There were lots of trade shows, a highly developed industry, where buyers and sellers could meet. It was easy for buyers and sellers to fly to Chicago where McCormick Place has trade shows constantly. It was also easy to ship exhibition booths around the country. Every business of any significance could get a lawyer to write or review contracts, and there was a well-developed legal system for dealing with problems that might arise. In short, there wasn't much standing in the way of small- and medium-sized businesses reaching a large national market if they had the right products at the right prices.

Some of the B2B exchanges argued that they could get the best prices for buyers. That was a great value proposition for the buyers. But the best price for buyers is the worst price for sellers. Sellers were reluctant to join these exchanges because, for them, it meant increased competition that would beat down their prices. The reluctance of one side to join a platform is not automatically a showstopper, of course. The B2B exchanges could have paid suppliers to join. That would have required the exchanges to generate enough value from solving frictions to benefit buyers, make a profit, and provide payouts to suppliers. Apparently, there wasn't enough value to go around to pay off the suppliers.[36] Most of the US B2B exchanges were similar to alibaba.com cn (later 1688, com.cn). They were like online malls. Unlike their Chinese counterparts, however, US sellers didn't need to use them to find potential buyers.

The B2B exchanges in the United States ultimately failed en masse because the friction they were trying to reduce wasn't significant enough to get enough buyers and sellers on their platforms. The value pie was too small. The buyers who joined early left disappointed because there weren't enough suppliers, and the early suppliers left disappointed because they weren't making enough profitable sales. The exchanges had trouble attracting other buyers and sellers to take their places because there weren't enough trades possible on the platform to make it worth their while to join. The exchanges couldn't grow, and because they couldn't get positive feedback effects from indirect network externalities working for them, they fizzled.

Clever Survivors

To be clear, there certainly were frictions in B2B dealings in the United States and other developed countries. They just weren't the same ones as in China, and they weren't as serious. They also weren't ones that many of the US B2B exchanges were set up to solve. And they certainly weren't large enough to support the valuations that the market initially placed on US B2B exchanges.

The frictions in the United States involved the back-office work of buying and selling. Large corporations did a lot of procurement by telephone and mail, and managed it with software programs running on mainframe computers that were primitive by the standards of the late 1990s. Most sellers sent out paper invoices. Buyers paid with paper checks that they sent through the US mail. Sellers wondered when their checks would show up, and often they didn't show up very quickly.

Companies like Ariba that focused on reducing *these* frictions for either side of the market were eventually able to attract enough buyers and sellers to survive. They provided an exchange platform so the two sides could do business with each other more efficiently. Ariba, in fact, started as a provider of modern software solutions for the procurement departments of large corporations. During the late 1990s, it was, in effect, doing for procurement what OpenTable was doing for restaurants—using modern software technology to solve specific one-sided problems.

Ariba realized that rather than connecting the procurement department of each buyer to individual suppliers, it could join them in a network. It opened ariba.com in 1999 as a network that moved from bilateral connections between buyers and sellers to multilateral connections among them. That got investors excited for Ariba's IPO. Caught up in the B2B exchange mania, its market cap rose to more than $40 billion in September 2000. It then fell to $1.1 billion by April 2001.[37]

After the dot-com bubble burst and the reality of B2B exchanges set in, Ariba went back to developing software solutions for the procurement departments of large buyers. It also started helping suppliers issue invoices and track their approval and payments. It took time for Ariba to have enough buyers and sellers on its network to support many transactions. By 2005, a decade after it had started, it began charging buyers and suppliers for transacting over its network as well as for the specific software solutions it sold them. SAP bought the reinvigorated company, one of the few B2B exchanges to emerge from the dot-com bust, for $4.3 billion in 2012.

Ariba had survived by focusing on solving very specific frictions faced by buyers and sellers, largely in operating their back rooms. "The B2B exchanges never really knew what they were going to do," according to Bob Solomon, a longtime Ariba executive, and the person who ran the network during most of the 2000s. "Ariba focused on using software to solve pressing problems for procurement departments, and later for suppliers. We eventually got enough buyers and suppliers on board to generate positive feedback effects and drive transactions through the platform."[38]

While Alibaba had quickly developed thick markets for narrow product categories, the US B2B exchanges had thin markets with few buyers and sellers. Alibaba secured critical mass, so that buyers attracted more sellers and sellers attracted more buyers, igniting sustained growth, while most B2B exchanges in the United States couldn't get critical mass and fizzled instead. We shouldn't underestimate how clever Alibaba was in building a sustainable business. Securing ignition is the hardest problem for multisided platforms to solve even if they are aimed at reducing a significant friction. Securing ignition is generally a race against time that most lose, though some win in spectacular fashion.

Chapter 5

Ignite or Fizzle

Multisided Platforms Must Secure
Critical Mass, or Else

N OW WHAT?
The three guys, all in their twenties, started working on
the website on Valentine's Day. People were posting short
videos on the web, like ones of the tsunami that had hit Southeast Asia a few weeks before, on December 26, 2004. But the clips
were hard to find. More videos were sure to come with the spread
of digital cameras, cheaper and faster broadband connections, more
and cheaper server storage, and better video software, particularly
Adobe's easy-to-use Flash 7.[1]

They had a first version of the website ready on April 23, 2005. It
was a simple place where people could upload videos and watch videos
that had been uploaded.[2] Except no one did either one.

It's not hard to see why. There was no reason why anyone should
come to their new website. There weren't any videos to watch. That's
because there wasn't any reason for people to upload videos to a
website that no one visited. Or, for that matter, had ever heard of.

This video-sharing website needed chickens, and eggs, and fast.
As happens with many great ideas, these guys weren't the only ones

who saw the promise of video on the web. Many start-ups, like theirs, were trying to figure out how to get uploads and eyeballs to watch them. So were some very large Internet companies. They were in a race to build traffic, even if they didn't necessarily know who else was in the pack.

Over the next year, the three guys—Chad Hurley, Steven Chen, and Jawed Karim—figured out how to secure a critical mass of people to upload videos and watch them. YouTube ignited and experienced truly explosive growth. Almost every other video-sharing site starting around the same time failed to get momentum and fizzled.

Solving the chicken-and-egg problem always looks easy in retrospect. In fact, it is one of the hardest problems any business ever faces.[3]

Critical Mass, Ignition, and the Coordination Problem

An entrepreneur who comes up with a new consumer product has to persuade retailers to stock it and then has to figure out a way to get consumers to buy it. If consumers don't buy the product, retailers won't keep it on the shelf.

On rare occasions, the product is so great that the main problem is keeping up with demand. That's what happened to Chobani when it introduced its Greek yogurt in the United States. More often, a company finds it hard to get buyers to try something new and to get enough of them to keep buying so that the company can make a go of it, even when the product is at least as good as its competitors.

A single-sided business, though, doesn't really face the "now, what?" question that faced Hurley, Chen, and Karim. The path forward may be difficult, but the direction is clear. When Hamdi Ulukaya was ready to market his first batch of Chobani yogurt, he knew he needed to get a retailer to stock it. That meant, as it turns out, persuading three small stores on Long Island that he had a good product and then hoping that consumers agreed.[4] It came down to consumer demand.

A multisided business, on the other hand, usually confronts the chicken-and-egg puzzle right away. A restaurant–diner matchmaker service, like OpenTable in 1998, would have seen a fogged-in thicket rather than a clear path forward. It would start by urging a restaurant to sign on. The restaurant owner loves the idea, but asks how many consumers the website has. If the answer is none, or few, the restaurant decides not to bother. The matchmaker encourages consumers to come to its web page. They love the idea too, just as they loved Chobani. But when they check out the page, they find that there are only a few restaurants or perhaps none at all. After one bad experience, consumers would be reluctant to try again, and they would likely warn their friends. There's a "coordination problem." Neither group will agree to use the service unless the other group does too.

Multisided platforms face this coordination problem because the fundamental product they are selling is providing one group of customers convenient access to one or more other groups of customers. There is no product for one group if the others don't show up.[5] Single-sided firms don't face this problem. They just buy the inputs they need, generally using well-developed supply chains, create their product, and try to generate demand for it. Chobani didn't need to worry about persuading the pasteurized milk it had ordered to show up.

Multisided platforms face another huge hurdle that is related to the coordination problem. They don't just need some customers from all sides to show up. They need enough to show up for it to matter. Without enough customers on all sides, a matchmaker is offering a lousy product.

Think about an individual walking into a nightclub, hoping to meet someone of the opposite sex. Many if not most people would turn around and leave if there were only a few potential partners. Nightclubs, like all multisided platforms, need to have enough participants from each side to produce the buzz that will keep participants from leaving and will get other people to show up.

"Critical mass" has become such a common business term that some may forget that it first became widely used in the 1940s to explain how much of certain forms of uranium or plutonium was needed to set off an explosive chain reaction. These so-called fissile materials are constantly emitting neutrons, and when a neutron hits an atom of one of these materials, the atom splits or fissions, emitting energy and two or more neutrons.

If there are enough fissile material atoms nearby, it is almost certain that these neutrons will split other atoms, thereby releasing more energy and producing more neutrons, and more splits. In very short order, this chain reaction causes the release of massive amounts of energy. In nuclear weapons, explosives are used to bring together enough fissile materials very quickly to exceed critical mass. It then takes only milliseconds for the number of neutrons splitting atoms to increase enough to create an explosion.

If there aren't enough nearby fissile atoms, too many neutrons fail to hit any, the chain reaction doesn't occur, and the whole thing fizzles. Physicists in the 1940s computed how much of each fissile material is the critical mass necessary for a chain reaction. For instance, a sphere containing 24.3 pounds (11 kilograms) of plutonium-239 does the trick.[6]

Business writers often talk about critical mass loosely, using the term to mean such things as how big a company needs to become to make money or to get costs down to a minimum. For multisided platforms, critical mass has a different, well-defined meaning, very similar to the one used in nuclear physics. It goes like this for a heterosexual nightclub:

The odds that any man and woman will like each other are low. A nightclub will become a success only if there are "enough" men and women at the club most nights so that club goers have a pretty good chance of meeting someone they like. The more people of the other gender, the higher the chances. Maybe some of them will pair off and stop coming, but others will hear good things about the club and will drop by.

There's a critical mass of participants when men and women both think it is worth coming, and at least as many new patrons want to come as old patrons want to stop coming. Below that point, though, either men or women or both don't find there are enough candidates to find matches. They stop coming and, just as in the physics of nuclear explosions, the thing fizzles. The nightclub owner needs to get the number of men and women just above critical mass to have a viable venue.

Matchmakers have more time than nuclear bombs to reach critical mass. How much longer depends on the business and the circumstances. There's nothing as definite as nuclear physics here. A lot of it comes down to momentum. Going back to the nightclub, if the early customers think it is good enough, and they find that the nightclub is doing a good job at getting new men and women to join, many will keep coming back and the nightclub's following will grow, and it will get to critical mass. On the other hand, without momentum, the longer a club lacks critical mass, the more people will perceive it as a dead spot to avoid, and the harder it will be to turn things around—not to mention the harder it will be to keep investors happy as the losses mount.

The economics of multisided platforms suggests some tactics for executing ignition strategies and avoiding the fateful fizzle. By studying multisided businesses, spread across many industries and over time, we can pull together many of the tactics that have worked in the past. In addition to doing that, we've also developed the theory behind ignition strategies to deepen understanding of the role of critical mass in multisided platforms.

Let's see how the YouTube guys did it.

Driving Traffic

First, they posted their own videos. They uploaded the first video on April 23, 2005—"Me at the zoo," an eighteen-second video of Karim in front of elephants at the zoo. They e-mailed friends and family to come watch and upload. Karim pleaded, "Can you help us spread the word? Since we just launched there are no girls in it . . . YET. Can you guys upload your own videos."[7] They had a dating component that suggested people could upload videos of themselves to attract the opposite sex.[8] They advertised on Craigslist, offering to pay women $100 to upload ten videos of themselves.[9] No one replied.

It was slow going over the next two months. Chen was "pretty depressed" in May, complaining, "Dude, we have like maybe forty, fifty, sixty videos on the site."[10]

They launched a new version of the website in June. It enhanced the viewing experience by making it easier to find related videos and to comment on videos. When they finally had enough videos, they were able to feature some of them. On June 14, these included "Kites," "Ibiza," "Bikes," and "Tim Sledding," all added the day before. They also had enough videos to create an index, but the list—which included tags such as "sad," "mallrats," and "malebear"—suggests how little they had to work with.

Over the summer, they launched several features that proved to be important for getting more people to upload and to watch videos. Most importantly, they enabled people to embed YouTube videos on MySpace, the most popular social network in the mid-2000s, and on personal blogs. That made it easy for people to make videos available to friends, thereby encouraging more people to create videos and upload them to the new site. It also made it easy for people to e-mail links to their favorite YouTube videos, including ones they had uploaded. These strategies increased the chances that people who wanted to upload and people who wanted to view would interact with each other.

By September 2005, the top bar on the YouTube website had tabs for Watch Videos, Upload Videos, and Invite Friends.[11] The second bar had MyVideos, MyFavorites, MyFriends, MyMessages, and My-Profile. The fourth bar, after the search box, had prominent buttons for Watch, Upload, and Share. YouTube had attracted enough videos that by September, the Watch button said, "Instantly find and watch 1000s of fast streaming videos."

Below these bars, "Today's Featured Videos" provided a list of popular videos. For each video, YouTube showed the number of people who had viewed it, linked to comments about it, and offered a five-star rating system. A few months later, right above the "Today's Featured Videos," it added a feature that showed recently viewed videos—"recent" meaning viewed a few seconds before.

The YouTube platform allowed people to upload pretty much anything they wanted. Some people uploaded clips of commercials that they found funny and portions of television shows. Someone uploaded "Lazy Sunday," a rap video that involved two white guys smuggling cupcakes into *The Chronicles of Narnia* movie, and it attracted more than five million hits. Another user's music video of the Mortal Kombat theme got more than twenty million hits. Some content owners complained that uploads of their shows violated their copyrights. YouTube had to take "Lazy Sunday" down.[12]

The site's traffic was driven by a very long tail of family, funny, and just plain stupid videos. Videos like "My Cat Stinky," while less popular individually, were nonetheless important in the aggregate.

For the results of YouTube's efforts at securing critical mass, see figure 5-1, which shows YouTube's daily reach (number of daily unique visitors per million people) between April 2005 and August 2006.[13] By August 2005, YouTube had a daily reach of around three hundred per million. Three months later, it had a reach of around a thousand per million. The number of videos uploaded each day increased from a

FIGURE 5-1

YouTube's daily reach

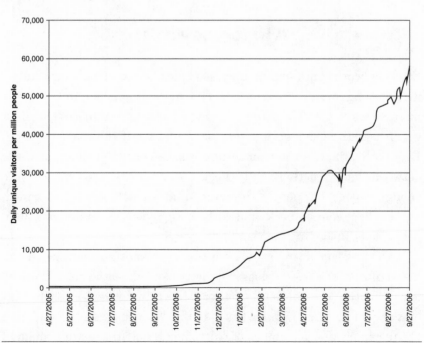

few a day to thirty thousand a day in May 2006. The stock of videos increased from forty to sixty in May 2005, to thousands in September 2005, to around 100 million by mid-July 2006.[14] The growth in traffic between April 2005 and August 2006 reflected the combined result of getting some people to come and watch videos and other people to upload them. The growth rate of traffic increased sharply between November 2005 and March 2006. YouTube *ignited* in that period.

We haven't said anything about YouTube making money. In fact, like Alibaba, it made the site free to both sides and focused on building up traffic. The founders knew that if they succeeded in doing that, they could open up the platform to advertisers. If advertisers knew that there was a critical mass of users, they would want to reach them, and that's where YouTube's revenue and profit would come from. That, in fact, is what happened, although it took longer for video advertising to take off than many anticipated at the time.

Google bought YouTube for $1.65 billion in October 2006. At that time, YouTube accounted for more time spent on the Internet than any other site in the United States.[15]

A Rigorous Model

YouTube worked at pushing up video uploads and video views during its yearlong march to ignition. The more it pushed uploads, the more views it got. The more it pushed viewing, the more uploads it got. It couldn't focus on just one side and expect the other to follow. Eventually, though, the momentum from the positive feedback effects between the two activities did most of the work. Because there were enough videos for people to watch, and enough new ones added, viewers kept coming back, and with enough viewers coming to watch, people kept uploading videos.

We've developed an economic model that shows in general terms how ignition works—or doesn't—for two-sided platforms.[16] The key feature is the "critical mass frontier" shown in figure 5-2. Each point on the critical mass frontier (such as the "3") consists of a number of Customer A's and a number of Customer B's. If there are enough of both then those participants want to keep using the platform. Moreover, in that case, there are so many of them participating that others want to join too. That results in ignition and self-reinforcing growth. There isn't a magic number of participants where this happens in practice. In the diagram it could happen at any of the points with numbers or any other point on the critical frontier. YouTube probably would have ignited if it had a somewhat different balance of uploaders and viewers. The critical mass frontier shows all the situations where there are just enough participants for growth. That's why we call the area to the top right of the critical mass frontier the "growth zone."

Below the critical mass frontier, however, in the shaded area, the platform is in deep trouble. If the platform gets stuck with too few of one type of customer, the other type will tend to stop using the platform. Moreover, new customers won't join. Unless something is done the platform will eventually go into a death spiral. That's why we call the area to the southwest of the critical mass frontier the "implosion zone." "The dead zone" would be another apt term for that area.

Figure 5-2 shows the challenge that a platform faces. The platform starts at the far southwest corner of the figure with zero participants on either side—just like YouTube did on its first day. It has to figure out how to push the number of participants up beyond the critical mass frontier. If it gets stuck along the way at low levels of participation, it will implode. That's what Steve Chen was worried about in May 2005 and what drove the YouTube guys into a frantic effort to get more uploaders and viewers. If YouTube had a large number of viewers with few uploaders, it would have failed, because people would have quickly seen most everything of interest and stopped coming. If "Lazy Sunday" had been all there was, even if it had driven massive traffic initially, it wouldn't have been enough to sustain growth. Similarly, if many people had uploaded videos and learned that nobody was watching, they would have stopped uploading, and the matchmaker would have fizzled. The YouTube guys figured it out. But most platforms, in fact, die on the arduous journey from the southwest corner to the frontier.

Ignition is not necessarily as hard for every platform as it is for the one depicted in figure 5-2. It is possible that a platform could ignite with a moderate number of participants on either side. In that case

FIGURE 5-2

Alternative critical mass constraints

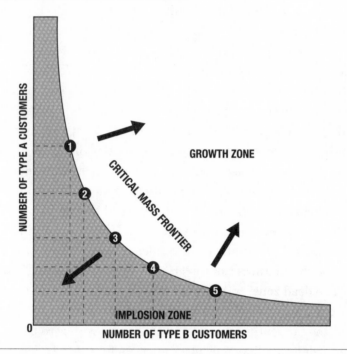

the critical mass frontier would be closer to the southwest corner. It might also be the case that participants on one side place a lot of value on having access to even a small number of participants on the other side. The situation shown in figure 5-2, however, is pretty typical in our experience.[17]

Either way, every multisided platform has to have a strategy for making the trek to the critical mass frontier from which they can survive and prosper.

Ignition Strategies and Tactics

Multisided platforms can adopt three main strategies for securing critical mass. The one that makes sense for a given company depends on the business it is pursuing and, to some extent, the particular circumstances in which it finds itself.

YouTube followed a *zigzag strategy*. It pushed participation by both sides simultaneously en route to critical mass. It didn't do this in lockstep. Instead, it engaged in multiple strategies to get more people to upload and more people to view. On some days, it likely focused more on one group than the other. Its upgrades in the summer of 2005 seemed aimed more at viewers than at uploaders, for instance. Alibaba also followed a zigzag strategy. It worked on getting Chinese suppliers and foreign buyers on board simultaneously when it first launched.

Some multisided platforms can, or must, use a *two-step strategy* to get to critical mass.[18] They persuade one group to join the platform, and once enough members of that group have done so, they persuade the other group to join. OpenTable ended up taking this approach to a significant degree. It focused first on signing up restaurants, and then, with enough of them on board, it recruited consumers. According to Chuck Templeton, it needed dozens of restaurants in each area offering each major cuisine to make sure consumers had enough to choose from to attract them to use the service.[19]

This strategy can work well for platforms that make money from advertising. They get people's attention—their eyeballs—by using various kinds of content as bait. If they manage to attract enough eyeballs, they can sell them in the highly developed market for advertising. Newspapers, magazines, and online publications of various sorts generally need to invest in content and attract eyeballs before they get interest from advertisers.

Many online attention seekers are three-sided platforms that combine a zigzag strategy and a two-step strategy. Their first step is a zigzag to get eyeballs. That's what YouTube did to get video uploaders and video viewers. Pinterest also did that to get people to pin pictures and to view pictures. Their second step is to get advertisers. YouTube showed its first video ad in August 2007 (twenty-eight months after its launch) and Pinterest in May 2014 (about fifty months after its launch).[20]

Some multisided platforms need to use a *commitment strategy* to get to critical mass. This approach is usually essential for platforms where one group needs to make investments to participate in the platform. Its members won't do that unless they have some guarantee that members of the other group with which they want to interact will show up. When Microsoft decided to enter the video game console business, for example, it had to persuade video game developers that there would be enough Xbox users for their games. Microsoft had to convince them that the Xbox was a great product, and it also committed to sell the Xbox at a low price as a way to persuade game developers that there would be demand for their products. [21]

Multisided platforms use a variety of tactics to implement these strategies. Self-supply is a common tactic to start. The platform supplies one side itself, rather than waiting for participants to join. Karim Jawed uploaded his "Me at the zoo" video, as well as videos of airplanes taking off, to create some initial videos on the new YouTube site. Apple didn't have an App Store, and didn't even make the iPhone available to developers, when it launched in June 2007, as we discuss in chapter 7. It put its own apps on the phone.

Getting some "marquee customers" on one side or both sides can help generate momentum. Shopping malls have perfected this tactic. They sign up stores that will attract a lot of foot traffic early on. The presence of these "anchor tenants" persuades smaller retailers to rent space at the mall because they anticipate that the marquee retailers will attract shoppers. Then when the mall opens, the anchor stores as well as the smaller retailers attract shoppers. Nightclub entrepreneurs use a variant of this tactic. They try to persuade a lot of "cool" people to come on the opening night. That generates buzz and creates momentum. OpenTable did this, too. By the time it got to New York, its third major city, it had started to go for the most popular restaurants in each city it entered.

"Make 'em believe," known more formally as shaping expectations, is perhaps the most common tactic used by multisided platform entrepreneurs. This sales job involves convincing members of each group that if they join the platform, members of the other group will be there too. If it works, this tactic builds valuable momentum.

Sometimes the vision, or the record of the entrepreneur, is enough. Max Levchin, one of the founders of PayPal and a highly respected innovator and entrepreneur, launched a novel and new consumer online transactional lending platform in February 2013, Affirm. He needed partners in the financial services sector to give him access to capital to lend to those consumers and merchants who would agree to accept Affirm as a method of payment. His reputation and success as a thoughtful innovator helped to secure both, which enabled him to get consumers on board.

Members of each group may believe that the platform proposition is so good that the members of the other group will believe, too. In other cases, the entrepreneur might stretch the truth and tell each side that the other side is already on board or exaggerate how far the platform has gotten in recruiting the other side. A more formal way to manage expectations is to get members of each group to sign conditional contracts obliging them to join the platform if the platform gets enough members of the other group or groups to join.

For all these strategies, it is important to remember the lesson that OpenTable learned. This isn't just a numbers game. Any new platform has to develop a thick market in which there are enough participants on each side that want to interact with enough participants on the other side. That often requires focusing efforts narrowly, as OpenTable focused on leading restaurants in only a few cities. PayPal used this approach effectively. It could have tried to persuade all online shoppers to get PayPal accounts and to persuade all the many online merchants that had started since 1995 to accept PayPal. It decided early on, however, that focusing its efforts would be far better.

According to one account, Luke Nosek, a key PayPal executive, had the crucial insight. "[eBay is] the busiest place for person-to-person interactions on the Internet. People from all over the Web come here to use this site. So, for PayPal to grow rapidly and expand all over the Internet, the quickest way to do that is to first grow on eBay!"[22] PayPal went on to develop a thick market on eBay, where it became the standard payment method. Eventually eBay bought PayPal.

Over time, PayPal has successfully expanded beyond eBay, so that many websites now take PayPal, and people are motivated to sign up for accounts even if they don't shop on eBay. As of the second quarter in 2015, around 78 percent of PayPal's volume occurred off of eBay.[23] Without the initial focus on eBay, it is doubtful that this online payments network would have ignited.[24] (Paypal and eBay split on July 20, 2015.)

The chicken-and-egg problem may seem unsolvable though successful platforms obviously figure it out. Most would-be matchmakers don't solve the puzzle.

Fizzles

Just look at all the video-sharing sites that started around the same time as YouTube, couldn't get enough momentum, and then fizzled. In May 2006, five video-sharing websites accounted for about 92 percent of traffic.[25] YouTube was one of them, as was Google Video. Google Video failed to attract significant traffic and was finally closed down in 2012.[26] It couldn't reach critical mass. Three other top-five competitors, Myspace Video, MSN, and Yahoo, still offer videos, but none is considered a significant video-sharing service. All likely survive as part of larger portals that feel they need to offer video sharing for credibility.

Brightcove's failed effort to ignite a multisided video platform illustrates how even well-funded start-ups with experienced entrepreneurs can get lost on the journey to critical mass.[27] Jeremy Allaire had served as the chief technology officer at Macromedia, the inventor of Flash, and had worked at a venture capital firm. He started Brightcove, having seen the promise of delivering TV over broadband Internet connections as an alternative to cable TV.

Brightcove wanted to provide a one-stop shop for Internet TV content providers, advertisers, and consumers. It planned to provide distribution services to content providers, including large ones like the *New York Times* as well as smaller ones that could make up the long tail; advertising, subscription, and other monetization methods that these content providers could use through Brightcove rather than having to create themselves; and delivery services to get content to consumers' personal computers, television sets, and mobile devices.

Brightcove adopted a two-step strategy like OpenTable's. It would first bring the publishers on board its platform by providing technology for delivering their content to various destinations. Content providers could upload content, have it encoded in the appropriate formats such as Flash, then put the content into players that they could make available to their own customers, using Brightcove's content delivery network. After getting a number of large and small publishers on board in this way, it opened the platform to consumers at brightcove.com.

The company encountered significant obstacles, however. Brightcove had become a successful technology provider to many premium video-content publishers. But those media businesses didn't want to help Brightcove build up its own consumer-destination site that would compete with them for eyeballs and the advertising revenue that comes from that attention. Brightcove had also focused its efforts mainly on securing premium content for which this conflict was particularly acute. It hadn't developed user-generated content from people who were happy just to make their videos available to everyone.

With limited content and significant competition, Brightcove had difficulty getting traffic. It couldn't reach critical mass, at least not in a time frame that was relevant to its investors and management. It shut down the consumer-destination site in April 2008. It switched to being a technology platform for premium content providers, and it has had some success in that one-sided business.[28] So far, it does not look as if it will follow in the footsteps of OpenTable and Ariba, both of which focused on building up one side for several years before launching successful two-sided platforms.

There is one important tactic that we haven't yet discussed. One of the things we've seen with all of the multisided platforms we've discussed so far is the importance of pricing. Alibaba, for example, gained incredible momentum in China by making access free for businesses to at least a basic version of its marketplaces. OpenTable found that it could reach critical mass by rewarding consumers but charging restaurants.

Companies usually need to stick with the pricing strategy they used during the process of getting to critical mass. The balancing act doesn't stop after they pass the critical mass frontier.

Chapter 6

Long Haul

How Balancing Prices Drives Value and Profits

D RIVING AN EIGHTY-FOOT EIGHTEEN-WHEELER BETWEEN Chicago and Seattle takes about three days. It's a nearly 2,100-mile trek, mainly on Interstate 90, heading north from Illinois, winding through Wisconsin, Minnesota, South Dakota, Wyoming, Montana, Idaho, and then across Washington almost to the coast of the Puget Sound. Along the way, the driver will likely visit at least one truck stop. There he can get a bite to eat, stock up on incidentals, fill his two-hundred-plus-gallon fuel tank with diesel, have a shower, and get some sleep.

Trucking is the most important way to move goods around the continental United States.[1] Fleet companies, some with hundreds of trucks, do most of the long-distance hauling.[2] Supporting these massive trucks and their drivers are sophisticated computer and communication systems. Among other logistical concerns, fleets have to track their drivers as they move across the country and make sure they get the best prices on fuel, since fuel—after the drivers—is their biggest variable expense.

The truck stop is an important component in the long-haul trucking system. Drivers refuel at least once on a 2,100-mile trip, but many gas stations are too small to accommodate an eighteen-wheeler, and not all carry diesel fuel.[3] And most drivers would like to eat, sleep, and shower during multiday trips. All told, there are more than twenty-five hundred truck stops near major highways, so that long-haul truck drivers usually aren't too far from one.[4] Many of the truck stops are parts of large chains, some of which, such as Love's Travel Stops, operate hundreds of them.[5] Across the country, every day, thousands of truck drivers pull into thousands of truck stops buying an average of about 100 million gallons a day at a cost of around $400 million a day.[6]

Most of them use a "fleet card" to pay. Truck drivers and truck stops can use it to settle up, and fleets can keep track of what their drivers are doing to keep their fuel costs low. Comdata, based outside of Nashville, Tennessee, invented the fleet card for long-haul trucking in 1981.[7] Since then, many other firms have started similar two-sided platforms for facilitating transactions between truck stops and fleets, executed by long-haul drivers. The same model has spread to short-haul trucking, which involves smaller trucks that often use gasoline instead of diesel. FleetCor Technologies, which now owns Comdata, and WEX, based in Portland, Maine, are two of the largest companies that provide fleet cards for long-haul and short-haul trucking.[8]

Over time, these fleet-card companies have had to make sure they priced their services right to both sides of their multisided platform to get both on board and to maximize the volume of transactions between them. This balancing act, which has been carried out during a period of tremendous changes in the trucking industry, illustrates some of the key principles of pricing for multisided platforms.

Dealing in Diesel on the Run

A truck driver takes Exit 67B off I-90 in Box Elder, South Dakota, and pulls into Love's Travel Stop, one of the three hundred truck stops this chain operates.[9] He can park his truck there overnight, get some sleep, and use one of its private showers to wash up. There's a convenience store and a chain restaurant, Hardee's, where he can get one of its famous Monster Thickburgers.

To fill up, he pulls his rig into the bulk-fueling lane.[10] To pay, the truck driver pulls out a plastic card with a magnetic stripe on the back that looks just like one of the debit or credit cards that you probably carry. Except that this card, which has a WEX Fleet One logo on the front, triggers a number of data streams that are much different from those triggered when a consumer makes a purchase at the local Walmart.[11]

WEX Fleet One generally allows a fleet to specify controls that prevent a truck driver from using the card to pay for things he shouldn't, such as beer, or at a truck stop that the fleet doesn't want him to patronize because its fuel is too expensive. It also provides the fleet with real-time data on where its driver has used the card and what he's trying to spend its money on.

If everything checks out, that card swipe sets several critical transactions in motion. WEX typically fronts the money for the truck fleet and pays Love's within about ten days.[12] It bills the fleet, which settles up a few days later. Because WEX might have advanced a few hundred dollars on this transaction alone, on an average day in 2015, the company had significant outstanding loans to the truck fleets using its service.

Chances are, the truck driver didn't just happen to pull into Love's. The fleets don't want their drivers to just stop anywhere. Responding to that need, the fleet-card companies have software that can direct a fleet's drivers to the nearest location with the best fuel prices. That's especially important for small fleets that can't afford to negotiate directly with the truck stop chains. WEX Fleet One probably served as a matchmaker between this particular truck driver for this long-haul fleet and this particular truck stop off of I-90 in Box Elder, South Dakota.[13]

The Balancing Act

Fleet-card companies, of course, would like to get paid for these services and make a profit. Each of these companies has to figure out the fees for the truck stops and the truck fleets. As in any other industry, the fleet-card companies have to worry about what their rivals are charging and how much their customers are willing to pay.

Unlike single-sided firms, each fleet-card company has to consider how its price to one group of customers affects the demand by the other group of customers. A fleet-card company that charged a higher price to truck stops would have a less desirable fueling network to offer fleets. A fleet-card company that charged a higher price to fleets would have fewer fleet customers and more trouble persuading truck stops to sign on.

Fleet-card companies have a pricing structure that balances these opposing forces. They typically earn the preponderance of their revenues from the truck stops rather than the truck fleets. WEX, for example, earns roughly three-quarters of its revenue from short-haul and long-haul trucking from truck stops.[14] Although rate structures vary, in a typical transaction, a fleet-card company might earn $2.00 from a transaction involving the purchase of diesel and other products by a truck driver at a truck stop. Of that $2.00, the truck stop would pay $1.50 and the truck fleet would pay $0.50, assuming it doesn't incur any finance charges from late payment.

The truck fleets pay a lower price mainly because they decide on whether a transaction is going to take place at all. If their drivers don't have fleet cards and permission to use them at a particular truck stop, that truck stop simply won't get any business from that fleet. Fleet-card companies therefore have strong incentives to price low to truck fleets to get their drivers to use the cards.

The large truck stop chains typically pay lower per-transaction fees than the smaller chains and individual truck stops. Of course, big customers get a break in many industries because a "yes" from a big customer brings more business than a "yes" from a small customer. But there's another factor at work in multisided platforms. Not only do bigger chains directly bring more business than smaller ones because they have more stores that they can commit to the fleet-card network, they can make the network more valuable to all truck fleets, and this brings the card network more business indirectly. With more total trucks affiliated, the card network is more valuable to all truck stop chains, including the tens of thousands of smaller ones. The bigger truck stop chains get rewarded for this contribution to the network's success, just as anchor stores at shopping malls get lower rental prices per square foot because their presence generates traffic for other stores, to which the mall can accordingly charge higher rents.

The fleet-card companies had to perform a delicate balancing act in setting their prices in order to make sure their prices attract both truck stops and truck fleets, and in the right proportion. They had to account for the strong positive feedback effects between these two sides. Finally, they had to make sure that they could make enough profit.

There's no way to know for sure whether fleet-card companies have struck the perfect balance. What we know for the larger players, such as FleetCor and WEX, is that with this pricing model they operate profitably, many truck stops accept their card, and many fleets issue their card to their drivers.[15] The fleet-card industry, following this basic pricing model, has made it possible for thousands of drivers to patronize thousands of truck stops every day and for fleets to manage one of the critical expenses of moving goods around the country.

Single-Sided versus Multisided Pricing

Of course, single-sided firms also establish price levels for their products. BMW, for example, has set the base price for the 2016 BMW 3 series in the United States at $33,150. Putting aside complications that arise because BMW sells multiple models, its pricing problem is relatively simple.

Like Goldilocks, BMW looks for a price that is just right: not too low or too high. Too low, and it sells a lot of cars but leaves money on the table. Too high, and it makes a lot on each car but doesn't sell many of them. To figure out the best price, BMW needs to answer only two questions: What does it cost to produce a car and ship it to a dealer? And how sensitive is consumer demand to price? If demand is very price sensitive, a lower markup over cost will make more profit because trying for a higher markup will sacrifice too much volume. If, on the other hand, demand is not very price sensitive, a higher markup will be better. Generations of Econ 101 students have learned the simple formula for finding the single-sided price that maximizes profit.[16]

In addition to its costs, in order to set the optimal price, a single-sided firm needs to know how price sensitive is the demand for its product? Of course, firms rarely know price sensitivity exactly. They may do market research to learn about it, or in principle at least, they can do simple experiments to find the best price. If BMW raises its price a bit and profits go up, it needs to keep raising price. If profits go down, on the other hand, it needs to lower price.

Because they are multisided platforms, the fleet-card companies, such as WEX, need to answer not just one but *four* questions: How price sensitive are truck fleets for fleet-card services? What about truck stop chains? How sensitive is the demand by truck fleets to participation by truck stops? And how sensitive is the demand by truck stops to truck fleet participation? WEX's problem is much more complex than that faced by a single-sided firm, and there are no simple market research questions or experiments that can reliably guide it to the optimal pair of prices. There is no substitute for a deep understanding of the firm's customers and for having good judgment.

Multisided firms need to consider the needs of the different customer groups that interact with each other on the platform. BMW sets one price to the one side of its business—car buyers—and that price will determine the demand for its cars. A multisided platform, in contrast, needs to recognize that the demand by any one group depends not only on the price, but also on the demand by the other group or groups it serves.

OpenTable had to take this into account when it set one price for diners and another one for restaurants. If a two-sided platform raises the price to one group, it gets fewer members of that group on board, which means that the platform is worth less to the other group. The platform must consider the fact that members of the other group might drop off, given that they have less access to the first group, and the firm would lose profits from that contraction. Of course, that would in turn lead to lower demand by the first group, then even lower demand by the second group, and so on. The right math takes all these positive feedback effects into account, and it sometimes yields counterintuitive prescriptions.[17]

As a two-sided platform, WEX needs to set prices for truck fleets and for truck stops together, because these two customer groups interact. Raising the price to fleets, for instance, will reduce fleet participation directly and, because truck stops care about fleet participation, it will also likely reduce truck stop participation. Both prices affect participation on both sides of the platform.

Price Level and Price Structure

What really sets two-sided platforms apart from single-sided firms is the importance of the *relative* prices they change their two sides. Matchmakers have to decide on both an overall *price level* and a *price structure*: how much to charge, and how much to earn from each side relative to the other side. For the truck driver transaction described earlier, the price level of the transaction was $2.00—$1.50 for the truck stop and $0.50 for the fleet. The price structure refers to the fraction of transaction revenue coming from either side.[18] In this case, the price structure was tilted toward trucks stops, which contributed 75 percent of revenue.

There are two sets of possible prices charged by a firm like WEX (see figure 6-1).[19] The per-transaction price to truck stops is denoted P^S, and the price to truck fleets is denoted P^F. Each line is the sum of the prices charged to each side, and the farther to the right the higher the total price. Points on a given line show the relative price charged to each side. The total price per transaction, P^T, is just the sum of these two prices: $P^T = P^F + P^S$.[20] Subscripts distinguish the prices at the points labeled 1 and 2. In this example the decrease in price results in a higher price for side S and a lower price for side F. In case 1, fleets pay a much larger share of the total price than do truck stops, while in case 2, their situations are reversed. If the firm began charging the prices at point 1 and then shifted to point 2, truck stops would likely complain that it had substantially raised its prices. In fact, the total price at 2, P_2^T, is lower than the total price at 1, P_1^T and the fleet price is also lower at point 2 than at point 1.

FIGURE 6-1

Price level and price structure for multisided platforms

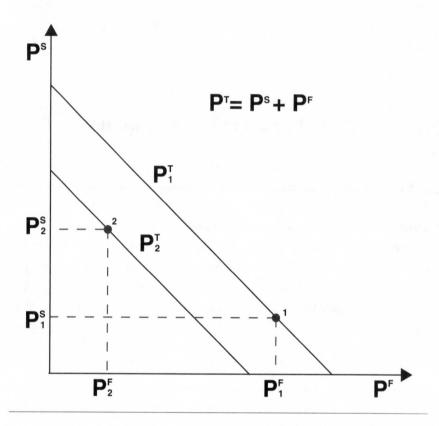

In both cases depicted in figure 6-1, one side pays substantially more than the other. While economic theory does not say that it is always optimal for multisided platforms to price this way, many do. They usually have a "tilted" pricing structure where one side seems to get a better deal than the other side. That's what we saw with fleet cards. The fleets paid one-quarter of the total price and truck stops three-quarters of it.

Setting the right price structure—the point on the downward-sloping lines in figure 6-1—is absolutely essential for running a viable and profitable multisided platform. The platform has to decide whether to adopt a flat pricing structure, so both sides are treated similarly, or a tilted pricing structure, in which one side does relatively better than the other. Sometimes, that means tilting the balance so far in favor of one side that the other side is paying 100 percent of the total price ($2.00 out of a $2.00 total price, for example). The second side could even pay more than 100 percent. That would occur if the first side got a $0.50 subsidy, for example, and the second side paid $2.50 to cover the subsidy; then the second side is paying $2.50 out of total price of $2.00.

Figure 6-1 describes a simple example and ignores the costs of actually serving customers on either side. In practice, in choosing a pricing structure, multisided platforms are looking at the profit margins on each side, given the costs of serving it, not just at revenues. Depending on the tilt of the pricing structure, the matchmaker may earn relatively more profit from one side than the other. As we mentioned in chapter 2, one of the remarkable things about multisided platforms is that sometimes they can make more profit by deciding to lose money on one side.

The Money Side and the Subsidy Side

Goldilocks could be sure of one thing while looking for just the right price for her single-sided firm. To have a chance of making money, she must set a price above her marginal cost, the cost of supplying another unit of output.[21] Clearly, she couldn't possibly make any money if she gave her product away for free.

That's not true for multisided firms. They can serve one group of participants for free, or even pay them to participate, and still make money. Google, for example, has never charged people to search, and its market cap as of November 20, 2015, was $527 billion, almost entirely from selling advertising to companies that want to reach the eyeballs its search engine assembles.[22] Some credit card companies give cardholders significant rewards when they make purchases with their cards. Their cardholders pay a *negative* price.

As we saw in chapter 2, many multisided platforms have a "subsidy" side, where the platform loses money for each participant that joins, and a "money" side, where the platform makes more than enough money to offset those losses.[23] For search engines, search advertising is the money side and organic search is the subsidy side, while for credit card transactions, merchants are the money side and cardholders are the subsidy side.[24] Platforms would prefer to avoid losing money on any side, but often that's not possible. If they didn't give participants on one side a free ride, or even pay them to participate, too few of them would get on board, and the platform wouldn't have anything to offer the other side.

We saw this with YouTube in the last chapter. In order to reach critical mass and maximize the size of its audience, YouTube didn't charge people to upload videos or watch them. Then it could deliver that audience to advertisers and get paid for it. Once that happened, it had to decide if it might make sense to raise prices to viewers, which meant weighing whether some viewers would watch less (or even stop watching at all) if they had to pay. If that happened, YouTube would make less money from advertisers that pay based on the number of viewers. The company had to measure the gain in viewer revenue against the loss in advertising revenue. For now, at least, it would appear that it has gone through this arithmetic and concluded that free is still the right price to viewers and uploaders.[25]

Some pundits talk about "free" as if it's a new business strategy. It isn't. Shopping malls, many newspapers, radio stations, broadcast television stations, yellow pages, credit cards, and many more matchmakers have followed this strategy profitably for many years. They probably did centuries and millennia ago as well.

The "free" strategy is just more common now because the Internet has enabled more rapid formation of multisided platforms and cheaper delivery of their services. For many online platforms, the cost of processing an additional transaction or managing an additional participant is very low, if not zero, so free is less of a stretch than it used to be.

Charging for Access

Platforms are almost always places—physical, or virtual, or both—that participants on each side need to get into before they can interact with participants on the other side. That often gives platforms the opportunity to charge participants for getting access to the platform as well as for interactions on the platform. Platforms that can observe both access and usage have to decide on an *access fee* and a *usage fee*. This adds another layer of complexity to platform pricing. Many matchmakers can use both of these prices to balance the demands of their customer groups, encourage interactions, and make money.

OpenTable, for example, charges restaurants a monthly fee for licensing the computer-based reservation system they need to get access to the reservation platform.[26] They pay $199 a month for the system. In addition to paying that access fee, they pay a $1.00 usage fee for every seat they fill through a reservation made on the OpenTable website. Diners do not pay an access fee or a usage fee— the whole thing is free for them, plus they get rewards (a negative fee) for usage.

To take another example, American Express charges cardholders an annual fee. That's an access fee to the cardholder side of the American Express network. American Express charges cardholders a negative usage fee; cardholders pay nothing to execute transactions and get rewards, just as they do from OpenTable. This encourages usage and makes accepting the card more valuable to merchants. Merchants don't pay an access fee; they can join for free. Having more merchants accept the card encourages consumers to carry it. Finally, American Express charges merchants a positive usage fee, around 3 percent of the value of each transaction. Cardholders value and pay for the option to use the card, while merchants value and pay for card usage in their stores.

At the Chestnut Hill Mall near Boston, there isn't an access charge for shoppers. Parking is free, and no one pays to go into the mall. But the retail stores there do pay an access fee—monthly rent for the space they occupy. Some of them may also pay usage fees, as many mall owners charge stores a percentage of sales volume. YouTube doesn't have any access fees for uploaders, viewers, or advertisers. Neither are there usage fees for uploading or viewing. There's just one positive fee—a usage fee for advertisers based on how many people view their ads.

The New Rule Book

Multisided platforms better get all these prices right. If they don't, they won't attain critical mass, won't make any money, and won't be in business long. Everything single-sided firms have to consider in making pricing decisions matters to multisided firms as well. But multisided ones have to answer several critical questions that single-sided ones don't worry about.

How sensitive is each group to price? This is all that matters to one-sided businesses, but it is just the starting point in analyzing matchmaker pricing. A platform can often charge a higher price to the group that is less price sensitive because it doesn't risk losing many customers that are valuable to the other group. Consumers are highly sensitive to prices for content on the web, for instance, and avoid sites with even small charges. Advertisers are less sensitive to pay-for-performance ad prices than to prices for other sorts of ads because they can make a significant margin when people click and buy.

Who needs whom, why, and how much? The answer is important for determining the pricing structure and whether to subsidize one group or another. Suppose members of the "desperate to meet" group place a very high value on getting access to members of the "be nice to meet" group. The platform might increase its profits by paying the members of the "be nice to meet group" to join, just to increase the number of members available to the "desperate to meet" group, which will then be willing to pay a high price for access. This provides a simple (if perhaps sexist) explanation for why nightclubs sometimes allow women in for free or offer them free drinks.

The Rosebar nightclub in Buenos Aires takes advantage of the differences between the sexes in an interesting (if even more sexist) way. The club has a VIP room with ample seating and free drinks. Any man willing to pay a very high access charge can go into the room, but only very attractive women are allowed in. And these women usually don't have to pay anything because they are invited by men in the club. The women can expect that most men in the room are well off, though some may be very unattractive.

Does one group control whether an interaction takes place? If so, since the platform won't get any usage unless the members of that group initiate an interaction, the platform may provide incentives—possibly subsidies—to get this group to use the platform. That's why American Express and OpenTable subsidize usage and why WEX Fleet One charges truck stops more than truck fleets.

This also helps explain search engine pricing. A consumer decides which search engine to use to look for reviews of new cars. The only way a car advertiser can reach that person at a time when that person is interested in new cars is to advertise on the search engine she chooses. Search engines have strong incentives not to charge searchers in order to be attractive to advertisers. Bing even provides "frequent flier" rewards just for staying signed in.[27] The search engines also share their revenues with other parties, such as websites and mobile handset makers, to make their engines the default choice for consumers.

In answering these questions, a platform needs to consider how to use access and usage prices. Platforms often do not charge access fees to a group whose participation creates positive indirect network effects, like merchants for American Express. When there are access fees, they are often combined with zero or negative usage fees, like for American Express cardholders. The platform collects a fixed fee but then encourages the participant to use the platform.

Monitoring costs are also important in setting access and usage fees. If it is costly to monitor usage or annoying to pay based on usage, it may be better not to charge a usage fee, even though an access fee doesn't reflect the platform's value to different users. The *Wall Street Journal* charges for access to its online content but not for stories read or time spent reading. Two people may pay the access fee, even if one spends a lot of time reading the *Journal* online, while the other one prefers old-fashioned newsprint and only reads online occasionally.

Despite all these complications, figuring out the right prices for a multisided platform isn't always difficult. Matchmakers that operate in competitive industries can more or less follow everyone else. A developer of a new suburban shopping mall really doesn't have any choice but to provide free parking and make its tenants the money side. An online media property knows that it probably can't charge people to view its site. Once it attracts enough viewers, its advertising rates will be determined in a highly competitive market.

On the other hand, pioneering multisided platforms may be free from competitive constraints but don't have models to follow when they launch. That was true for OpenTable and Alibaba. They were either smart or lucky and got their pricing right at the start. But just because a platform gets its initial pricing right, there is no guarantee that the balance they've struck between their sides will remain optimal. Circumstances in the market may change, as they did in the fleet-card business.

The Balancing Act on a Moving Train

Until the 1970s, truck fleets gave their drivers cash at the beginning of each trip to pay for fuel and other things along the way. If a driver ran out of cash, the fleet would wire him money. In the early 1970s, Comdata introduced a product that worked like a check to make this process easier.[28] Fleets paid Comdata a fee for each check transaction, and Comdata provided guaranteed payment to the truck stop for free.[29] This structure made sense. Comdata could deliver value to the truck fleets only if truck stops agreed to cash its checks.

Pricing in the fleet-card industry evolved from this early check model. Comdata issued the first fleet card and was followed by other firms. By offering to direct traffic from the fleets they had signed up to truck stops that agreed to pay a higher fee, the industry moved from the fleet-pays model to a flatter pricing structure in which the truck fleets and truck stops paid similar shares of the total per-transaction price.[30]

Then, in the late 1990s, the long-haul trucking industry came under severe economic pressure from rising fuel prices and increased competition. The fleets became much more sensitive to fleet-card prices. On the other side of the platform, there had been extensive consolidation among truck stops, giving a handful of large chains significant bargaining power.

In response, around 2000, the fleet-card companies moved from a relatively flat pricing structure to the tilted pricing that we see for most multisided platforms. Prices fell on average for the truck fleets and increased for the truck stops. The large chains got less of an increase than the small independents because of their importance in providing value to the truck fleets.

Over the course of more than forty years, the fleet-card companies—all of which had to respond to the same competitive pressures—have moved from a pricing structure in which truck fleets paid and truck stops were subsidized, to a relatively balanced structure, and then to one in which truck stops contributed considerably more to revenue than fleets.

Newspapers have also had to rebalance their prices over the last several decades. These two-sided platforms use content to attract readers and then make those readers available to advertisers. Print newspapers make money by charging readers for monthly subscriptions or for single copies at the newsstand and by charging advertisers for ads mixed in with the news or in the classified ad sections. Readers have generally paid less than the cost of printing and distributing their papers, though. They were the subsidy side, and the advertisers were the money side.

This business model started unraveling in the early 2000s with the explosive growth of the web, as we discussed in chapter 3. Online competition on both sides made readers and advertisers more sensitive to price. Newspapers responded in part by rebalancing their pricing.[31] Reader revenue accounted for no more than 20 percent of total newspaper revenue from 1997 through 2007. This percentage increased rapidly thereafter, and in 2013, reader revenue accounted for over a third of total revenue. Behind this trend are declines in both advertising revenue and circulation, coupled with increases in the prices readers pay that have kept reader revenue fairly stable. The ratio of reader revenue to average daily circulation rose by 34 percent over the 1997–2013 period and by 17 percent from 2007 to 2013 alone.

While this rebalancing has helped stabilize newspaper revenue, it has not been enough to save many US newspapers, as we discussed in chapter 3. Just as indirect network externalities can drive explosive growth, operating in reverse, they can make decline inevitable. When ad revenue declined, newspapers could spend less on content to attract readers and had to raise newsstand and subscription rates, thus reducing readership and thereby becoming even less attractive to advertisers.

Before they select a pricing policy, many businesses must choose how many sides to have on their platform or even whether to be a matchmaker at all. For example, on January 9, 2007, when Steve Jobs stood on stage at the Macworld convention to announce the advent of the iPhone, he had decided to operate it as a single-sided business where Apple provided everything including the apps. At that point, he only had to worry about how much to charge for the device itself. As you probably know, Jobs later changed his mind.

Chapter 7

Beyond the Castle Walls

Building a Platform and Ecosystem
That Can Create Value

T HE MOBILE PHONE LOOKED LIKE A RUNAWAY SUCCESS IN 2005. More than 1.5 billion people had one.[1] Mobile carriers were adding subscriptions at a rapid clip, and sales of handsets were keeping pace. The mobile phone was one of the most successful consumer products ever introduced.

The future seemed to look bright for the industry that year. The feature phones that most people had were only useful for making phone calls and sending text messages, but they were being replaced with phones with chips that made them handheld computers. These "smartphones" still had a small market share in 2005, but their numbers were growing rapidly. As faster mobile broadband connections became available, smartphones could be used to browse the web and stream music. The expectation was that eventually almost everyone would have one of these handheld wireless computers. That would put the power of computers and the power of the Internet into the hands of billions of people around the world. At least, that was the dream.

In fact, for those who really knew what was going on, the mobile phone business was a mess. Smartphones had rudimentary operating systems compared to those of personal computers. Most developers had given up writing apps for them. Every mobile carrier operated a walled garden for the handsets it offered: software developers needed to get a carrier's permission to put their apps on the carrier's phones. Most countries had several mobile carriers. Software developers had to do hundreds of contentious deals to get global deployment. They also needed to customize their apps for dozens of different handsets with different operating systems and hardware configurations.[2] The frictions that software developers faced were massive and stopped most from developing or distributing apps.

These new phones were smart, but their intelligence was being squandered. Unless something was done, it wasn't going to get any better.

Early in 2005, Apple and Google—two of the companies with the most at stake—set out to reduce the frictions that made "the software industry for mobile phones . . . one of the most dysfunctional in all technology."[3] Their efforts serve as a good illustration of how businesses design platforms and then nurture ecosystems in which those platforms can thrive.

There isn't a single best way to do this. In fact, these two tech giants succeeded with very different approaches. But each company applied the same general principles, and that's where we start before showing how the two of them, based nine miles apart in Silicon Valley, got their mobile operating systems on almost every smartphone in the world.

Creating Healthy Ecosystems

Multisided platforms are seldom self-sufficient fiefdoms where everything that's required for creating value takes place within the moat-protected castle walls. Matchmakers have to pay a lot of attention to their business environments. Their surroundings usually affect how easily platform participants can get together for valuable interactions.

To create a successful shopping mall, for example, a real-estate developer has to think hard about where to build it. The mall site must be convenient not only for shoppers but also for trucks making deliveries. That is, the site must have a good road system surrounding it. If such a system doesn't already exist, the developer may have to work with local governments to create it and may be required to pay some of the costs.

Roads are not the only things beyond the perimeter of a mall that can affect its ability to create value. If the surrounding towns are affluent, that can make a difference as to whether the mall wants to locate there and to its business model. If the region agrees to make the mall a stop on a major bus route, that could increase traffic to the mall. A regional economic decline, on the other hand, could reduce the mall's sales.

An ecosystem consists of all the people, businesses, institutions, and other things that, because they interact with each other, affect the value a platform can create. The ecosystem of Microsoft's Windows includes computer manufacturers and software developers, but also makers of mouse pads, keyboards, DVDs, surge protectors, and a host of other products, as well as providers of training and maintenance services.

For better or worse, the participants in an ecosystem depend on each other. A successful mall can boost business for nearby stand-alone retailers and restaurants, for example, while a vibrant community can help a nearby mall. On the other hand, the fact that Windows 8 wasn't popular with users was unpleasant for all firms in the Windows ecosystem.

Pioneering platforms have to make sure that they understand the ecosystems in which they are going to operate. They may have to devise specific incentives to encourage support from that ecosystem or to persuade participants to act in ways that benefit the platform and the ecosystem as a whole. Alternatively, they may decide to do without some potential third-party participants and solve some problems themselves. OpenTable, for example, could have waited for other companies to develop table management software and then try to build a business using their software to make reservations for restaurants and diners. It didn't have time to wait for that to happen, however, and it also needed an immediate way to recruit restaurants.

The Single Life

Any business needs to decide what it will do within its castle walls and what it will rely on partners or suppliers in its ecosystem to do. A fundamental choice for some businesses is whether to be single-sided or to be a matchmaker, and thereby give up some control to other members of the ecosystem. Of course, some businesses, like OpenTable, had little choice but to be matchmakers. Others, however, must decide whether to start out as a multisided platform or a single-sided firm, and some reverse their initial decision later on.[4]

Single-sided firms don't face the complex problem of getting to critical mass by attracting both chickens and eggs, but they can't use indirect network effects to trigger explosive growth. YouTube had some difficult months trying to decide how to get uploaders and viewers on its platform, as we have seen, but once it got enough of each, each group attracted more of the other, and YouTube's only serious problem was getting enough capacity to handle all the traffic. Other video-sharing sites faced the same problem, failed to solve it, and fizzled.

As we mentioned in chapter 6, one approach to attaining the critical mass necessary for a viable matchmaker is to start out as a single-sided enterprise. Palm was essentially a single-sided company when it launched the Palm Pilot personal digital assistant (PDA).[5] It avoided the problem of attracting app developers to a pioneering device by developing and installing a suite of apps itself. When the Palm Pilot became successful, Palm was able to become a multisided platform by attracting third-party app developers and hardware manufacturers.

In retailing, single-sided firms clearly have more control over their customers' experience, but they pay for it by having to raise more capital and incur higher operating costs. When Zappos decided to switch from being a mall for shoe manufacturers to being a one-sided online shoe store, for instance, it had to carry an inventory of shoes and handle shipping to customers itself, rather than relying on shoe manufacturers to perform these and other functions.[6] Similarly, Netflix has decided to operate as a single-sided provider of video content online. It pays producers of movies and television shows a fixed fee for the rights, often for several years, to stream their content to subscribers. The producers don't have any direct interaction with the subscribers. Like Zappos, with this single-sided approach, Netflix is completely in control of its customer relationships.

As a platform that enables drivers to deal directly with riders, Uber relies on its drivers to make some decisions that a single-sided firm might make for them. Uber drivers can decide when to drive and what to drive—subject to some constraints to ensure it is a good vehicle. But Uber controls the prices the drivers can charge. Technology has made it possible to apply versions of Uber's model linking service providers to customers in a wide range of other areas. For example, HourlyNerd competes with traditional management consulting firms by linking businesses and experts. And Coursera competes with traditional universities by linking teachers and students.

The kind of control that platforms of this sort maintain over service providers shapes providers' incentives, and these effects must be taken into account in designing the platform. For instance, if tomorrow Uber allowed drivers to set their own fares, competition among drivers would likely lower fares in the short run. This would make riders happier, as long as they could get rides. But lower fares would make driving less attractive, drivers would likely leave Uber, and a system with lower fares but fewer cars might well be less attractive to riders.[7] Multisided platforms have to consider the impact on the value of the platform of controlling some things itself and ceding control of other things to platform participants.

Amazon, unlike eBay, decided to start as a single-sided firm. For many years, Amazon was just a reseller, no different than Walmart. When it started as a bookseller in 1994, it bought books from publishers and resold them to consumers. It did not connect readers with publishers directly, something that a two-sided platform would do. As it expanded out of books, Amazon initially followed the same single-sided reseller model. From electronics to toys, Amazon bought goods, put them in warehouses, and then sold them to consumers.

Amazon's initial decision made sense for what it was trying to do in the United States. Unlike China, where Alibaba initially set up Taobao as an online mall, there was a well-developed offline US retail market. But consumers still had to spend time going to stores, and brick-and-mortar stores have space constraints that limit their inventory. There are millions of books in print at any one time, but no store could realistically have them all on its shelves.

Amazon provided a "vast selection online"—more than 2.5 million titles as of 1997—and made it easy for people to order them.[8] People had access to more titles than a bookstore could offer and didn't have to leave home to buy them. Amazon extended this same model based on scale and convenience to the other categories of merchandise it sold.

When Amazon launched Amazon Marketplace in 2000 and allowed third-party sellers to reach consumers through its website, it mainly relied on those other members of its ecosystem to decide what products to offer at what prices. But, as we note in chapter 9, it has exercised some degree of control on Marketplace participants by imposing rules against various sorts of bad behavior.

A Little Bit Single, A Little Bit Multi

Entrepreneurs often don't have a stark choice between being only a single-sided firm or only a multisided platform.

Microsoft, for example, operates Windows as a three-sided platform. Developers have created more than 16 million apps for Windows, which has increased the value of the platform to users, and competition among computer makers has dramatically reduced the price of computers using Windows for end users.[9] But Microsoft also operates a single-sided business right alongside this platform. It develops apps for the Windows operating system.[10] One of those apps—Office—accounted for more revenue than Windows itself in 2013.[11]

Windows is an example of a *vertically integrated platform*, depicted in figure 7-1. There are two groups of customers, A and B, just as there were in our basic description of a two-sided platform shown in figure 1-1. But in the case of this platform, the Customer B's are complementary products, such as QuickBooks, that Customer A's can use with the platform. The platform operator supplies some of these complementary products, just as Microsoft does with Office. Some vertically integrated multisided platforms, like Microsoft, operate significant businesses in competition with other participants on the platform.

By 2014, more than two million third-party sellers were using Amazon Marketplace to reach consumers. Consumers who search

FIGURE 7-1

A vertically integrated platform

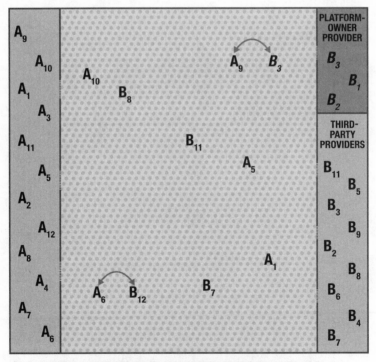

The platform facilitates interactions between two types of
participants, A and B. *B* indicates products or services provided by
the platform owner, and B indicates products or services provided by
third parties that are unaffiliated with the platform owner.

for items on Amazon see offers from Amazon's store and from the third-party stores. By 2014, more than 40 percent of the items sold on Amazon came from the third-party sellers.[12]

Amazon is an example of a hybrid *reseller platform*. In this case, as depicted in figure 7-2, one company operates a platform that helps connect consumers and sellers (like Amazon Marketplace), and a traditional store that buys from third-party sellers and resells their merchandise directly to consumers (like Amazon's direct to consumer business).

Amazon and Microsoft are examples of businesses that have blended significant single-sided and multisided businesses. Some multisided platforms are just a little bit single; they have a small degree of participation on one side as a supplier or reseller. Microsoft's

FIGURE 7-2

A reseller platform

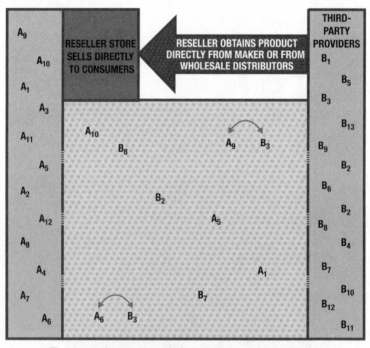

The same entity operates a platform that helps connect producers
and consumers who then do deals and a store that buys from
producers and sells to consumers.

Xbox Studios publishes games for its Xbox platform. Some single-sided platforms are just a little bit multi; they provide a platform for competitors to reach their customers. Tencent, for example, earns most of its revenue from providing games for its users, but it allows third-party game developers to use its system as well.

When, Where, and How Many

Pioneers have to decide how many sides to have for their platforms, when to open up each side for participation, and, in some cases, with what configuration to start the platforms. We don't want to suggest that successful pioneers usually start with a master plan. More likely, they make some of these decisions as they go along and, if they are lucky or good, discover the right strategies for ignition and growth as events unfold in the marketplace.

Facebook, for example, started with a social network at Harvard University in February 2004. This two-sided platform connected senders and receivers of messages. It then expanded the social network to include other colleges, high schools, and eventually everyone, in September 2006.

Facebook became a three-sided platform in mid-2004 when it started selling advertising. It had advertising revenues of only $382,000 that year. Apple and Victoria's Secret signed on in 2005. Other advertisers followed. Facebook's user population grew explosively, and it invested in developing tools for advertisers. Its advertising revenue reached almost $11.5 billion in 2014.[13]

Three years after its launch, in May 2007, Facebook announced a software platform developers could use to create apps, which opened up a fourth side. Some developers, like Zynga, wrote games such as Farmville, which drove significant traffic. It created a fifth and sixth side by allowing businesses to set up brand pages and send messages to, and receive messages from, people on Facebook. Figure 7-3 shows the architecture of this six-sided platform as of 2015.

Adding more sides to a platform may increase the number of positive, indirect network effects, which could increase growth-driving forces. But it also creates a more complex business model. Microsoft, for

FIGURE 7-3

Facebook's six-sided platform

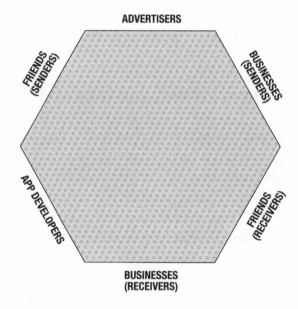

ADVERTISERS

FRIENDS (SENDERS)

BUSINESSES (SENDERS)

APP DEVELOPERS

FRIENDS (RECEIVERS)

BUSINESSES (RECEIVERS)

Note: Facebook connects friends with each other, enables advertisers to send advertisements to "friends," enables businesses to send and receive messages from friends, and enables app developers to create apps for friends and businesses and for friends and businesses to use those apps.

instance, has had to deal with a large number of personal computer manufacturers, each with their own preferences and objectives, while Apple has been able to optimize how its Macintosh hardware and software work together.

Sometimes, what looks like a potential new side, isn't. Microsoft approached a number of firms seeking to have them manufacture the Xbox game console, just as third parties had manufactured all the computers running the Windows operating system. No manufacturers were interested, however, since consoles are the subsidy side of video game platforms. Microsoft has ended up manufacturing the consoles itself.[14]

It Seemed Like a Good Idea, But . . .

In early 2005, Apple and Google faced all the issues we've described. What should they do to create a healthy ecosystem for their mobile phone businesses? How many sides should their businesses have at the start? Should they be single-sided, multisided, or a mix of both? When should they open up new platform sides? Others had already started multisided platforms in the smartphone space. Perhaps they could learn from them.

Symbian was the smartphone operating system leader in 2005. It began in 1998 as a joint venture by several handset makers and a small software provider in London to develop an operating system for smartphones.[15] The handset makers worried that if they didn't create their own operating system, Microsoft would control the dominant mobile system, and they would have to license it, just as personal computer makers had to pay for Windows.[16]

Symbian's strategy appeared to work at first. Its operating system was installed on almost 60 percent of smartphones sold between 2004 and 2008.[17] That was 5.5 times more than the Microsoft mobile operating system. Handset makers sold almost 78.7 million Symbian smartphones in 2007.[18] Developers had written around 10,000 Symbian apps.[19] As of 2006, six of the largest handset makers, including Nokia, which sold half of the phones in the world, owned and supported Symbian.[20] It looked everything like a successful two-sided business.

Below the surface, though, Symbian was paralyzed by frictions. It had become an accomplice in creating the mess that Apple and Google wanted to clean up. Symbian couldn't do much to reduce those frictions, however. The way it was constructed meant that its software providers couldn't introduce the sorts of innovations that were driving the personal computer and web economies.

To begin with, each of Symbian's handset-maker owners wanted to differentiate its own products. Given its ownership and governance structure, Symbian had to go along. It developed multiple user interfaces for the handset makers, which could then choose among these and customize them further. Between the differences in software environments and phone features, software developers couldn't just write an app for Symbian as they could for the Mac OS or Windows for desktops. They had to tailor their apps for each handset maker. According to one former executive, "the mixed platform control—between Symbian and its handset companies—meant that developers often had trouble finding the right information about APIs [application program interfaces] or other development questions."[21]

In addition, Symbian's handset-maker owners were beholden to the mobile carriers that distributed more than 90 percent of mobile phones.[22] The handset makers had to go through them if they were to have a chance to sell a significant number of phones. Nokia, for example, was barely present in the United States, despite being the leader elsewhere in the world, because the large mobile carriers in the United States wouldn't sell its phones.[23]

Symbian was obliged to reflect the interests of its owners. It was in no position to stand up to the carriers. That made it hard for Symbian to roll out new features for its operating system. Each mobile carrier had restrictions on what Symbian handsets could do. "I remember one case where there were 10,000 requirements to get Symbian products onto that one carrier's network," according to a former Symbian executive. "A typical carrier requirement would [be] anything from do or don't include Wi-Fi support to where things showed up on a menu."[24] Symbian couldn't build a new release and roll it out globally to its handset-maker partners. It had to engage in many individual negotiations with carriers and make modifications to the operating system as a result.

Symbian also wasn't in a position to help software developers in their negotiations with the mobile carriers to make their apps available on Symbian phones. Even software developers that worked for the mobile carriers had problems. A senior Android developer recounted his experience working for Orange, a UK-based mobile carrier. He couldn't get the company to approve a mobile phone app because it would cannibalize its thirty-year-old legacy technology.[25]

The Symbian experience showed Apple and Google that just starting a two-sided platform and securing customers on both sides wouldn't be enough. The platform would also have to nurture a healthy ecosystem around it. Symbian couldn't do that. If anything, Symbian contributed to making its ecosystem more dysfunctional.

In 2005, when Apple and Google started looking into how to reduce the frictions in the mobile phone business, it wasn't obvious what sort of platform they should build or how they should go about nurturing a healthy ecosystem around it.

Maybe One Side Is Enough

Steve Jobs, having created a highly successful music business around the iPod, was worried: "The device that can eat our lunch is the cell phone."[26] People wouldn't need iPods if handset makers built music players into them. To protect its music franchise, Apple put together a partnership in 2005 that included Motorola, to manufacture a phone with a built-in iPod, and Cingular (then the largest US carrier, which became AT&T Mobility in 2007), to distribute it. They released the ROKR in September 2005. The reviews were not kind.[27] Sales were disappointing.[28] "Jobs was furious," according to his biographer.[29]

Apple decided to make a phone itself. Sixteen months later, on January 9, 2007, Jobs previewed the iPhone to the world.[30] Apple designed the phone and then outsourced its manufacturing. All the phones Apple sold were iPhones. It had total control over its handsets.

The company developed a mobile operating system, iOS, which adapted the Mac OS operating system used in its Macintosh personal computers to the new mobile device. No other handset makers were allowed to use it. Apple also adapted several of its desktop apps, such as iTunes, for iOS, developed some new ones like Calendar, and included Google Maps and YouTube on every iPhone.

No other app developer was able to get access to the iPhone. "[Jobs] didn't want outsiders to create apps for the iPhone that could mess it up, infect it with viruses, or pollute its integrity."[31] (Developers could, however, write web-based apps that worked with the Safari browser on the iPhone.)

Finally, Apple entered into exclusive contracts with a single mobile carrier in each country to distribute the iPhone. The contracts were long—four years in the case of AT&T, Apple's partner for the iPhone in the United States. In return for exclusivity, the carriers essentially gave Apple complete control over the handset. Based on the consistent iPhone interface, carriers did not seem to be allowed to block Apple apps or features, and they couldn't install their own apps. Exclusivity didn't come cheap for Apple in the United States. Since AT&T's share of US mobile connections in the second quarter of 2007 was only 26.2 percent, the iPhone wasn't available to 73.8 percent of subscribers unless they switched carriers.[32]

The iPhone was thus a single-sided business when Apple made the first iPhone available on June 29, 2007. Apple made the handset, the operating system, and most of the apps. It just needed to get the subscribers of the mobile carriers, the ones it did exclusive deals with, to buy its new phone.

Herding Cats

Larry Page was as worried about the mobile phone as Steve Jobs, but for a different reason.[33] Google made its money serving ads on the web that people accessed from desktop computers. With the explosion in mobile devices, Page thought it was clear that most people were eventually going to move from fixed to mobile devices.

Google had experience developing apps for mobile phones and knew it was a nightmare. It had to develop for hundreds of handsets and carriers. If people started using mobile phones instead of personal computers, Google, and everyone else who had become accustomed to a smooth experience online, would have trouble. Google was also concerned that Microsoft would extend its dominance in personal computers to mobile phones.

In the spring of 2005, Page met with Andy Rubin, an entrepreneur who had a vision for cleaning up the mess in the mobile phone industry and had started developing a platform to do so.[34] The idea was to create a mobile operating system provided under an open source license so that anyone could take it and modify it, and any handset maker could install it for free. Within weeks, Google decided to buy the company and its software, both called Android, and to bring Rubin and his team on board to help the search-engine giant shake up the mobile phone business.

Rubin and his team had made great progress by the end of 2006. They needed to make sure that the operating system could support innovations on the handset and that the handset could support innovations in the operating system. While Google wasn't planning to make its own phone, it did develop two prototypes for the software development team to use. They were called "Sooner" and "Dream." The Dream had a touch screen; the Sooner didn't. As of early 2007, the Sooner launch was scheduled for the fall of 2007, while the Dream was still in early stages.[35]

A few days into the new year, Jobs previewed the iPhone, with its large touch screen and cool looks. Google scrapped the Sooner and reached for the Dream.

Google had planned to create partnerships within the ecosystem to launch Android. Apple's strategy made this easier. The handset makers didn't have an operating system that would enable them to compete with the iPhone. Symbian and Windows Mobile weren't up to the task.[36] Mobile carriers that didn't have long-term exclusive deals for the iPhone were faced with years of competing with a rival that did.

On November 5, 2007, ten months after Jobs previewed the iPhone, and four months after its release, Google gave the world a peek at Android. What it showed, though, wasn't a phone with hot features and cool apps. It was a framework for organizing the ecosystem and a consortium called the Open Handset Alliance (OHA).

Mobile carriers and handset makers were leery of getting locked into any single operating system. Google used a commitment strategy to solve this problem. It released Android under a license that enabled anyone to use the system for free and to modify it if they wanted.[37] The handset makers didn't need to depend on Google to update the system. Anyone or any coalition could build its own version of Android. "Free" was an attractive price for the cost-conscious handset makers. Until Android, the cost of the operating system and other software was about a fifth of the cost of a handset.[38] A free operating system could lower the price of the handsets and stimulate adoption.

Google's decision to make Android available under an open source license, however, risked creating the same fragmentation that had held Symbian back. There was what economists call a collective action problem. In total, the mobile carriers and handset makers would benefit from a standard operating system that could attract many apps and users. Individually, each would benefit from making its operating system slightly different from the others to attract more users who liked its distinctive features.

To remedy this, Google organized a coalition of handset makers, mobile carriers, software developers, and other members of the ecosystem. They all agreed to maintain a standard version of Android. Google developed a certification process to ensure that handset makers complied. That way, handset makers could ensure users and developers that apps developed for the standard version of Android would work on their devices. Google had assembled thirty-four members of the OHA by its launch announcement. *That*—the organization of the ecosystem—was its big news on November 5.

A week after the OHA announcement, the company made the Android system available to software developers, along with a developer kit to help build apps. It even set up a contest for the best apps, with a deadline of April 14, 2008, and put up $10 million in prize money. It also made its own popular apps, such as Google Maps, available after porting them to the new operating system, to enhance the value of Android phones. Thus, Google started with a multisided platform.

Google still had the mobile carriers and their walled gardens to deal with. For many mobile carriers, Apple's arrangements with their competitors softened their resistance to ceding control.[39] In the United States, for example, Verizon, which had had an unfriendly relationship with the search giant, encouraged Google to provide a phone that would enable it to compete with AT&T's popular iPhone.[40] Google softened up the carriers even more by giving them most of the commissions from distributing apps.[41] One by one, the walls came down, and the carriers signed on.

When it came to deploying phones, though, catching up with Apple was hard. The first Android 3G phone, the HTC Dream, released on October 22, 2008, achieved only moderate success against the 3G iPhone that had been released that July. The real battle wasn't to start until November 6, 2009, when the very successful 3G Motorola Droid appeared.

Two Is Better Than One

After the June 2007 iPhone launch, Jobs reconsidered his opposition to third-party apps. Eventually, and after discussions at four board meetings, Apple decided to permit them.[42] Jobs announced this move in an open letter to developers on October 17, 2007.[43] The company released its software development kit in March 2008 and launched its App Store in July 2008. Developers could only get their apps to users through Apple's App Store, and Apple got to decide whether to make an app available. It developed strict standards and processes for testing and reviewing apps. A year after its launch, the iPhone was a two-sided platform connecting users and app developers.

It turned out that third-party apps were important for getting users interested in both new smartphones. Apple and Google both invested great effort in stoking the supply of third-party apps, touting how many they had, and making it easy for users to get them. In 2015, Americans spent 71 percent of their time with apps when using their smartphones.[44] Handset makers made investments in other operating systems at the same time they were working with Android. We suspect that one reason they did not sell many phones based on those operating systems is that there were very few apps for them. Google succeeded in getting a thriving community of app developers around Android, as Apple did around the iPhone's iOS.

A Healthy Ecosystem and Explosive Growth

Apple and Google took different approaches to building mobile platforms and organizing the surrounding ecosystems, but together they eliminated the major frictions that existed in the mobile phone business in the 2000s. Software developers can now write apps for iOS and Android and distribute those apps to people worldwide regardless of their mobile carrier. By and large, mobile carriers don't get in the way anymore. They aren't able to prevent users from getting whatever apps they want. Apple and Google also make sure those apps run on most handsets using their operating systems.[45]

Both platforms enjoyed explosive growth, driven significantly by the positive feedbacks between app developers and users. Figures 7-4 and 7-5 show the growth of mobile phone subscribers and apps for each operating system. By 2015, more than 452 million people were using iPhones around the world and 2.47 billion people were using Android phones.[46] The iPhone had about 1.5 million apps available, and Android phones had about 1.6 million. The head counts of users and apps don't tell the whole story, though. As of late 2015, consumers spent about twice as much time using apps on iOS devices than on Android devices, and app developers favored iOS devices because that's where they were most likely to get paying users.[47]

Symbian rapidly fizzled. The final blow came when Nokia dropped it in favor of Windows Phone (the successor of Windows Mobile) in 2011. Microsoft acquired Nokia's handset business in early 2014 and has invested in making its operating system more consumer friendly. However, only about 3 percent of smartphones sold in the first half

FIGURE 7-4

Global smartphone installed base

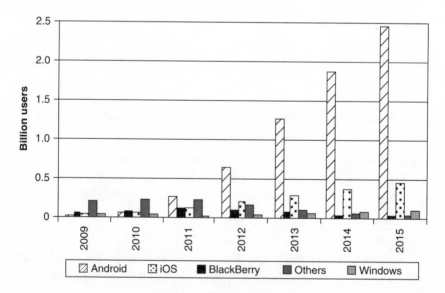

Source: Canalys, "Worldwide Smartphone/Mobile Phone Installed Base Forecast (Consclidated)," June 2015.

FIGURE 7-5

Number of apps by app store

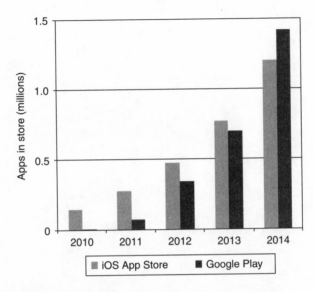

Source: "App Stores Growth Accelerates in 2014," appFigures Blog, January 13, 2015,
http://blog.appfigures.com/app-stores-growth-accelerates-in-2014/.

of 2015 used the Windows Phone operating system, and only about
385,000 apps were available for it.[48]

Apple and Android have been more successful than others at
making their multisided platforms for smartphones attractive to
users and developers. Much of that has to do with the inner workings
of the platforms. This chapter has looked at how multisided platforms
establish the perimeters of their platform to deal with the broader
ecosystem beyond. Next we go inside the platform walls and consider
what multisided businesses had to do to increase the quantity and
quality of interactions among the participants in the platform.

Chapter 8

Interior Design

Building Platforms to Maximize Activity and Value

THE UPSCALE AVENTURA MALL IS A FEW BLOCKS FROM THE BEACH in a suburb north of Miami. People from the surrounding area and visitors from around the world love it. It has even been described as "shopping heaven."[1] It has more than 300 stores, including six anchors, spread out over 2.7 million square feet on three levels.[2]

This chic collection of stores, the largest mall in Florida and the third largest in the United States, opened its doors in April 1983. A quarter century before, Harry Soffer, a mall developer from Pennsylvania, and several other investors bought more than 785 acres of land in South Florida. Soffer put his son, Donald, a Brandeis-educated football player who turned down the San Francisco 49ers to work for his father, in charge of developing the property. Donald Soffer and his team built a new town called Aventura, a golf course, luxury condominiums, and eventually the mall, which had 1.2 million square feet when it opened. They have worked since then to expand the mall and enhance its allure.[3]

They also had to design the mall so as to maximize its value to the stores, to shoppers, and, ultimately, to its owners. That meant figuring out the right mix of stores and negotiating deals with them.

It also meant working on the interior and exterior layout of the mall. In doing this, they could draw on decades of learning from other mall developers, going back to the Southdale Center, the very first modern shopping mall, which opened in Edina, Minnesota, in 1956 and was designed by the pioneering retail architect, Victor Gruen.[4]

All matchmakers, whether they operate physical or virtual places, face these same sorts of decisions. They need to figure out how to design their platforms to increase the chances that participants will be able to find each other and engage in mutually beneficial exchanges. They must construct the platform, whether from bricks or lines of code, and often develop tools that participants can use to find valuable matches.

The art and science of doing this varies from business to business. The new economics of multisided platforms, however, has identified certain basic principles that almost always apply. After we've discussed those principles and looked at an important example, we'll return to the mall.

Making Markets Thick

If you want to sell the antique cookbook you found in your grand-mother's attic on an online auction site, get a good price for it, and do it quickly, there have to be enough people who visit that site who are interested in buying antique cookbooks. If the site doesn't have very many people participating in it regularly, the chances are pretty slim that there's going to be someone interested in your cookbook. The more people that use the auction business, the better the chances.

eBay developed a "thick" market for obscure things. As it got larger and developed a reputation for being a good place to buy and sell obscure things, more people came to it to buy and sell obscure things. You'd have pretty good luck selling your antique cookbook on eBay. Back when people were selling junk at local flea markets, you probably wouldn't have been able to unload the cookbook or, if you did, to get much money for it. Local flea markets were too small. They were thin markets.

Successful platforms are designed to create thick markets. Consider stock exchanges. If you want to buy ten thousand shares of IBM common stock at the market price on June 27, 2016, at 11:30 a.m. EDT, there have to be enough sellers offering enough shares at the market price for you to do that, and if you want to unload ten thousand shares around that time, there need to be enough buyers.

Stock exchanges have traditionally relied on firms designated as "market makers" to make sure that markets are thick. Market makers are one side of the exchange platform, and ordinary investors—buyers and sellers—are the other side.[5] Each market maker would be responsible for one or more stocks. Whenever the market is open, a market maker would be required to post prices at which it would buy up to a stated number of shares of each of its stocks—the bid prices—and at which it would sell up to a stated number of shares of each of its stocks—the offer prices.

Market makers have to be compensated for performing this function. They bear risk, since they are required to take positions in stocks based on others' decisions—to buy ten thousand shares of IBM because somebody else just learned bad news about the company, for instance. Exchanges provided that compensation in part by designing the "tick size" for the exchange. The tick size is the fraction of a dollar in which bids and asks are made; it is now one cent on US exchanges, but it used to be measured in one-eighths of a dollar or 12.5 cents.[6] Bid prices must be below the corresponding offer prices by at least the tick size.[7] Market makers get to keep the spreads between bid and offer prices. A higher tick size makes market making more attractive. It also makes buying and selling stock more costly. To make sure the market is thick enough, with enough participants on both sides, the exchange has to balance those two effects in choosing the tick size.

Small Can Be Beautiful

Stock exchanges are not the only multisided platforms that have to make sure there are enough participants on each side who could benefit from getting together with participants on the other side.

To do this effectively, matchmakers must account for heterogeneity among participants on both sides and for the fact that participants' interests and desires may change over time. In general, each platform participant must have enough options so he or she can find a good match, given what he or she is looking for at any particular time.

Multisided platforms often have to choose between having a larger, more inclusive design or a smaller, more exclusive design. Successful matchmakers don't all make the same choice. The recruitment business for employers and workers is a good example. Some online platforms such as Monster allow every employer looking for workers and every person looking for a job onto their platform. They design large. Other platforms such as specialized recruiters focus on matching a limited number of prescreened employers and job seekers. They build their reputation on bringing good candidates to employers and good jobs to seekers. They design small.

Just getting lots of participants on all sides doesn't necessarily lead to an attractive platform.[8] Matchmakers need the *right* participants. A restaurant reservation platform needs to have enough of the right restaurants, in the right city, at the right time. It can't make up for this deficit by having many restaurants that aren't relevant to the people making the reservations, as OpenTable found.

Platforms sometimes add value by limiting their size. They focus on collecting the particular types of participants they want to connect with each other. Often they do this through a platform *screening device* that selects the right participants on one side. Then they seek the relevant group of participants on the other side who want to connect with that narrow group. Screening tends to make the platform smaller by discouraging participants who are not quite right from joining.[9] But it makes it easier for those who pass the screen to find a good match. The platform has fewer participants, but it can charge them more because it is generating better matches and more value for its participants.

One way to screen participants is by offering something that only the "right" participants want. *Hoist* magazine, for example, has articles of interest to overhead crane operators. It then sells advertising aimed at this group to companies that sell equipment that would appeal to them and their employers. That's much more efficient and cheaper for sellers of crane-related equipment than putting an ad in *People* magazine.

Another way to screen participants is to create a signal that certain participants should join and others shouldn't. Doing so in a way that works and avoids seeming discriminatory means setting just the right vibe.[10] FarmersOnly.com, for example, is a dating site that is designed to attract "single country gals" and "local farmers and cowboys" looking for potential partners. The company name makes its profile clear, and its home page pictures a couple standing in a pile of hay under a banner that says, "Single in the Country." By screening out "city folks" who "just don't get it," this dating site helps to create a thick market for country folks who want to get together.[11]

Multisided platforms may have another reason for limiting how big they are if the participants on one side do not like competing with each other.[12] The more competitors, the lower the value of the platform to each of them. Recall from chapter 4 that one of the problems the B2B exchanges had is that they created such intense competition that the suppliers didn't want to join. Some platforms limit the competition on one side to make the platform more attractive to that side. That then makes it easier to recruit members on the other side, something that then raises the overall value of the platform.

On the other hand, some platform participants are so attractive that other participants on the *same* side benefit from the traffic they generate.[13] Platforms can develop more attractive and valuable markets by getting more of these "marquee" participants. A mall does this by charging a low rent to stores that will attract lots of shoppers, who will walk past and perhaps buy at the other stores in the mall. A nightclub does the same thing by letting the hottest men and women jump the line to get in. While a particularly attractive man is competition for other men, other men are likely to figure that he will attract more than one appealing woman.

Yet another reason for limiting a platform's size is congestion, which can make it difficult for participants to search for and interact with each other. Physical limits require entry restrictions.

Popular nightclubs restrict the number of people who can get in, not just because they want to focus on the cool people. In addition to fire-code regulations that limit crowds, the nightclub needs to make sure people can move around and interact.

Platforms can reduce the effects of congestion by making it easier for participants to connect with each other faster.[14] It can take a long time for taxicabs and riders to connect in major cities. Some people who call for taxis end up hailing one because of uncertainty about when and whether the driver will show up. Ride-sharing apps, such as Didi Kuaidi, reduce this problem by using technology to enable drivers and riders to connect quickly and confidently. Search engines, to take another example, design their results pages to make it easier for people to find relevant organic and sponsored search results. Showing people too many items on one page makes it harder for people to find things, since each additional item adds congestion.[15]

Searching and Matching

A platform's design must do more than help get enough of the right participants. It also has to make sure interactions happen between them. After all, that's why the participants have joined the platform and how the platform owner makes money.

Matchmakers can often facilitate interactions by organizing participants around a standard that they all agree to use. The smartphone operating systems we discussed in the last chapter provide standard ways for app developers and users to interact. Software developers receive specific instructions, incorporated into "software development kits," on how to design their apps to work with each operating system. Twitter adopted a maximum 140-character statement as the standard method of communicating on its micro-blogging platform.[16] That told message receivers what to expect and message senders what to do. Although people could send multiple tweets to create a longer message, the platform was set up to encourage people to compress their message into the 140-character limit.

Certain physical platforms have devised ways to help participants look for good partners. A successful nightclub has an interior designed to make it easy and appealing to mingle. At farmers' markets or other bazaars where buyers enter, look for merchandise that interests them, and then negotiate with the seller, stalls are arranged to increase the odds that merchants get foot traffic and buyers find things they want to buy.

A platform *signaling device* provides a simple way for participants to find each other. Modern payment card networks did this with the "card bug" and the "acceptance mark." Merchants are supposed to post an acceptance mark in prominent places when they agree to take a card associated with a particular branded network such as Visa. Card issuers print a card bug on their plastic cards to signify that transactions made with that card are processed over the indicated network. A consumer whose US bank issues her a debit card with a Visa bug on it then knows that she can use that card at a petrol station in the south of France that has posted a Visa acceptance mark.[17] The acceptance marks were especially important signaling devices in the early days of the payment card industry, when relatively few merchants took cards.

Some platforms have highly complex computerized algorithms for matching participants. Google Search, with its sophisticated algorithms for matching keywords, websites, and advertising, is perhaps the most famous. Modern securities exchanges are based on computerized platforms for matching trades efficiently. Advertising networks can almost instantly match people and advertisers based on their characteristics so that websites can present ads that are relevant to each individual reader.[18]

Many platforms provide search and matching tools that, in terms of the level of sophistication, lie between the primitive approaches taken by nightclubs and the big-data approaches taken by search engines. Most Internet-based platforms, for example, have search buttons that people can use to look for participants on the other side. These are sophisticated enough to allow a YouTube user to find a crazy cat video or a diner to locate a Mongolian restaurant in the Chicago metropolitan area with a table available at 9:00 p.m. next Thursday.

Balancing Externalities

Oddly, many multisided platforms are in the business of matching up participants who ordinarily wouldn't want to get together. What is remarkable is that they have figured out ways to do this that makes everyone happy and generates profits.

Meet Annie, a confirmed couch potato, and Jack, the owner of Jack's Used Cars. Jack (and other advertisers) would like to present messages to people like Annie, because doing so will raise sales. But Annie, like most people, doesn't want to receive those messages. In fact, she may find advertising so annoying she would pay to avoid it, watching only HBO or Netflix, using DVRs to skip ads, and using an online ad blocker like AdBlock.

Here's a simple model to explain why it makes sense to push an unwilling participant (Annie) together with a willing one (Jack). Assume Annie would pay $5 not to have to watch ads for Jack's company. Jack, however, would pay $20 to get those ads in front of Annie. These two are not meant for each other—or so it would seem.

But there's a potential gain from their interaction. A platform could pay Annie $10 to view Jack's ad. Annie is then ahead $5 ($10 minus the $5 cost of doing something she'd rather avoid). The platform could charge Jack $15 for access to Annie's TV. Jack goes for this and is ahead $5 too ($20 minus the $15 commission). The platform makes $5 in profit ($15 fee from Jack minus the $10 payment to Annie). Everyone is better off.

Those economics drive the design of advertising-supported media businesses. Media businesses create content that they use to compensate people for receiving advertising messages. Instead of the platform paying Annie to meet Jack, it provides Annie with valuable content in exchange for listening to the possibly annoying ad from Jack's Used Cars. Feature articles in magazines, news and entertainment in daily newspapers, music and talk shows on radio, search-engine results, and television shows are all forms of subsidies—you could also call them bait or bribes—to attract viewers. Successful media businesses make enough money from advertisers to cover the cost of their content and make a profit.

Some advertising-supported media go further. They make it difficult to avoid the ads even at the cost of aggravating the reader.

Vogue, for example, buries the table of contents in the midst of many pages of ads at the beginning. The magazine then has many full-page ads that are unnumbered so that it is difficult to flip through the magazine to find a particular story.

Yet *Vogue* is successful because this is a good deal for both the reader and the advertiser. The reader bought a glossy magazine filled with articles she wants to read and perhaps even many advertisements she wants to look at. The price she paid at the newsstand probably doesn't cover the cost of printing and distributing the magazine, never mind the cost of generating the articles. Even though the design causes her some inconvenience, she is better off. The advertisers benefited from being able to reach her because it increases the chance that she will buy one of their products. And, of course, *Vogue* makes money by figuring out how to design a platform to get fashion-conscious women together with advertisers who want to reach them.

Platforms also engage in *search diversion*.[19] Karen wants the fastest, easiest way to find what she is looking for—a new pair of shoes for herself. But Maggie's Dog Boutique won't get a chance at any of Karen's attention because Karen just doesn't know what she is missing, even though she has a dog. A physical or virtual commerce platform might be able to come up with a design in which Karen is encouraged to at least consider Maggie's Dog Boutique.

Shopping malls are the leading practitioners of search diversion, but e-commerce sites often use a variation of this tactic by providing lots of suggestions for other things you might want to buy, based on your history or what you are currently considering. These recommendations can be distracting and may lengthen the shopping experience, but if they are well done, they may stimulate sales and increase customer satisfaction.

Anyone who visits a mall will see all these economic principles in action. So let's return to Aventura.

A Tour of the Mall

The Aventura Mall is on Biscayne Boulevard in Aventura, Florida.[20] From the main entrance, a shopper can drive to one of six major parking lots, each in front of one of the six anchor stores. JCPenney and Nordstrom are at one end of the mall and Bloomingdale's is at the other end. Sears is on one side, and Macy's and Macy's Men's & Home Furniture are on the other side. For a mall map of the first level, see figure 8-1.

Shoppers can enter the mall in various ways. They can go into one of the anchor stores directly. If they want, they can just shop there and go back to their cars in the nearby parking lot. Many shoppers, of course, go from an anchor store into the mall. Some might park outside an anchor store and walk through it to the mall with no intention of buying anything at that store. Shoppers can also go directly into the mall without passing through one of the anchor stores.

FIGURE 8-1

Map of Aventura Mall

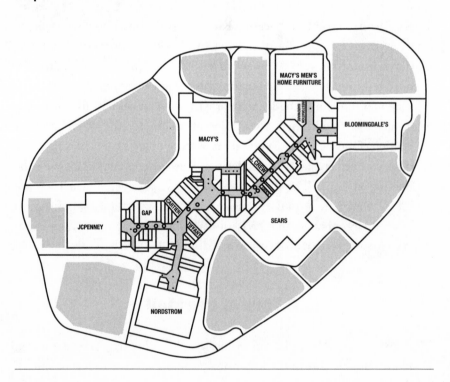

The mall has a center court with a three-story atrium. That leaves a large common space on the first level and a hallway that extends around the perimeter on the interior of the second level. More than 300 stores, such as Cartier and Adidas, are located off the common area on the first floor and along the second-floor hallway. There are a dozen dining places, such as Johnny Rockets, throughout the mall, as well as a food court with seventeen food vendors located in an open area with seating. The third level has an AMC movie theater.

The Aventura Mall "is not just for shopping and dining," according to its website. "It's also a place to be entertained." In addition to the movie theater, it hosts a regular farmers' market in the atrium, a pet-adoption event, and a chocolate festival. The center court is heavily decorated for the Christmas holidays, with a Santa's Village and more than a million sparkling lights.[21]

Selecting Stores

The design of the Aventura Mall is a very conscious one. The mix of anchor stores and the inclusion of the AMC theater are intended to attract different groups of people. The fact that the mall has a Bloomingdale's and Nordstrom also signals that it is a high-end mall. Each of the anchor stores likely draws a significant number of shoppers that the other stores wouldn't attract. The combination of these stores is meant to increase the number of shoppers who come to the mall mainly to shop at one of those anchors. The mall directory lists Aventura's non-anchor stores in twenty-two different categories. Some categories, such as card and gifts, have only one store, while others have many.

Consumers have a significant range of choices for shopping, although the stores are skewed more toward high-end places. This mall has both a Tiffany & Co. and a Cartier. It describes itself as a "Luxury Shopping Destination" on its website. A Google summary says that it is "an upscale super-regional shopping mall." The reviews describe it as a "chic" mall with "high-end shops." It attracts crowds of shoppers.

The selection of anchor and smaller stores provides a signal to shoppers.[22] Shoppers know to go to this mall for upscale shopping.

"Definitely not the type of mall where you come if you're trying to find some bargains," according to one visitor.[23] On the other side, since upscale retailers know that Aventura Mall has foot traffic with the kind of people who would likely buy from them, many luxury brands have stores there. The result is that both stores and shoppers are likely to find good matches.

Mall Layout

The physical design of the mall and the locations of its stores determine how people walk through it and what stores they encounter. The map in figure 8-1 shows that the mall isn't designed to minimize the amount of time people take to walk between stores. A consumer who wants to compare sweaters at Bloomingdale's and at Nordstrom has the longest walk. The perimeter walkway on the second level, around the atrium, eliminates the possibility of choosing the shortest distance as the crow flies.

The Aventura Mall is designed to encourage people who want to shop at multiple stores to walk a lot. "Take your walking shoes," noted one visitor, "you will need them."[24] Encouraging foot traffic means more people pass by each store and increases the odds that a consumer will come in and buy something. Stores benefit from this; shoppers don't. Some malls go even further by putting the up and the down escalators on opposite ends of the mall.

Store locations in the mall seem to follow some logical patterns. Stores that tend to attract similar types of shoppers are clumped together. The corridor leading to the Nordstrom stores is lined with luxury stores like Cole Haan, while the corridor leading to JCPenney has more down-market stores like The Gap. Tiffany and Cartier are located opposite each other. There is no corridor leading to Sears and few significant brands are nearby, reflecting the fact that it isn't a feeder of significant traffic to the luxury stores.

By locating similar stores close together, they attract more traffic—what is known as an agglomeration effect—while also increasing competition between them. These location decisions were likely made in concert with the stores, particularly the anchor stores, which have considerable bargaining power. Presumably, the agglomeration effects outweighed the competition effects for Tiffany and Cartier.

The Aventura Mall impresses visitors as a "beautiful and classy place."[25] That doesn't happen by accident either. Mall operators have to make sure that stores do their part to keep up appearances and provide good service, because that affects everyone. They also have to make sure that people behave themselves. To make their platforms nice places for their participants they need to have and enforce rules and, as we see next, most do just that.

Chapter 9

Fakesters and Fraudsters

Governing Bad Behavior by Platform Participants

LINDSAY LOHAN GOT BUSTED IN LATE 2008.[1] IT WASN'T FOR DRIVING drunk, doing coke, or lifting jewelry. Facebook caught the actress posting under an assumed name, a violation of its policy. The social network didn't kid around. It didn't offer probation, house arrest, or a nice jail cell as the City of Los Angeles did two years later. It just kicked her out. "All I can think is," she wrote on her blog, "WHO is running this site? And how can they just 'disable' my account without first, sending me a warning notice, or AT LEAST asking me some account verification questions."[2]

Expelling the star of *Mean Girls* was all in a day's work for Facebook's "User Operations" staff, which polices this massive community. Their work shows. Facebook is a much nicer place to hang out than was MySpace, the previous behemoth of social networks, which one commentator called a "vortex of perversion."[3] In addition to banning those who use fake names, Facebook exiles those who show too much skin, harass people, engage in hate speech, and even those who call someone a jerk.[4] It takes a lot of people to patrol a village as big as Facebook. Around the time Lindsay Lohan got caught out, Facebook had about 150 employees, almost a fifth of its workforce, looking for offensive content and misbehavior.[5]

It may seem odd for a private company to have a whole operation that polices, prosecutes, and punishes its own customers. But it makes sense when you think of Facebook as a community. One of the ways Facebook adds value is by providing a nice place for people, businesses, celebrities, advertisers, and developers to get together and interact.

Just as in any community, members can do bad things to each other. It turns out that Facebook has a lot of company when it comes to imposing rules on customers and kicking them off the property when they don't obey. Many multisided platforms have policies about things that participants better not do . . . or else. They punish participants that violate those rules. That includes bouncing them off the platform for good.

Lohan, in fact, belongs to a rogue's gallery of platform scofflaws that ranges from some of the most admired companies in the world to some very nasty people. Good governance is a critical component of operating a successful matchmaker.

Behavioral Externalities

If Lohan lived alone on a desert island, she couldn't harm anyone but herself by driving under the influence. There'd be no one to sideswipe. Once other people come to live on the island, though, there is a possibility that each of them could harm the others or maybe even help the others, Lindsay included.

Economists say there's an "externality" when people aren't compensated for providing a benefit to, or aren't punished for inflicting a harm on, other people. If Lindsay plants a beautiful garden near her hut, one that neighbors can also enjoy, that is a positive externality, but there's no externality if she harvests coconuts and sells them to her fellow islanders for bananas. She's helping them, but getting paid for her initiative. There is a negative externality if she makes a lot of noise shaking the coconuts down, annoys her new neighbors, and maybe even wakes them from their sleep.

We've introduced certain kinds of externalities already, when discussing indirect and direct network effects in earlier chapters. *Indirect* network externalities arise in a multisided platform when the value of the platform to members of one group is affected, usually positively, by the participation of members of another group, as when the value of OpenTable to diners is increased when more restaurants participate. *Direct* network externalities arise when the value of the platform to members of one group is affected, positively or negatively, by the participation of members of that same group, as when increasing the number of men in a singles bar (holding the number of women constant) makes the bar less attractive to each man.

The externalities we're concerned with here originate from the *behavior* of participants on matchmakers, not from the fact of their participation or the number of participants. Having Lohan on the island may, by itself, make her neighbors happier or sadder or not affect them at all. Her noise making or gardening, however, could have significant effects on their happiness. We'll call these sort of effects *behavioral externalities* to distinguish them from the network externalities with which this book is primarily concerned.

The ability of community members to impose behavioral externalities on other community members is one reason why societies adopt laws and regulations; establish police, courts, and authorities; and erect prisons for the worst offenders. Governments everywhere prohibit a wide range of behaviors that cause negative externalities, from littering to murder. They fine people, toss them in jail, and worse.

Multisided platforms are communities, too. Their whole reason for being is to provide a place for participants to get together. They are, in many respects, like villages, cities, and countries. Because there are lots of behavioral externalities that can increase or decrease a matchmaker's value, they need rules to make sure people and businesses that participate on the platform behave themselves. Successful platforms nurture the positive behavioral externalities and minimize the negative ones, particularly by discouraging participants from behaving badly.

Behaving Badly

Lohan hardly committed a capital offense by using a fake name for her Facebook page. It is easy to see why a celebrity might want to do that to interact with her friends while keeping her privacy. Allowing people to use fake names, however, can cause problems for others. Some people may just not like using a social network where some people aren't real. More seriously, there are real concerns that people could disguise their identity to do bad things. Sexual predation and online harassment are common problems.

Sadly, some members use social networks to inflict emotional distress, which can lead to suicides. A highly publicized case involved the use of MySpace by one Lori Drew to retaliate against a young girl, Megan Meier, who had a disagreement with Drew's daughter.[6] Using a fake account under which Drew assumed the false personality of a teenage boy, Drew orchestrated an online romance with Meier, had the fake boy become hostile, and eventually suggested that Meier kill herself. Soon after, Megan committed suicide.[7]

The full gamut of bad behavior that we encounter in society, as citizens, consumers, and merchants, can happen on multisided platforms. Participants sometimes engage in offensive behavior. Some post obscene material, engage in hate speech, or are just plain annoying. Of course, people lie about their age or their weight on dating sites.[8] Hooligans can trash a web-based community just as they can trash a shopping mall or a nightclub.

There is fraud and misrepresentation. Merchants, for example, sell counterfeit goods or take payment but then do not ship the goods.[9] That was one of the problems Alibaba tried to solve in China by putting payments into escrow until the purchasers actually got the product they had ordered and could inspect it.

Interactions become risky when platform participants aren't trustworthy. It is hard to know who is concealing information, promising more than they can deliver, or engaging in other shenanigans that maybe aren't illegal but are just opportunistic. Hidden information may produce the famous "lemons problem" associated with used-car markets. Sellers know whether a used car is a lemon—one with many problems—but buyers can't easily figure out which cars are lemons and which aren't. Buyers pay less for all cars because of the risk. But, then, people with good cars don't sell them because the price is too low. As a result, even more of the cars for sale are lemons.

Platforms can deal with this problem by preventing low-quality entrants from joining. Steve Jobs was worried that the iPhone would attract low-quality apps that would decrease the value of the platform. Apple solved this by imposing quality control on the apps it would make available in its App Store. This sort of quality control requires platforms to invest significant efforts into investigating participants and kicking out bad ones. Limiting a platform on one side to participants that exceed some threshold of quality necessarily limits the number of participants on that side.

Opportunistic behavior is a common problem that platforms have to deal with. Brokers on exchanges, for example, are often tempted to engage in what is called "front-running." Suppose a broker receives an order to buy so many shares of British Petroleum (BP) that its price is likely to be driven up. The broker would front-run by buying BP stock for its own account first, then placing the client's large order, then selling the BP stock it just bought and profiting from the client-induced price increase. Front-running hurts the client who is likely to have to pay more. All exchanges have rules against this practice and staff charged with detecting it.

In another example, online merchants trick people who pay with credit or debit cards by engaging in what is known as "drip pricing."[10] Once people spend the time going through the online checkout process and enter their card information, the merchant adds a surcharge for paying with plastic, assuming that buyers will be so far along in the transaction that they won't cancel it. Payment card networks have historically banned merchant surcharges; the drip-pricing problem has arisen in countries, such as the United Kingdom and Australia, that have required card networks to allow surcharges.

Bodily harm can occur on platforms as well. Sexual predators have used Craigslist to meet people they have raped or killed.[11] This concern is obvious when strangers travel together in automobiles. The French ride-sharing service BlaBlaCar, which has 20 million members in nineteen countries outside the United States, has taken great pains to deal with this concern. It verifies members' identities, requires them to supply photographs, and has drivers and passengers rate each other after every trip. Because women are likely to be particularly concerned, it has a "ladies only" feature that allows women to elect to travel only with other women.[12]

Negative behavioral externalities of the sort we've discussed here reduce the value of a matchmaker. They make participants less likely to join and more hesitant to engage in interactions even if they are on board. Platforms have strong financial incentives to limit this sort of bad behavior.

Of course, matchmakers lack some of the tools that governments use to deal with negative behavioral externalities. They can't get warrants to inspect private property, interrogate participants, or put people in jail. What they can do is act swiftly in identifying problems and dealing with them. The City of Los Angeles took years to put Lindsay Lohan behind bars for more than a day, despite repeated arrests for drunk driving and other offenses. Facebook could just disable her account.

Sometimes governments can't do anything, and platforms have the only available recourse. When Lori Drew engaged in her reprehensible activity, there were no laws on the books against it in the state of Missouri where she lived.[13] A social network could at least try to monitor these kinds of actions and, if nothing else, ban the user for life. Indeed, government laws and regulations may be so ineffective at dealing with bad behavior that they provide an opportunity for multisided platforms to create value by devising and enforcing rules.

Follow the Rules

That situation existed in England in the early 1700s, at the start of the Industrial Revolution. People had been trading shares of company stocks for many years and had more recently begun using option and futures contracts to speculate on future stock prices without actually buying shares.[14] The courts had decided that trading in options or futures was a form of gambling, however, and wouldn't enforce those contracts.[15] In fact, in 1734, the British Parliament passed Sir John Barnard's Act, which made trading options or futures illegal, though there doesn't seem to have been much prosecution.

According to Ranald Michie's history of the London Stock Exchange, "it was . . . left to the market participants themselves to create a code of conduct that enforced the conditions necessary for trade. Even without the legal impediments . . . those who participated actively in the market would seek to find a solution to their own problems among themselves."[16] Even though investors couldn't use the courts to enforce options or futures contracts, there continued to be active trade in them throughout the 1700s. That would not have happened if fraud had been rampant. In order to maintain market activity, honest brokers worked hard to protect investors from fraudsters, with no help from the courts.

Early in the eighteenth century, trade in stocks and related securities came to be concentrated in Jonathan's Coffee House, near the commodities exchange. At first, brokers who had reneged on contracts were physically ejected from Jonathan's. But as the market grew and Jonathan's became more crowded, there was apparently no way to keep ejected brokers from returning later when no one was watching the door. In response, the leaders of the market wrote the names of fraudsters on a highly visible blackboard to warn investors and other brokers.

During the rest of the century, leading brokers tried various ways of keeping fraudsters out so that they could offer investors an honest trading venue. After some time and several business models, they finally got it right on March 3, 1801.

The London Stock Exchange opened that day, but only to members who paid a significant fee.[17] The new exchange adopted a set of rules and regulations. According to Michie, "[a]dherence to these rules and regulations was monitored and adjudicated by a committee, including full-time administrative staff, and enforced by the threat of expulsion from the market."[18] Most of the regulations focused on creating trust among members, particularly involving payment and delivery. As a late nineteenth-century treatise put it:

> [The London Stock Exchange's] main objects appear to be the easy and expeditious transaction of business, and the enforcement of fair dealing among its members. To these ends . . . a set of results formed for the admission and expulsion of members,

and for the control of their conduct both between themselves and towards the public.[19]

Ever since, stock exchanges have adopted rules and regulations for ensuring that participants do not impose negative externalities by, for example, failing to fulfill their obligations or using opportunistic and nefarious methods for manipulating prices.[20]

Multisided platforms adopt rules and regulations even when platform participants could turn to the courts. Some of them adopt very extensive rules to do so. BlaBlaCar, for instance, has a particularly detailed set of "Terms and Conditions," violation of which is punishable by suspension or termination of membership.[21] And eBay has a link on its home page to a "Rules & policies" page, which in turn provides links to detailed policies on various matters.[22] According to the company, "Our policies are designed to create a safe and fair environment for all eBay members." eBay prohibits everyone from using profanity, misrepresenting their identities, or trying to consummate transactions outside of eBay.

eBay closely regulates transactions. It requires buyers to pay for items they commit to buy, prohibits them from bidding on things they don't intend to buy, and allows them to retract bids only under specific circumstances. It prohibits buyers from manipulating prices; they aren't supposed to help a seller by bidding the price up so that others will pay more.

Sellers have to sign a contract with eBay that imposes even more restrictions on them. eBay prohibits them from failing to deliver a product they've sold, from posting false or misleading content, and from manipulating prices. They can't sell some types of items on eBay including pornographic material, firearms, and counterfeit copies.

Some matchmakers carefully guard the gate to the platform to ensure that participants who could harm others don't get on board in the first place. As we noted earlier, any developer who wants to put an app on Apple's App Store, which is the only way they can realistically get their app to iPhone users, has to follow an extensive set of rules and regulations.[23] According to Apple, "[i]f your App doesn't do something useful, unique or provide some form of lasting entertainment, or if your app is plain creepy, it may not be accepted." (Apple also pulls apps that make it into the App Store if it decides later that they violate its rules.)

The company points to the negative externality that bad apps create: "We have lots of serious developers who don't want their quality Apps to be surrounded by amateur hour." And so, "[i]f your App looks like it was cobbled together in a few days . . . please brace yourself for rejection."

Deception is also out of bounds: "If you attempt to cheat the system (for example, by trying to trick the review process, steal data from users, copy another developer's work, or manipulate the ratings) your Apps will be removed from the store and you will be expelled from the developer program."

Getting apps through the approval process is "more challenging than ever," according to a blogger in charge of submitting apps for his company.[24] He found that the top reason for rejection is that "your content is boring." Apple responded to one submission by saying, "We found the experience your app provides is not sufficiently different from a web browsing experience, as it would be by incorporating native iOS functionality." The second top reason is "your design/layout needs a facelift." According to Apple, "Apple and our customers place a high value on simple, refined, creative, well-thought through interfaces."

Policing platforms, particularly sprawling global ones with millions of users, can require much effort. Internet-based multisided platforms have developed tools to help participants penalize members from engaging in bad behavior. The five-star rating system is common now and seems to be effective.[25] Uber passengers and drivers can rate each other, for instance, as can passengers and drivers brought together for longer trips by BlaBlaCar. In all these cases, passengers can decline rides from drivers with low ratings, and drivers can decline to pick up passengers with low ratings. These ratings provide incentives for participants to follow the rules, provide good service, and behave well.

Get Out and Stay Out

Most nightclubs have a device for enforcing rules: the bouncer— usually a big muscular guy. He tosses people out—sometimes literally—if they violate the rules by grabbing women, pulling out a knife, or throwing bar stools. He's also the guy who keeps out undesirable people. Given the potent mix of hormones and alcohol in many clubs, the bouncer provides the only way to maintain a nice environment where people want to socialize.

Ejecting participants is the ultimate threat that enables matchmakers to enforce their rules and reduce bad behavior. Many platforms make sure they are in a position to do this. They, too, have a "bouncer"—which might be based on software rather than brawn—to exclude participants who could harm the platform community.

OpenTable, for example, has a "no show" policy. Diners are required to cancel reservations they make through the platform at least thirty minutes in advance as a courtesy to restaurants.[26] The company advises people about its list of terms and conditions, to which diners must agree in order to use its platform, that it will monitor their cancellation behavior. It will cancel their accounts if they don't show up more than four times in a twelve-month period.

Platforms don't always choose to go to this extreme. Google, for example, imposes sanctions that usually stop short of permanent exile. In responding to a search request, its search engine gives more weight to websites to which many other websites link and that have keywords that are relevant to the particular request. It has rules, though, that prohibit websites from trying to inflate their rankings artificially. Websites aren't supposed to use "link farms" that charge websites for providing link or "doorway" pages that trick web bots into thinking that the website has more relevant keywords than it actually does.

In 2011, Google discovered that JCPenney was inserting keywords for its products in thousands of websites that linked back to jcpenney .com. This strategy catapulted the company's products to the tops of many search results. As a penalty, Google punished the company by manually lowering search rankings for its products for about ninety days.[27] While JCPenney had been the first result on the first search page when consumers searched for "Samsonite carry on luggage," during the penalty phase, it fell to the seventh page.[28] This penalty essentially knocked JCPenney off the search engine while it was in force, since hardly anyone ever goes that far down the search listings. That's known in the website business as going to "Google Jail."[29]

Having the right rules and enforcing them can make all the difference for a multisided platform. But sometimes the right rules are not at all obvious. The back-to-back demise of the two largest social networking sites in the United States shows the importance of having rules about "friends" like the sultry Tila Tequila.

Friendsters, Fakesters, and Fraudsters

Early on, Friendster looked like it was going to own the social networking category. Launched in March 2002, it grew rapidly, signing on more than three million users by November 2003.[30] Back then, most of the social networking sites were focused mainly on dating. But, as Jonathan Abrams, Friendster's founder, put it, they were "too anonymous and creepy."[31] Users couldn't rely on the posted information about people. Abrams pointed out that "[w]ith JDate, a guy is almost bound to be twenty pounds heavier or twenty years older than he is in his photo."[32]

Friendster decided to take a different approach. "We're trying to make the process more accountable," Abrams said.[33] The idea was that people would link to friends of friends. "People will put a more accurate picture of themselves on Friendster because you know your friends will see it."[34]

Unfortunately, the new social network hadn't anticipated that people would create fake profiles. The site was inundated with "fakesters" who made up fictional personas for themselves. According to Danah Boyd, a sociologist who has followed social networking from the beginning, "[f]akesters were created for famous people, fictional characters, objects, places and locations, identity markers, concepts, animals, and communities."[35]

While some of these were amusing and lovable, they made it hard to use the site for serious social networking.[36] Some of the fakesters attracted massive traffic, which congested the site's limited server capacity. One of them was a young Vietnamese model, Thien Thanh Thi

Nguyen, who called herself Tila Tequila. She attracted a large follow-ing in part by posting provocative photos of herself.

Friendster decided to send the fakesters into permanent exile.[37] But then, the fakesters organized themselves and attempted to reinsert their profiles. Friendster deleted Ms. Tequila's account several times. The fakesters also sought revenge on Friendster by having fraudsters masquerade as real people. Friendster's growth slowed considerably.

During this time of turmoil, a new social network, MySpace, launched in August 2003.[38] Its founders thought that Friendster was making a mistake in preventing people from having fake identities.[39] It welcomed the fakesters. Tila Tequila and many others abandoned Friendster and joined MySpace.[40]

MySpace grew very quickly, overtook Friendster, and was one of the most heavily trafficked sites on the Internet and the largest so-cial networking site in the mid-2000s.[41] But its "Everything goes!" policy soon caused problems. It did not require or encourage people to provide reliable information. That attracted minors who lied about their ages, as well as child sex predators who sought them out. The site didn't discourage people from having user pages with "partial nu-dity, obscenity, crude sexual jokes, and other objectionable content."[42] MySpace gained a reputation as a "vortex of perversion."[43] It was like the red light district of the web.

Nevertheless, a large number of people liked the risqué nature of MySpace. On the other hand, advertisers—who provided the principal source of revenue for MySpace—did not.[44] They didn't want to risk displaying their brands on pages with sordid content. MySpace re-sorted to using advertising networks to sell ads because it couldn't get major brands to buy space. Ad networks target people with ads based on what they know about those people and what they are looking at on the web page. Perhaps inevitably, many of the ads were for products and services that only advanced MySpace's seedy reputation.

Facebook, which started in February 2004, took a very different approach than either Friendster or MySpace. It adopted strict rules to prevent bad behavior, despite being started by and initially targeted to college students. Like Friendster, it focused on creating a platform for people to manage their relationships with friends. But Facebook required people to use their real identities. It initially limited access to the site to people with valid university e-mail accounts ending in ".edu," starting with harvard.edu accounts. It then expanded to selected groups, including businesses with identifiable e-mail addresses. When it opened to the world in September 2006, Facebook had five hundred regional networks based on e-mail addresses that tied the users to known organizations.[45]

This approach made it more difficult for people to use fake identities on Facebook. But it was still possible.[46] The company deleted the pages of people, like Lindsay Lohan, who violated its policies. But, by the time it had to start doing this, virtually everyone on Facebook was real because of the e-mail policy, and it had established the vibe that Facebook was the social networking site for real people who wanted to stay close to their real friends.

Facebook has also taken active steps to limit negative behavioral externalities on its site that would limit its appeal to new users and to advertisers who are considering inserting messages on its pages. Its terms of service prohibit various actions, including bullying, intimidating, or harassing any user; and posting content that is "hateful, threatening, or pornographic, incites violence; or contains nudity or graphic or gratuitous violence."[47] *Newsweek* called the Facebook employees in charge of this the "porn cops":

> User Operations looks at all content that users say is harassing (via "report this" links spread liberally throughout the site) or that shows drugs, nudity or pornography. It also maintains an extensive "blacklist" of forbidden names that cannot be used to make new profiles, like Batman. Some of this monitoring is quite small beer: you're not allowed to call someone a "jerk" on Facebook if someone reports it. Employees also vigorously enforce their "real-name culture."[48]

The treatment of negative behavioral externalities was a major factor in the rise and fall of Friendster, MySpace, and Facebook. Friendster had the right idea, but didn't put enough attention into designing the system for imposing and enforcing rules. MySpace thought that rules didn't matter. It was wrong. Even if people were happy coming to the site, advertisers weren't, and that strangled the money side of the platform. Bad behavior still happens on Facebook, just as it happens in every community. But this matchmaker with 1.55 billion monthly active users as of September 30, 2015, has devised and developed a system of rules and an enforcement division to make it as nice as can be.[49]

In this chapter and the preceding five chapters, we have taken a close look at some of the key decisions that multisided platform business must make. We now turn to the special challenges faced by platform pioneers and their investors. As they make the journey toward the critical mass frontier, how can they know whether they have made a wrong turn and need to adjust, whether they should abandon the trip, or whether they are about to cross the frontier into the growth zone? Let's follow one of the most successful matchmakers of all time on a recent trek.

Chapter 10

Fizzle or Sizzle

Making Smart Bets on New Matchmakers

FORTY-THREE MINUTES INTO THE APPLE LIVE EVENT, ON September 9, 2014, after introducing the new iPhone 6, Tim Cook announced he was going to talk about an "entirely new category of service" for Apple.[1] A thick wallet with cash and cards sticking out appeared on the screen behind him. "Our vision is to replace this."

According to Cook, people in the United States "scramble" for their cards about 200 million times a day, and they "go through what is a fairly antiquated payment process." A video showed a woman paying for some clothes. She fumbled for her plastic card in her pocketbook, presented it to the clerk, who then asked for identification. The clerk swiped the mag-stripe card through a clunky-looking terminal. Apple's CEO noted that the widely used mag-stripe card was based on a fifty-year old technology, wasn't secure, and was easy to lose.[2]

Cook then unveiled Apple Pay. He showed the same woman paying for her clothes, but using her iPhone 6. She held up her phone to a small elegant device on the counter, and she was done. It was fast and simple. Cook showed it one more time, "in case you blinked and missed it." "It's so cool," he exclaimed before passing the microphone to Apple exec Eddy Cue to dive into the details.

Six weeks later, on October 20, Apple turned on its new payment service. At the start of that day, not a single consumer had Apple Pay.[3] Users first had to activate it on their iPhone 6s. On the other side, most retailers didn't have the devices they needed to process payments with it. Apple was facing the sort of chicken-and-egg problem that some matchmakers crack and see their businesses sizzle, and that most don't, which makes them fizzle. The company needed to get both consumers and merchants on board and using the new service. Apple was no novice when it came to igniting multisided platform businesses. What were the odds that it would succeed?

What we've learned about multisided platforms in the last six chapters—from friction to rules—helps predict whether any particular new matchmaker will fizzle or sizzle. This guidance can help investors, including entrepreneurs themselves, determine whether their bet on a new multisided platform will pay off and whether they will need to change course during their early days as they see how things unfold. Anyone who is thinking of partnering with a platform, or joining one, would also benefit from knowing how much of a chance that platform has.

The Checklist

Starting a new shopping mall or magazine is pretty cut and dried, even though both are matchmakers. So many of these businesses have been started that it is pretty clear what makes them work. Launching a successful mall or magazine might be hard, and the venture might fail, but at least there's a well-known road map to follow.

That's not true for pioneers. They can't look at how similar matchmakers cracked the chicken-and-egg problem, figured out the right pricing balance, or designed their platforms to solve the myriad of externality problems these sorts of businesses face. All Apple really knew when it designed its payment service was that the companies that had tried starting mobile payments in the United States—including Google and a joint venture of three of the four largest mobile carriers in the country—were struggling.[4]

While there is no step-by-step guide for creating a successful multisided platform, we can at least come up with a checklist of things that a pioneering matchmaker should consider before it sets out—a list of key questions that it must answer. These questions aren't only relevant for entrepreneurs. A platform pioneer usually has to persuade many people to share her vision, from family and partners in the new venture to employees, who risk being jobless if the start-up fails. She also has to convince desirable participants to invest in joining the platform.

Platform pioneers are sometimes employees of large companies. They have to convince senior management, and sometimes the board of directors, that the platform can succeed. Microsoft employees had to persuade Bill Gates and others that it was worth investing in the Xbox.[5]

Anyone who is on the other side of a would-be pioneer's sales pitch should ask some tough questions, because as we've emphasized throughout, building a multisided platform business is fraught with danger. Most don't take off. Perhaps that's because their leaders make bad design decisions or because there is no way to crack this particular chicken-and-egg problem. Here are the six key questions we ask start-up matchmakers, particularly would-be pioneers, and recommend that you also use:

1. What's the friction, how big is it, and who benefits from solving it?

2. Does the platform design reduce this friction, balance the interests of participants on all sides, and do it better than other entrants?

3. How hard is the ignition problem, and does the entrepreneur have a solid plan for achieving critical mass?

4. Do the prices necessary for ignition and growth enable the platform to make money?

5. How is the matchmaker going to work with others in the broader ecosystem, does it face related risks, and has it dealt with them?

6. Is the entrepreneur ready to modify her design and ignition strategy quickly in response to market reactions?

There's a lot of meat behind these questions, meat that anyone quizzing a matchmaker entrepreneur, or an entrepreneur checking whether he has thought through what he is doing, should get into.

What's the friction, how big is it, and who benefits from solving it? Every successful matchmaker is formed in response to a significant friction that prevents market participants from getting together efficiently. Figuring out what those frictions are and how a multisided business can eliminate or substantially reduce them is the first and most important task for an aspiring platform pioneer. The bigger the friction, the greater the value the platform can potentially provide, the greater the opportunity for getting participants on board, and the greater the chance for the platform to make money. Knowing which type of participants benefits the most from eliminating that friction can guide decisions on ignition strategies as well as on pricing.

Sometimes, as with OpenTable, the platform drastically reduces a clear market friction, and the issue is whether the friction is big enough to enable the platform to earn adequate revenue to cover all the costs of launching and running the platform. In other cases, the platform pioneer has identified a new way for participants to interact—one that no one recognized because there was no way to do it. People and restaurants were already making and taking reservations before OpenTable came along. People really weren't sharing videos much before YouTube started. As a result, YouTube couldn't be sure how much value it would provide by facilitating video sharing, since video sharing had been effectively impossible. It turned out that people really wanted to share videos when they could, and that YouTube eliminated a significant friction.

As we've noted before, in our experience, the biggest mistake platform entrepreneurs make is to embrace the "if you build it, they will come" fallacy. No, they won't, unless the platform solves a big problem for participants and unless the entrepreneur cracks the chicken-and-egg problem. Without a significant friction to address, no matter how great a platform's technology, there is no case for investing.

Does the platform design reduce this friction, balance the interests of participants on all sides, and do it better than other entrants? Unfortunately, the answer to this question is usually no. Looking carefully at how the platform is designed to reduce the friction it addresses can provide clues as to the likelihood of success.

We saw that with YouTube. There were many entrants, from start-ups to giants, that had the same general idea about Internet video at about the same time. Few survived, and those that did are now puny next to YouTube. They all saw the friction; they just didn't have a great way to reduce it. Maybe they chose bad designs or had the wrong pricing structure or didn't figure out how to work with other actors in the broader ecosystem.

How hard is the ignition problem, and does the entrepreneur have a solid plan for achieving critical mass? Just because it is possible to design a platform that could create great value if participants join doesn't mean that it is possible to secure enough of a critical mass for that platform to ignite it. Unless she can figure out how to solve the critical mass problem, even an entrepreneur who has identified a significant friction and a platform design that could reduce it substantially won't succeed.

A platform doesn't generate any value for anyone unless the right participants join it and, until they do, the platform is a dud. Once a platform or any business gets a reputation for being a dud, it is hard to recover, particularly with impatient investors. Matchmaker novices often don't recognize how difficult it is to solve this chicken-and-egg problem. The entrepreneur must be realistic about the challenges involved and have developed tactics for getting enough of the right participants, in the right proportions, on board before her money runs out or the platform's reputation has been trashed because it hasn't enabled enough interactions.

Do prices necessary for ignition and growth enable the platform to make money? The answer to this question is related to the answer to the friction question. If a matchmaker generates enough value, the value pie will likely be big enough to get participants to join, to fund any subsidies necessary for getting the most desirable (marquee) participants, and to make money. If it requires substantial subsidies to get participants on one side to join, the entrepreneur should be able to explain why the participants on the other side are going to pay enough to both support those subsidies and generate a profit, and why the high prices necessary on the other side to cover costs won't limit the growth of the platform.

This problem is easier for advertising-supported platforms, where there is a well-developed market for selling access to viewers. For those types of matchmakers, the entrepreneur just needs a convincing story about how the platform will secure the advertising revenue necessary to support the cost of creating the content or other platform features that attract those viewers.

How is the matchmaker going to work with others in the broader ecosystem, does it face related risks, and has it dealt with them? The importance of the broader ecosystem varies across platform ventures. But unless the platform pioneer has examined what goes on outside the walls of her platform, she won't know whether the platform and its participants depend on other members of the ecosystem, and whether those other members could get in the way of ignition and growth. Apple and Google were both very aware that the success of their smartphone operating systems depended on mobile carriers, and they each devised strategies to deal with them. Brightcove, which we discussed in chapter 5, had to ditch its plans for a multisided video platform in part because it hadn't factored in how the complexities of the media ecosystem made it difficult to crack the chicken-and-egg problem.

Is the entrepreneur ready to modify her design and ignition strategy quickly in response to market reactions? All businesses should learn from and respond to the market, of course. But doing so is especially critical for multisided platforms, which need to achieve balance on multiple dimensions. In particular, attaining critical mass is often such a hard problem that, in practice, plans that made sense at the start need to be adjusted in the face of evidence on how possible participants actually behave. When Chuck Templeton had trouble selling his reservation management system to restaurants reluctant to make large investments, he pivoted quickly to charging a small installation fee and a monthly rental fee for his system, and restaurants began signing up. Just like a skateboard rider, the would-be pioneering matchmaker has to make constant adjustments to its surroundings.

Warning Signs

The countdown begins after launching a multisided platform. Either the platform will reach critical mass before its time runs out and it will ignite, or it won't and it will implode. There's no standard time limit for this race, but in our experience, platforms often make it in the first couple of years or they never do. They don't have much time, simply because participants will stop coming if the platform doesn't deliver for them. The platform will then lose value and will have difficulty attracting many new or former participants, as well as investors.

During this ignition phase, the platform pioneer, as well as others who are invested in the success of the platform, can monitor movement to critical mass. Warning signs may suggest that the platform design needs to be tweaked or radically overhauled in order to secure ignition.

If the platform has trouble early on attracting participants to one side or both sides and can't even get the early adopters who are willing to try almost anything, it is in trouble. When YouTube launched its platform, not much happened. That led the founders to redesign their video-sharing site. If a platform has trouble persuading marquee players—those essential for getting to critical mass—to join, something needs to be done. Once it had gotten some experience in San Francisco and Chicago, OpenTable went to great lengths to sign up the marquee restaurants in each new city. Its investors should have slept better when the most popular restaurants signed on, just as they should have worried greatly if those restaurants wouldn't.

Diagnosing when a platform is close to being dead in the water at the outset may be fairly easy, though the cure may not be obvious. But once the platform starts getting participants and activity increases, it becomes much trickier to figure out whether growth is fast enough to reach critical mass before time runs out. The entrepreneur and those invested in the platform should be concerned if the number of participants on both sides and the amount of activity on the platform aren't accelerating. Another symptom of serious problems is that early adopters are defecting because they have concluded there isn't enough value for them to stick around. The failure to close deals with marquee players provides an additional warning signal. If a platform isn't growing momentum behind it, it's probably in trouble.

After a year or two, most matchmakers should see an inflection point where there's a sharp acceleration in growth and the platform feels as if it is "taking off." If the platform is still struggling to get critical mass after this much time, then it faces a serious risk of an imminent fizzle. OpenTable's investors encountered this problem after almost three years. They were burning through a lot of money and decided to radically, and successfully, change the company's ignition strategy. They switched from "grabbing all the eyeballs" (sign up lots of restaurants) to a "go narrow/go deep" approach (first create thick markets in a few cities).

More often, in our experience, if a platform hasn't ignited after a couple of years, either it implodes as participants drop off because there's not enough value, or investment capital dries up in the face of uncertainty over whether the platform will ever succeed. When eBay attempted to expand its business into China, it had trouble attracting enough retailers and buyers to interest either side, and it had to give up its expansion plans.

Apple Pay Organizes Support

In 2014, there was a well-developed ecosystem for consumer payments in the United States. Along with cash and checks, there were credit and debit cards.[6] The average person over the age of 18 had 2.4 cards. Many merchants accepted these cards; consumers could pay with them at millions of locations.[7] Americans used them a lot, as Tim Cook pointed out: more than 200 million times a day for a total of $4 trillion of purchases a year.[8]

Debit and credit cards involve three major groups of businesses in the United States and many developed countries.

First, there are four major card networks that ultimately make it possible for consumers to pay with a card and for merchants to receive payment. MasterCard and Visa work with banks to issue the cards and with banks and other companies to service merchants. American Express and Discover issue cards themselves and usually work with consumers and merchants directly.

Second, in the United States, there are more than ten thousand commercial banks, savings banks, and credit unions. Most Americans have their checking accounts with one of these financial institutions. Almost everyone gets his or her debit card from one of them. The larger banks also issue credit cards.

Third, a variety of companies like First Data Corporation and Vantiv work with merchants to accept payments, provide point-of-sale terminals for cards, and process payments. Smaller merchants usually rely on one company that provides them with everything they need. Larger merchants with multiple locations often work with several different providers.

Apple decided to work closely with the card networks and banks for its Apple Pay network, and all of the major networks except Discover were on board when Apple Pay launched. To set up Apple Pay, consumers use one of their existing credit or debit cards that is associated with one of those networks. Apple wanted to make it easy for consumers to load their cards into the system and developed a way for users to sign on by taking a picture of their card. They worked with banks to do the rest of the work to get the card into their system. The banks agreed to pay Apple 0.15 percent of the value of transactions on their cards done through Apple Pay (15 cents for every $100).[9]

Apple, the card networks, and many of the large banks worked together to promote Apple Pay. The large banks agreed to promote it to their users, and Visa, MasterCard, and American Express promoted it as well. This meant that from the beginning, Apple had much of the payment card ecosystem organized around its new payment method and invested in its success.

The card networks and the large banks were behind Apple Pay for at least three reasons. They believed that people would switch from paying with cash to paying with cards if they could use mobile phones to pay conveniently. They were also concerned that the other mobile payment schemes under development that bypassed payment card networks and thus would compete with payment cards could take off. Finally, the banks, widely viewed as boring while also being blamed for the financial crisis, liked being associated with the cool, innovative Apple brand.[10]

Apple Pay's First Year

Not just anyone could use Apple Pay when it launched on October 20, 2014. Users had to have the new iPhone 6. Older models didn't have a "near-field communication" (NFC) chip that made it possible for people to just wave their phones near a terminal. And iPhone 6 owners couldn't just use it anywhere they could use cards. They could only use it if the merchant had a terminal that could read wireless signals from NFC chips.

Luckily for Apple, the new iPhones sold very well. Around 29 million people in the United States had either an iPhone 6 or an iPhone 6 Plus by the end of 2014, and more than 70 million people had them by the end of September 2015.[11] That is, around 15 percent of Americans between the ages of eighteen and sixty-five had an iPhone 6 by the end of 2014 and 35 percent by September 2015.[12] Almost all those people had a payment card and could activate Apple Pay if they wanted.[13]

At the time of Apple Pay's launch, however, most merchants didn't have terminals that could accept it. Very large retailers were most likely to have the terminals because many were in the process of upgrading as a result of security and other issues. But, of the top one hundred retailers and restaurants in the country, a group that accounts for 36.5 percent of sales for the retail industries, including restaurants, only ten had terminals that could take Apple Pay. That group accounted for 10.7 percent of sales made by the top one hundred retailers, and therefore 3.9 percent of all retail sales.[14] The retailers that were not among these very large retailers, and that collectively accounted for the remaining 63.5 percent of all retail sales, were less likely to have Terminals that took NFC. The millions of small merchants—the mom-and-pops—were especially unlikely to have them.[15] "The truth is, today, no one uses NFC," according to an executive at a company that provides payment technology to merchants, speaking in the early fall of 2014.[16]

As a result, when consumers shopped, they found that they couldn't use Apple Pay at most places they went. One reporter who tried found, "For now, though, contactless payments feel like a novelty. Among the retailers I visited that didn't take Apple Pay were Best Buy, Walmart, the local Ace Hardware store, Dollar Tree, the US Post Office, Safeway, An-Jan pet store, O'Reilly Auto Parts, and Taco Bell."[17]

Apple adopted a "go broad/go shallow" strategy. It covered the entire country. But within any geographic area, the company's choice of technology limited the number of people who could use Apple Pay, because they needed new iPhones, and limited the number of merchants that could accept it, because most needed new terminals. Apple ended up with many thin markets but no thick ones.

Early on, there were signs of trouble. About a month after Apple Pay launched, it was Black Friday in the United States—the day after Thanksgiving when shoppers usually go in droves to the stores to begin the holiday shopping season. Many people had already bought new iPhones and were carrying them that day.[18] Hardly any of them used Apple Pay when they bought something at stores that took it.

As of Black Friday, November 28, 2014, only 9.1 percent of the iPhone 6 users had installed Apple Pay on their phones.[19] And even this small fraction of early adopters weren't that active. About half (50.5 percent) didn't use it when they were at a terminal that accepted it during their shopping that day. For a typical transaction at a terminal that took Apple Pay, only one out of twenty iPhone 6 users (4.6 percent, which is 50.5 percent of the 9.1 percent who had it) who could have adopted Apple Pay and used it, did so. That low usage wasn't because they didn't know whether the merchant took Apple Pay. Many merchants that took Apple Pay highlighted the fact that they accepted it. Their terminals usually had the Apple Pay logo on them, indicating that it, along with other payment methods, was accepted.

Nonetheless, the news wasn't all bad for Apple. Many of the people who had tried Apple Pay were enthusiastic about it. Only 1.8 percent said it was difficult to use, and only 14 percent claimed it was confusing, while 52.6 percent said it was amazing and easy to use. Of the latter group, 42.1 percent said they would use Apple Pay "every chance I get," and another 35.1 percent would do so "when I remember that I can." These early adopters were quite satisfied.

Over the next year, the number of people with new iPhones that could use Apple Pay increased dramatically. But the percentage of people who had ever tried Apple Pay didn't increase much. In October 2015, a year after the launch of Apple Pay, only 16.6 percent of people with an iPhone 6 had ever tried it. More alarming for Apple, the percentage of people who used it when they could had plummeted from 50.5 percent in November 2014 to 30.7 percent in October 2015. A year after launch, out of 100 users, about 17 had ever tried it and out of those 17 just 5 used it when they could.[20]

Over the course of the year more people got the new iPhone model so that more people in total had Apple Pay set up on their phones and used it when they could. The number of people who probably had Apple Pay on their phones increased from roughly 2.7 million in November 2014 to 11.7 million in October 2015.[21] As a result, the likelihood that an American adult would use Apple Pay at a terminal that accepted Apple Pay increased from 0.7 percent in November 2014 to 1.8 percent in October 2015.[22]

When it planned Apple Pay, the company had reasons to believe that more retailers would have the slick NFC terminals that Tim Cook showed at the September 2014 announcement. The payment card networks in the United States had told merchants that to reduce fraud, they had to install terminals that took "chip-and-pin" cards in addition to mag-stripe cards. If they didn't install those terminals by October 1, 2015, the merchant, rather than the card issuer, would bear the cost of fraud. Very large merchants installed the new terminals because of this liability shift and because of fraud concerns. The chip-and-pin terminals, also known as EMV terminals, generally have the capability of taking contactless payments. So if a merchant has a chip-and-pin terminal, it can generally turn on NFC.

However, installing these chip-and-pin terminals and redesigning computer systems and business processes to accommodate them is costly. In addition, it is more cumbersome to dip a card into a chip-and-pin reader—you have to stick the card in and then wait for the transaction to be approved before taking it out—than to swipe. Many merchants have weighed the costs of making the switch against the cost of fraud and decided not to upgrade for now. Then, many of the merchants that have installed chip-and-pin terminals have decided not to turn on NFC because doing so would further increase cost and inconvenience. Apple, however, might have banked on the prospect of consumers coming in and wanting to use Apple Pay to tilt the calculus in favor of spending money on the modern terminals and flipping on NFC.

By October 2015, although the situation at merchants had improved for Apple Pay, most still didn't have terminals that could take contactless payments. Twenty-three of the top one hundred retailers, including restaurants, accounting for 19.8 percent of sales of the top one hundred, had made NFC terminals available to customers.[23] But the very large retailers that can take Apple Pay only accounted for 7.2 percent (0.365×0.198) of retail and restaurant sales. Except for these mega retailers, NFC is far less common. And so far, the prospect of taking Apple Pay has not resulted in a rapid movement toward making NFC terminals available at the point of sale.

Although hard data is not available, the fraction of retail sales that takes place at terminals that can take Apple Pay was probably somewhere around 10 percent in October 2015. Apple Pay accounted for about 1.8 percent of the value of transactions at those terminals that month. It therefore accounted for about .18 percent—18 out of 10,000—of all card-based transactions at retail stores after a year.

Apple Pay Diagnosis, One Year In

It was apparent in the two back-to-back videos that Tim Cook showed on September 9, 2014, that Apple would face challenges in igniting its new mobile payment service. The first video suggested that there was a significant friction paying with plastic cards at the point of sale. The woman in the video had to dig into her pocketbook to find her card. Then the clerk insisted on identification. The clerk swiped the card twice, apparently because it didn't work the first time.

Most people in the United States don't, in fact, have this sort of experience. They know where their cards are. Merchants seldom ask for identification, especially when people use their debit cards with a PIN. For smaller transactions, merchants just swipe the card. They don't require a PIN or even a signature.[24] It is really fast. Even for larger transactions, clerks and customers make card transactions so often that they get it done pretty quickly. Apple Pay therefore doesn't appear to reduce a significant friction for most card users or merchants.

The second video shows how the design of the Apple Pay made it difficult to solve the chicken-and-egg problem. For Apple Pay to work, the shopper needed to have not just a smartphone, and not just an iPhone, but a new iPhone—the iPhone 6. That design decision resulted in about 65 percent of American adults being unable to use Apple Pay almost a year after it was launched.[25]

The department store also had to have decided to switch to the new terminal technology. Given that installing and integrating the new terminals into its payment processing systems would take some time, that design decision resulted in Americans being unable to use Apple Pay at 77 percent of the one hundred largest retailers in the country and at an even higher percent of smaller ones one year after the launch of Apple Pay.

The consumer and merchant both needed new technology because Apple decided to use NFC in its Apple Pay program. And on launch, Apple Pay didn't attract enough devoted users to persuade merchants they needed to invest in new terminals or in altering their check-out process. One large retailer noted in June 2015 that "the company hasn't adopted Apple Pay . . . because not even a 'small percentage' of its customers have asked for it."[26] This lack of consumer interest limited the positive feedback between the two sides of the Apple Pay platform and prevented the "cool" new payment method from gaining momentum. Apple Pay had difficulty getting to critical mass.

Starbucks, by contrast, launched a mobile payment app in 2011 for use in its stores. A "quick response" or "QR" code, which carried the consumer's payment credentials, appeared on the smartphone screen when consumers went to pay. This worked with all major smartphones. Consumers pointed the phone at a QR code reader at the checkout counter at Starbucks. Virtually all Starbucks shops already had one of these.[27] By the end of its first year, more than 2 percent of the transactions at Starbucks were made using its smartphone app. That had increased to 16 percent by 2014.[28]

Apple Pay could still ignite. Merchants are gradually installing new point-of-sale terminals that have the capability of accepting NFC. That will reduce the cost to merchants of adopting Apple Pay, although they will still need to decide to turn on that technology. Greater merchant acceptance of Apple Pay could stimulate more consumer adoption and use over time. Meanwhile, as iPhone users gradually replace their old iPhones with new ones, the number of consumers that could use Apple Pay will increase. In several years, then, a much larger portion of Americans will be able to use Apple Pay, and they will be able to do that at a much larger portion of merchants. Over time, positive feedback effects could kick in and get consumers and merchants more interested in Apple Pay.

Apple could also change its strategy. It could take steps to increase positive feedback effects and enhance the likelihood of ignition. It could, for example, develop additional features for Apple Pay that address more substantial frictions than just paying at the point of sale. It could also give retailers incentives to make NFC terminals available to consumers. Apple could also move to QR codes or some other approach that increases the portion of merchants that could accept it. Samsung Pay, which was available on Samsung 6 phones as of September 2015, has technology that enables people to use it at older mag-stripe terminals.

Unlike most platform pioneers, Apple Pay has a large enough bank account and a strong enough reputation to weather a slow ignition phase and eventually reach critical mass. OpenTable took about six years to get off the ground, and its patient investors stood by its side. Apple could certainly stay the course, too. On the other hand, Apple faces the risk that another player will come in and introduce a mobile payment solution that will ignite quickly. Therefore, if we were investors in Apple Pay, which we aren't, we wouldn't necessarily write it off, but we would be quite concerned. Given Apple's strategy and the results to date, we also wouldn't advise other mobile payments entrepreneurs to give up. Clearly, the game's not over here.

No multisided platform is guaranteed real success, even with a big bank account and persistence, if it isn't solving a big enough problem. The flip side of that proposition, though, is that a matchmaker can grow explosively if it succeeds in eliminating a big enough friction. On the day that Tim Cook announced the launch of Apple Pay in September 2014, about ten thousand miles southeast of San Francisco, in Kenya, most people were already using mobile phones to send and receive money. That was thanks to platform pioneer that figured out how to secure fast ignition and, in doing so, leapfrogged traditional banking and payments.

Part Three

Creation, Destruction, and Transformation

Chapter 11

Moving Money

How a Matchmaker Leapfrogged
Banking and Brought Financial Inclusion
to an Impoverished Country

I N 2006, KENYA WAS ONE OF THE POOREST COUNTRIES IN THE
world. GDP per capita was only $2,156, about 5 percent of that in the
United States.[1] Travel around the country was difficult, expensive,
and dangerous.[2] There were only 558 bank branches in this entire
country of 36.3 million people, placing it 164 of 203 countries ranked
by the World Bank.[3] Only one in seven people had a bank account, and
for those who did, it was often too expensive to use frequently.[4]

Many households were separated over long distances. Often, a
husband or son moved to Nairobi or another city, while the wife or
parents stayed behind in rural areas. Family members typically
had to work multiple jobs just to survive. Those in rural areas often
farmed or raised cattle but depended on money from their urban
relatives to make ends meet.[5] They faced a constant challenge of
moving cash, Kenyan shillings, across the country, a process that
was fraught with frictions.

People traveled, on average, about 200 kilometers (124 miles) to
deliver or pick up cash, or relied on friends or family to make the journey.[6]

That was expensive, time consuming, and treacherous. Some used bus companies or taxis to bring the cash from city to village, but trusting a third party was also risky. The driver might steal the cash or might be robbed along the way.

Less than ten years later, in 2014, more than 84 percent of Kenyan mobile phone users, including many of the very poor, were able to use their mobile phones to transfer money to each other, to pay their bills, and to pay at stores.[7] People can now also use new financial services available through their mobile money accounts to save money and take out loans, and many do.[8] Increasingly, stores are accepting mobile money for payment.

The way this happened in Kenya is a remarkable story of how a company figured out how to ignite a multisided platform in trying circumstances, to massively reduce important market frictions, and to provide financial services to millions of impoverished people. And it is a story of how multisided platforms—M-PESA and other mobile money schemes that have started in Kenya and elsewhere—are leapfrogging traditional industries. Kenyans don't need to rely on banks for many financial services. And while it is too soon to tell, Kenyan merchants and consumers may end up using mobile money instead of traditional payment cards and point-of-sale equipment.

The Birth of a Platform

The first mobile network operators entered Kenya in the mid-1990s at a time when few people had landlines. One of them, Safaricom, was operated by Telkom Kenya, then the monopoly landline phone system in the country. Vodafone, based in the United Kingdom, took over its management in 2000 and acquired a 40 percent equity stake.

Over the next decade, Safaricom and its smaller rivals installed cell towers throughout the country, developed 2G networks that provided phone service but not Internet connections, and enrolled subscribers. By 2006, about 7.3 million Kenyans, out of an adult population (fifteen years and older) of about 20.7 million, had mobile phone subscriptions. About 73 percent of those used Safaricom.[9]

In the early 2000s, Vodafone was looking into ways to use mobile phones to bring financial services to people who didn't have ready access to bank accounts. In its exploratory work in Kenya, it found that moving money between people was a major problem. In collaboration with Safaricom, Vodafone began working to develop a multisided platform to solve this problem.

Since smartphones weren't available in Kenya at the time, Vodafone developed a mobile money platform that would enable people to use their feature phones to send and receive "e-money." The e-money reflected debits to the sender's account and credits to the receiver's account. The system puts account details onto the phone subscriber's SIM card and uses SMS to transmit the details of the transactions between phones. Safaricom adopted this mobile money platform for Kenya. Using the Swahili word for money, *pesa*, it called the mobile money platform M-PESA and set it up as a subsidiary of Safaricom.

M-PESA needed more than this technology, though. Kenyans needed a way to exchange cash for e-money that they could send, and M-PESA had to figure out a way they could exchange e-money for cash at the other end, since that's what they needed to pay for virtually everything. That required a network of physical locations where people could put cash in to the mobile money system and take cash out.

Building a network of specialized cash-in and cash-out (CICO) agents that would cover the country, particularly its rural areas, was unattractive to M-PESA for the same reason that banks found it uneconomical to build many rural branches: volumes would be too low at many locations to cover fixed costs. M-PESA had to attract a network of physical CICO agents that had already established businesses generating revenue streams that could help cover fixed costs.

Thus, M-PESA had to develop *two* intersecting two-sided platforms and get both sides of both platforms on board. It needed a mobile-money platform to send and receive e-money, and it had to get both senders and receivers on board that platform. It also had to attract a CICO network of physical agents, some of whom would mainly convert cash into e-money and some of whom would mainly convert e-money into cash. It had to solve two chicken-and-egg puzzles.

How It Works

A Safaricom subscriber needs to go to a CICO agent to set up an M-PESA account. The CICO agents are typically small shops, gas stations, bank branches, or post offices that offer these services as part of their businesses and that can thus make a profit on relatively small volumes of M-PESA transactions.[10] The agent records personal information about the subscriber, replaces the SIM card in the subscriber's phone, and provides him a PIN for accessing the account. To obtain e-money for his account, the subscriber hands cash over to the agent, and the agent uses the M-PESA system to deposit e-money in his account.

To send e-money, the subscriber needs to type in the mobile phone number of the recipient, the amount of money he wants to send, and his own PIN. The recipient gets the money in her e-money account almost instantly. The recipient can then go to a CICO agent to withdraw the money in cash. She enters the agent's number, the amount of the withdrawal, and her PIN. The agent uses the M-PESA system to reduce the balance in the recipient's e-money account and gives her the withdrawal amount in cash. Meanwhile, the sender's e-money account is debited. Both the sender and receiver get SMS receipts for these transactions.

M-PESA receives and pays various fees during this process. While the company doesn't charge the sender anything to put money into his account, it charges a fee to send money and another to receive it. M-PESA pays the CICO agents a commission for each new customer they sign up and for cash-in and cash-out transactions.

The Start-Up Problem

The M-PESA system sounds great, just as OpenTable and other successful multisided platforms do, with twenty-twenty hindsight. But a moment's reflection reveals just how difficult it was to get this mobile money platform off the ground.

Suppose a young man working in Nairobi signs up for M-PESA so he can send money to his parents. The service is worthless to him unless his parents are willing to use the service. One might think that getting recipients on board would be easy, but in practice, it wasn't. And, as we saw for YouTube, the need to get both sides on board in order to make the platform valuable for either one—the chicken-and-egg problem—is the key reason two-sided platforms are generally harder to get off the ground than single-sided firms.

While some people are mainly senders and others are mainly receivers, most people probably use the M-PESA system both to send and to receive money. Thus, senders and receivers aren't groups of different people; they are people playing different roles at different times. When playing different roles, the same person or business may care about different aspects of the system and may be more or less willing to pay to use it. A student working part-time in Nairobi may regularly send his parents—farmers in a rural village—money for groceries, for instance, and they may occasionally send him money on special occasions. Similarly, most M-PESA agents both get and give out cash, even though some do more cash-in and others do more cash-out.

The need for cash-in and cash-out outlets compounded the M-PESA start-up problem. Senders can't use the platform if they can't put cash in, and receivers won't use the platform if they can't get cash out. So the mobile money platform would be dead in the water without physical agents. But moving cash to and from rural areas is costly, and holding it in anticipation of withdrawals has both costs and risks. Since M-PESA pays agents only for transactions, a shop needs to make sure there is enough demand from senders and receivers before it signs up to be an agent.

As a result, this multisided platform works in practice only if there are enough senders and receivers transferring money between each other and enough agents who are providing cash-in and cash-out services where these senders and receivers are located.

How this multisided platform could get anyone to sign on is not at all obvious. Senders won't sign on without receivers; neither will sign on without agents; and agents won't sign on without senders and receivers moving money. The amazing thing about pioneering multisided platforms like M-PESA is that they figured out how to solve this difficult coordination problem.

M-PESA's Balancing Act

Because so many stores in Kenya were already working with Safaricom to sell airtime along with other products, M-PESA was able to leverage those stores for its new service. That required deciding on a compensation system, selecting and recruiting stores, training their personnel, and supervising them. It also required convincing potential agents that when M-PESA launched, they would have enough customers to make investing in the business worthwhile.

At its launch in 2007, M-PESA had signed up 307 shops and other agents. It made sure that they were represented in all of Kenya's seventy district headquarters, so that most people would be reasonably close to a CICO agent where they could buy e-money and cash it in.

In setting up the CICO network and expanding it, M-PESA had to balance two conflicting forces. Senders and receivers would value having more agents nearby. That argued for recruiting more agents and increasing the density of stores throughout the country. But if there were too many CICO agents in a given area, they would compete for the same customers, reducing profits from being an agent. That's the direct *negative* externality problem we introduced in chapter 2, and it gave rise here to the sort of balancing problem that matchmakers regularly confront.

Given the number of senders and receivers on the e-money platform, M-PESA needed to ensure that there were enough customers per store to make the business potentially profitable for all. Stores that found the M-PESA business not worth the trouble would likely either drop it or devote little effort to it, annoying senders and receivers in both cases. When M-PESA launched in March 2007, there were roughly 68 registered users per agent, and by the end of the year there were more than 850.[11]

M-PESA chose to expand the number of agents in tandem with the growth in senders and receivers, which ensured that stores had sufficient incentives to join and stay on the CICO network. Of course, it also ensured that the stores could receive transaction fees that were high enough to make it worthwhile for the stores to devote attention to M-PESA customers.

Some Kenyans were more often senders, and others were more often receivers. To get a significant volume of transactions flowing through its system, M-PESA needed both kinds of people. That required another balancing act, some aspects of which we've seen several times. Given the internal migration and employment patterns in Kenya, senders were disproportionately located in the urban areas, and receivers were disproportionately located in the rural areas. To make sure both types of customers were on board, M-PESA made sure it had agents who could register people and provide both cash-in and cash-out services throughout the country, including the important rural areas.

M-PESA adopted a pricing model that would encourage senders to recruit receivers. It was possible to send e-money to anyone in the country who had a mobile phone number. But the mobile money platform made it much more expensive for registered users to send money to people who were not also registered users. For example, it cost 30 Kenyan shillings (KShs) to send KShs 35,000 to a registered user and it cost KShs 400 to send that same amount to an unregistered person.[12] That price structure provided strong incentives for senders to persuade those to whom they wanted to send money to register for M-PESA. Table 11-1 summarizes M-PESA's fees as of 2009.[13]

TABLE 11-1

M-PESA's fee structure, 2009 (in KShs)

Transaction type	Transaction range		Customer charge
	Minimum	Maximum	
Deposit cash	100	35,000	0
Send money to registered M-PESA user	100	35,000	30
Send money to nonregistered M-PESA user	100	2,500	75
	2,501	5,000	100
	5,001	10,000	175
	10,001	20,000	350
	20,001	35,000	400
Withdraw cash by registered M-PESA user at M-PESA agent outlet	100	2,500	25
	2,501	5,000	45
	5,001	10,000	75
	10,001	20,000	145
	20,001	35,000	170
Withdraw cash by registered M-PESA user at PesaPoint ATM	200	2,500	30
	2,501	5,000	60
	5,001	10,000	100
	10,001	20,000	175
Withdraw cash by nonregistered M-PESA user	100	35,000	0
Buy airtime (for self or other)	20	10,000	0

Platform Ignition

When M-PESA opened its doors in March 2007, it had some members of all sides on board. An intense marketing campaign had persuaded people to register for M-PESA accounts, and it had successfully recruited CICO agents across the country. It had solved the initial coordination problem. Yet that did not guarantee its success.

M-PESA tried to get people to subscribe by emphasizing how the platform could solve a single major friction for them. It focused on "Send Money Home." Its award-winning commercial shows a young man in a suit and tie at his desk at work.[14] He picks up his mobile phone and selects "M-PESA" and then "Send Money" from the menus. The commercial then shows Kenyan shillings shooting out of the phone and landing in the apron of a woman who could be his mother, working on a farm. She pulls out her phone, which says she has received KShs 1,000 from John on June 3, 2007. The voice-over is "You can send pesa fast and safe using Safaricom's new service."

Several charts reveal how M-PESA did during these dangerous early months. Figure 11-1 shows the number of registered users and the value of transfers that took place over the thirty-six months from the service's launch in March 2007 to February 2010.[15] The number of registered users increased dramatically during this period and, in parallel, so did the value of transactions on the e-money platform.

By February 2010, there were 9.7 million registered users (42 percent of people over the age of fifteen) and $678 million in transactions monthly. Given Kenya's size and wealth, that volume of transactions was significant: on an annual basis, it amounted to 20 percent of GDP.[16]

The number of agents also grew rapidly. Figure 11-2 shows the number of CICO agents over this same time period, as well as the growth in transaction volume. The number of agents grew from the initial 307 in March 2007 to 25,394 in February 2010.

Figure 11-3 shows transaction volume per agent and registered users per agent. During the first few months, the agents' economics improved, on average, as the number of registered users per agent grew. From mid-2008, though, the number of agents grew a bit more rapidly than the number of registered users, so that both transaction

FIGURE 11-1

Registered M-PESA users and value of transactions in US$

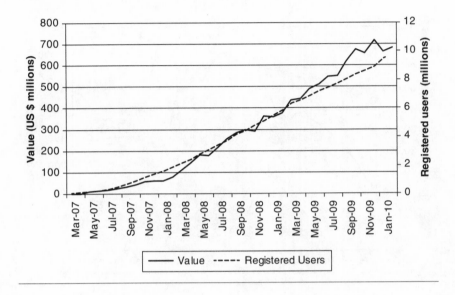

FIGURE 11-2

CICO agents and M-PESA transaction volume

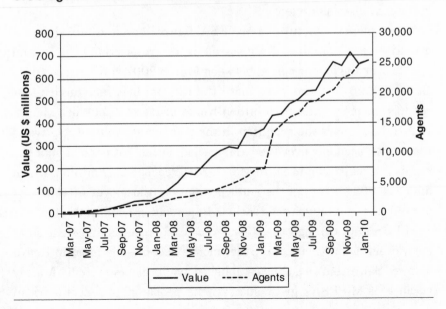

FIGURE 11-3

M-PESA transaction volume per agent and registered users per agent

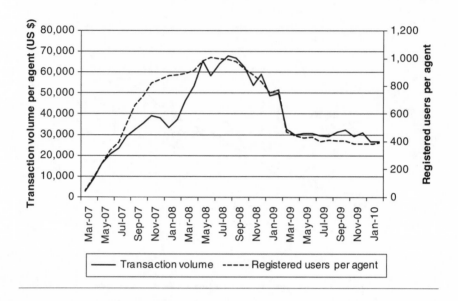

volume per agent and registered users per agent reached their highest values in the first half of the year and decreased until early 2009. After the decrease, they stabilized at about $25,000 and four hundred registered users per agent.

To complete the picture for M-PESA, figures 11-4 and 11-5 show the evolution of the number of registered users, transaction volume, and agents over the longer period between March 2007 and March 2015.[17] By March 2015, there were more than 25 million registered users conducting more than $2.5 billion worth of transactions per month. Figure 11-6 shows the evolution in the transaction volume relative to the overall economy over the same period. Other data shows that the number of registered users in March 2015 reached 25.7 million, which amounted 99 percent of the adult population (those over fifteen), and annual transaction volume reached 45 percent of GDP in 2014.[18]

M-PESA got through the treacherous early months and went on to enjoy overwhelming success. Other mobile network operators in Kenya followed Safaricom's lead and established mobile money systems. Mainly because of M-PESA's great success, the people of this poor African

FIGURE 11-4

Number of registered M-PESA users and transaction volume between March 2007 and March 2015

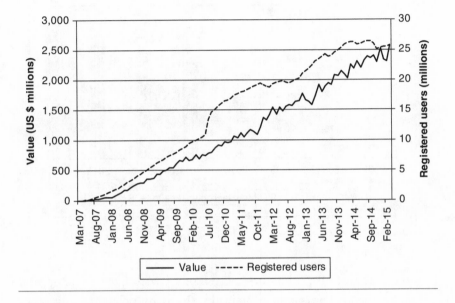

FIGURE 11-5

Number of M-PESA/CICO agents and transaction volume between March 2007 and March 2015

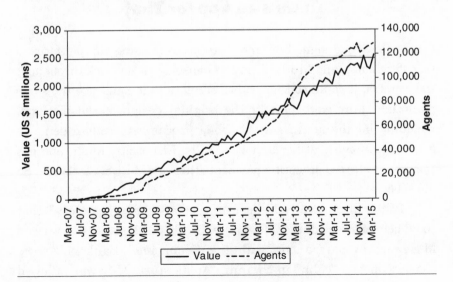

FIGURE 11-6

Annual M-PESA transaction volume as a percentage of GDP

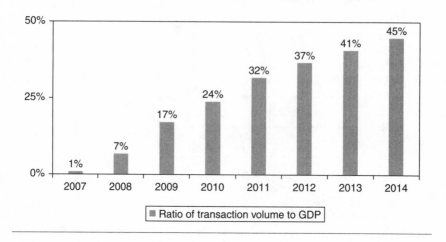

Ratio of transaction volume to GDP

country of only 44.9 million are more likely to use mobile money, and to conduct more transactions monthly, than the people of any other country in the world.[19] But M-PESA's success was far from inevitable.

There's an App for That

Once people had signed on and were actively using the platform to transfer money, and M-PESA had its dense agent network throughout the country, it could consider other services that could use the same platform. Many were part of the original design of the platform, including buying airtime with mobile phones rather than going to a shop and paying utility and other bills. Electricity, water, and gas companies started accepting payments through M-PESA accounts. So did schools.

M-PESA also selectively opened its platform to "partners" that could help provide additional services. In late 2012, M-PESA launched M-Shwari in partnership with the Commercial Bank of Africa. (*Shwari* means "calm" in Swahili.) At its start, M-Shwari allowed users to save as little as one Kenyan shilling and earn interest of 2 percent to 5 percent and to receive short-term loans of between KShs 100–20,000 ($1.15–$230), payable within thirty days, at an interest rate of 7.5 percent. By early 2015, the Commercial Bank had lent KShs 24 billion ($271 million). In early 2015, the KCB Bank Group launched a program in partnership with M-PESA. This program allowed users to access loans of between KShs 50 and KShs 1 million ($0.565–$11,300), due in one to six months, at interest rates between 4 percent and 12 percent.

M-PESA and the other mobile money schemes replace many of the services that traditional banks would provide. People can use mobile money as they would a depository account. They can obtain access to that account through CICO agents instead of bank branches. And they can get various financial services through their mobile money account. Although the mobile money schemes collaborate with banks for some things, they make banks irrelevant for many other things.

M-PESA, on its own, introduced a payments system in mid-2013. Lipa Na M-PESA enables brick-and-mortar merchants to receive payments from M-PESA users (*Lipa Na* means "pay with" in Swahili). Merchants establish an account and get a till number. When a shopper wants to make a purchase, she enters the till number provided by the merchant on her phone and goes through a set of prompts to authorize the debit from her e-money wallet. After the transaction is complete, M-PESA sends a confirmation message to both merchant and customer.[20] M-PESA then credits the merchant account.

Merchants constitute yet another side of the M-PESA platform. As of December 2014, more than thirty-two thousand merchants had signed up for Lipa Na M-PESA. This mobile payments service could possibly leapfrog traditional payment cards in Kenya and eliminate the need to install point-of-sale terminals around the country. Since people already have mobile money, and many don't have access to banks, there is seemingly not much room for debit cards. Most merchants have the ability to accept payment using mobile phones, so why would they want to buy the expensive physical point-of-sale terminals that are used in countries where most consumers use cards?

As of late 2015, M-PESA consisted of four intersecting two-sided platforms: (1) a sender–receiver money-transfer platform; (2) a registered user–CICO agent platform; (3) a financial services-to-registered-user platform; and (4) a registered merchant–registered user platform. All four platforms intersect with the registered user, who relies on her phone to interact with all the other sides.

Africa Rising

M-PESA has shown the way for countries in the rest of Africa to bring financial services to people across the income spectrum, from the poorest rural farmer to rich urban executives. Mobile money schemes have started in thirty-seven of fifty-four African countries.[21] So far, though, in only eight nations, shown in Table 11-2, have these schemes cracked the chicken-and-egg problem and obtained significant growth and penetration.[22] Others are sure to follow, though, since M-PESA, as a pioneering platform, has shown a way to do it successfully and has demonstrated that successful mobile money schemes can speed up economic development by leapfrogging traditional banking and payment cards.

TABLE 11-2

African countries where mobile money schemes took off

Country
Côte d'Ivoire
Ghana
Kenya
Rwanda
Somaliland
Uganda
Tanzania
Zimbabwe

Note: Mobile money has taken off in Somaliland, which is part of Somalia; it is currently not recognized as a country, however.

Source: Based on data presented in Evans and Pirchio, "An Empirical Examination of Why Mobile Money Schemes Ignite in Some Developing Countries but Flounder in Most," 18.

The economic development of Africa, long an impoverished and stagnant continent, is a complicated story and involves much more than mobile money. But these multisided platforms, building atop the spread of feature phones and cell networks, have proved extremely important in providing financial services in the countries where they have ignited so far. They have eliminated the need to extend physical bank branches throughout very rough terrain—in terms of both roads and risks—and have provided an economic model that delivers a much lower cost of service than banks are able to offer.

The mobile money platforms have drastically reduced the amount of time and money that people have to spend moving cash. Those transfers are an absolute necessity for dispersed households in which part of the family, often women, back in a village can't support themselves. They have made families less susceptible to income shocks. One study found that the use of M-PESA enabled Kenyan families to maintain consumption in the face of negative income shocks, while those who didn't use this money transfer service saw household consumption decline by 7 percent when shocks hit.[23] Mobile money has also increased the circulation of cash, enabled many to borrow and save, and increased household liquidity. While there are no studies yet documenting the impact of these services on economic development, it would be surprising if the impact were not significant.

Mobile money platforms cannot counter the violence and political instability that still holds African countries back. But, by providing a faster and more secure way of moving money over long distances using e-money, and by eliminating frictions and reducing transaction costs, they have made life notably easier for many families and businesses.

Mobile money platforms in developing countries may slow the growth of conventional banking systems, but they aren't likely to threaten their existence or force those systems to reinvent themselves. In contrast, multisided platforms in developed nations often pose serious threats to established industries. Like retailing.

Chapter 12

Gone Missing

How Multisided Platforms Are
Transforming Retail

WHERE IS EVERYBODY?

It's Saturday, December 6, 2014, eighteen shopping days before Christmas, in Boston. The economy is doing well. Yet the stores on Newbury Street, a high-end shopping area, the nearby Copley Place mall, and department stores like Saks Fifth Avenue just don't seem that crowded. It's not our imagination, and it's not just Boston.[1]

RetailNext, which has sensors that track visits at a sample of retailers, mainly department and mall stores, found that the number of visitors declined by 8 percent between 2013 and 2014.[2] People who used to come into the stores to walk around, to look at prices, to meet friends, and maybe to buy weren't coming as much. Foot traffic—that's what retailers call it—had fallen.

The less crowded aisles in brick-and-mortar stores are a symptom of a "gale of creative destruction" that is sweeping over the 894,000 American retail stores that sold more than $3.6 trillion of merchandise in 2014.[3] Multisided platforms, turbocharged by the six technologies we described in chapter 3, are behind this gale. They are changing how people shop and buy and, in doing so, are transforming American retail. Already we've seen the mass extinction of whole categories of retailers, while others are trying to figure out how to reinvent themselves to survive.

This ongoing story is important in its own right, but also for insights into other industries that face matchmaker threats to their survival. It's not a simple story, and it won't have a happy ending for everyone.

The Creative Destruction of Retail

Retail chains are shutting down stores. In 2014, more than 125 retail chains, including department stores, announced they would be closing more than 6,400 stores.[4] Sears shut down 339 stores in 2014, including its flagship store in Chicago.[5] The tween clothing store Delia's, which started as a catalog company in 1993 and expanded into mall stores, announced it was shutting all of its almost 100 stores at the end of 2014.[6] Ninety percent of the American population used to live or work within minutes of one of the 5,000 RadioShack stores, where they could get a wide variety of electronic goods. Bankrupt, the company is closing almost 2,000 stores, with possibly more to come.[7]

Luxury malls, like the Aventura Mall we discussed in chapter 8, are still attracting crowds. Many other malls, especially down-market ones, are deserted. A *New York Times* article described the situation at the Owings Mills Mall in suburban Baltimore during the 2014 Christmas shopping season: "Inside the gleaming mall here on the Sunday before Christmas just one thing was missing: shoppers."[8] Many other nonluxury malls are struggling to rent space and attract shoppers.

Retailers aren't just shedding space by closing stores. Some are also making their stores smaller.[9] "Brick-and-mortar stores' traffic declines have retailers rethinking the store format and considering smaller footprints," according to Shelley Kohan, who teaches at the Fashion Institute of Technology.[10] Best Buy has rented excess store space to other retailers and shaved the size of its new stores by 20 percent.[11]

This disappearance doesn't have a simple explanation. To understand how turbocharged multisided platforms are transforming retail, we must first solve a mystery. Where did those shoppers go?

The Case of the Missing Shopper

They didn't all go online. Physical retail still accounted for 93.6 percent of retail sales in 2014. That is a decline of only 2 percentage points, from 95.5 percent, since 2010.[12] Clearly, there wasn't a stampede to online shopping that could explain the decline in foot traffic.

Nor did shoppers buy a lot less. US Census data shows that per capita spending at physical stores increased 2.2 percent between 2013 and 2014, from $13,299 to $13,595. The increase in sales from the economic expansion more than made up for the slight loss in sales to online between those two years.

What has changed is that consumers visit fewer stores today than they once did. On an average mall-shopping trip in 2007, they went to five stores, compared to an average of only three in 2014.[13] Shoppers don't buy merchandise at every store they go to. They sometimes look around, check prices, and compare merchandise, but then maybe go to another store to buy. Americans are looking around less, and that's why foot traffic is falling.

And that's where online shopping has made a huge difference. Americans no longer need to go to physical stores to see what products are available or to compare prices. They can search for items, compare them, look at reviews, and check prices online. They are going to online matchmakers, such as eBay and Amazon, and online retailers to get that information. Most large physical retailers have websites that display the products that are available in their stores. People can compare a retailer's products virtually rather than make a trip.

They also rely on various online tools for figuring out what to buy and where to buy it. They could use general search engines such as Google Search and specialized ones such as Yelp. Online media, such as cnet.com and consumerreports.org, provide a lot of information, and social networks such as Facebook and Pinterest provide reviews and recommendations as well.

Smartphones also have specialized apps such as AroundMe that suggest where people should shop, given their current locations. Or they can get notifications from stores that they're near. They can also compare prices using apps such as PriceGrabber. When they are on a shopping trip, they can make decisions on where and whether to buy without going to as many stores. They can also navigate physical space more efficiently using GPS and mapping software on their phones. That likely means that stores get fewer window shoppers and fewer people who decide to stop in a store they just happen to be passing by.

The growth of smartphones has had a significant impact on shopping. Online search and discovery previously meant sitting in front of a computer, most likely at home or at the office, using a browser. With smartphones, consumers can engage in search and discovery any time and any place they want, including on shopping trips. Between 2011 and 2015, the percentage of American adults with smartphones increased from 35 percent to 68 percent.[14]

Canary in the Coal Mine

One could argue that these changes in how people shop and buy don't really matter for physical retailers. Two decades after the birth of the commercial Internet, physical stores still account for most retail sales. All those predictions about the death of brick-and-mortar stores have proved wrong.[15] Those traditional retailers could make even more money in principle since they don't need as much real estate.

Sadly for traditional retailers, however, the aisles in American stores are like the canaries in coal mines. The fact that they are getting quiet signals a dangerous problem: traditional brick-and-mortar stores may not be in danger of extinction, but the businesses that run them are.

For decades, physical retailers, from small boutiques on Main Street to massive shopping malls in the suburbs, have designed their businesses to encourage people to come in, browse, and discover, and then to buy and carry the merchandise home. That has dictated the size of their stores, how they are laid out, their marketing, their prices, and much more.

Those business practices don't make as much sense when all a consumer wants to do at a brick-and-mortar facility is pay and pick up his merchandise as efficiently as possible. Innovation has given consumers better ways to shop since they don't need the services that traditional retailers provide, and they can shop at big-box stores and pay lower prices. Not coincidentally, there has been a steady and substantial increase in the relative importance of warehouse clubs and other supercenters since around 2000.[16] Innovation has also given retailers better ways to sell. But that doesn't make it easy for many of them to figure out what to do.

The Three Waves of Retail Disruption

Turbocharged multisided platforms are behind three waves of disruptive innovation that have changed how people shop and buy. This is well beyond the simple "sexy matchmaker kills boring single-sided business" story, though.

The first wave of disruption came from the expansion of fixed broadband providers. These businesses connected American households and Internet content providers. These foundational platforms enabled the online companies described earlier to connect vast numbers of people and businesses.

Some of those companies, such as Google and eBay, were also multisided platforms. Others, such as Walmart's single-sided online store, were, in effect, apps that ran on these foundational platforms.

The second wave of disruption came from the expansion of mobile broadband providers and the spread of smartphones with sophisticated operating systems. These multisided platforms made it possible for people to access web-based companies almost anywhere and almost anytime. They also provided foundational platforms for apps that made it easier for people to search and discover merchandise.

Many of these apps, such as Groupon's mobile app, are multisided platforms that connect advertisers and consumers.

The third wave of disruption, which is just beginning to break, involves the integration of the online and offline worlds. With GPS in their phones, people can rely on apps that help them navigate and do things in physical space, relying on code that lives partly in the Cloud and partly on their mobile devices. Apps in the virtual universe can interact with people in the physical universe as long as people let apps know the location of their smartphones. Physical stores are beginning to use this functionality by installing wireless devices in their stores that track people as they enter and move around.

If you look behind what is changing how people shop and buy, and how physical retailers are responding to those changes, you will find a multisided platform or an app running on one. Matchmakers are powering the gale of creative destruction sweeping traditional retail.

Business Survival in the Face of Platform Threats

People who live in the paths of hurricanes have choices. Make sure their houses are built to withstand powerful winds. Place boards across the windows to help get through the latest storm. Leave the area until the storm has passed. Sell the house and move somewhere safer. Or stay home and live for the moment.

Businesses face similar choices. Their decisions are more challenging when multisided platforms are behind the forces of change. As we saw earlier, businesses have to worry about threats coming from new multisided platforms as well as the businesses they power. Personal computer operating systems, for example, enabled developers to create word processing software that, along with cheap, fast, small printers, obliterated the typewriter industry. To take another example, smartphones with cameras, powered by smart mobile operating systems, have reduced the demand for cameras because they make it easy to take and share photos.

Traditional businesses face a particularly potent threat when they find themselves competing with the subsidized side of a multisided platform. Online media, for example, provide content free to viewers. As we discussed in chapter 3, that placed physical newspapers, which earn revenue from readers as well as advertisers, in a very difficult position. Many newspapers have closed, and many others are struggling to survive.

Traditional businesses facing such threats are simultaneously hit with an improved way of doing things, a radically different pricing model, indirect network effects they can't duplicate, and sometimes a global reach they couldn't possibly obtain on their own and with which they can't compete.

While the solution isn't appealing to executives and investors, sometimes the best these businesses can do is to milk their assets and prepare for an inevitable exit. The companies that published Yellow Pages, which enabled people to search for businesses in a thick paperback book, didn't really have any ability to take on the search engines. They simply lacked the necessary assets and skills.

Competing with a pioneering platform isn't always hopeless, though. American Express is one company that made an impressive pivot to do so. In 1950, the company was most famous for its Travelers Cheques, which it had introduced around the turn of the century. Travelers could use them to pay most merchants in the United States and to purchase foreign currency at banks abroad. Travelers Cheques were guaranteed if they were lost or stolen, which was especially convenient for foreign travel.

That year, Diners Club introduced the first charge card. It quickly became a serious threat to Travelers Cheques, which weren't as convenient for consumers or merchants as this newfangled means of payment. The charge card platform grew explosively, and Diners Club was soon accepted by many of the same travel and entertainment merchants that took Travelers Cheques. In response, American Express launched its own charge card in 1958. The card was a success, in part because American Express knew a lot about the payments business, and it had a base of consumers and merchants as well as a network of travel offices in major cities abroad.

New multisided platform ideas often provide opportunities for established businesses. During the 1950s and early 1960s, many US banks started credit card schemes. But most had trouble getting a critical mass of merchants and cardholders, in part because regulation prevented them from operating nationally or, in some cases, even statewide. They couldn't compete with American Express, which wasn't a bank and could operate through the United States as well as abroad.

Then, in 1966, MasterCard and Visa started national card networks. By joining one of these networks, a bank that issued cards got access to all the merchants that took that card brand, and a bank that signed up merchants got access to all the network's card-carrying customers. MasterCard and Visa ignited. Their success enabled many banks, including small ones, to operate profitable card programs.

For traditional retail, there isn't a simple guide for survival in the face of the emergence of turbocharged multisided platforms. The possible responses vary across the diverse categories of retailers, from jewelry to electronics to groceries; retailer sizes from small stores to large department stores; for single-sided stores versus two-sided malls; and across many other dimensions for this huge assortment of businesses. The video store segment illustrates both a missed opportunity for survival and provides a lesson on why many traditional retailers just can't make it.

Extinction

Video rental stores have closed en masse in the United States. There were 18,739 of them in 2005. Eight years later, in 2013, 83 percent were gone. Blockbuster, once the largest chain, shut its last three hundred US stores in early 2014. It might have survived but didn't even try to pivot. Smaller chains and individual stores really had no option but to accept their fate.

Mail-order DVDs took sales from video stores starting in the 2000s. Netflix was the pioneer. Its customers could select and order DVDs online. The service offered far more video titles than any physical store could possibly stock: its catalog had more than fifty-five thousand titles by 2005.[17]

The web apps used by the mail-order businesses provided many features that video rental stores couldn't easily replicate. These apps enabled people to search quickly for movies to watch. Using data analytic capabilities, they could use people's viewing habits to suggest new DVDs.

For many video rental stores, though, the fatal blow was the rise of video streaming. Consumers could get access to most movies and television shows over the Internet from home or wherever they had a broadband connection. They got instant gratification—no need to wait for the DVD to arrive—and didn't have to deal with sending videos back. The streaming movie providers, such as Netflix, had apps that ran on increasingly fast, fixed broadband networks. They worked on browsers, as apps on mobile devices, and on Internet TVs and set-top boxes like Roku.

Blockbuster should have seen this coming. The ability of web-based platforms to remove frictions and attain massive reach was apparent by 2000. That year, when Netflix approached it to partner, however, Blockbuster's executives "just about laughed us out of their office," according to Barry McCarthy, Netflix's chief financial officer at the time.[18]

By the early 2000s, it was clearly just a matter of time before technology made video streaming possible. In 2001, Reed Hastings, Netflix's founder and CEO, told *Billboard* that Netflix expected to have a robust streaming catalog in a decade.[19] Netflix bided its time with its mail-order rental business while broadband speed improved and used the time to work out a number of technical and business issues. It launched its video streaming service in 2007. By the time Blockbuster closed its last stores in 2014, Netflix had more than 44 million streaming subscribers.[20]

Blockbuster could have embraced the world of turbocharged multisided platforms and the apps that powered them earlier. Indeed, the possibility of video streaming led many entrepreneurs to launch video sharing sites in the mid-2000s, as we saw in chapter 5. With its huge scale and knowledge of its many regular customers, Blockbuster might well have been able to make the shift. Of course, it faced the problems all incumbents have. It may have lacked the technical and business skills that enabled Netflix and others to succeed. Or, like many successful firms facing disruptive innovation, it may just have been too wedded to the approach that had made it successful.[21]

Video streaming of movies and television shows is a capital-intensive national business requiring significant scale. Smaller video rental stores couldn't have pivoted to operating streaming video services. Instead, some have tried to diversify into selling coffee or party supplies.[22] Others have stayed the course, perhaps simply unwilling to accept that there's a gale set to knock their shops down. Shortly after Blockbuster's final exit from operating physical stores, an owner of an independent video rental store cheerfully told *Time* magazine, "People are getting tired of sitting home and having everything fed to them. This is a place to go and wander around. We've had people get married from meeting here."[23] The odds of his survival do not look good.

Death Spiral

Having a platform business powered by indirect network effects, like shopping malls, is great, until those network effects work in reverse. That's what's happening to some malls that aren't focused on high-income shoppers and luxury stores.

People outside of Baltimore used to go to the Owings Mills Mall to shop at Boscov's department store, a regional favorite. They would walk around the mall and go into other stores. Then Boscov's closed its Owings Mills store. Fewer people came to the mall. That made the mall less attractive to smaller stores, and even less attractive to shoppers. The same thing happened when the mall lost two other anchor stores, Lord & Taylor and Sears.

By the Sunday before Christmas 2014, there weren't many shoppers and there weren't many stores. The *New York Times* reported, "A few visitors walked down the long hallways and peered through locked metal gates into vacant spaces once home to retailers like H&M,

Wet Seal, and Kay Jewelers."[24] That creates a bad vibe for the shoppers who do come. "It's depressing," one shopper said.

Nonluxury shopping malls were struggling even before smartphones changed how people shopped. In fact, while about fifteen hundred enclosed shopping malls were built between 1956 and 2006, not a single one was opened between 2007 and 2013.[25] The more recent changes in how people shop and buy have added to their difficulties. Large department stores are closing some anchor stores at malls, as happened at Owings Mills. Other chains are closing some of their stores, too. That results in the mall losing foot traffic.

Here's where the bad side of positive indirect network effects come into play. Just as increases in participation on the platform can result in accelerating growth, decreases in participation can result in accelerating decline. Positive feedback effects magnify small changes. A decline in foot traffic or the departure of a store can lead to a downward spiral.

That's so common in the mall business that there's a name for the result—"a dead mall." There's even a virtual cemetery for them—deadmalls.com. Sadly, a tour around deadmalls.com, which also tracks department store closures and dying as well as dead malls, provides a poignant view of what's happening to the traditional retail industry.

As of 2014, about one of five shopping malls had vacancy rates of 10 percent or more—a signal of trouble—and more than 3 percent had vacancy rates of 40 percent or more—a sign of impending death.[26] Unfortunately, once a mall has entered a death spiral, there isn't much hope. Mall operators, of course, know this and they are figuring out how to stay alive.

Retail Reinvention

Malls may close, stores may downsize, and more retailers may declare bankruptcy. Brick-and-mortar stores aren't, however, going to go the way of the typewriter. An A.T. Kearney survey of twenty-five hundred shoppers in 2014 found that many consumers prefer physical stores for looking for things, for trying them, and for buying them. Millennials liked online the most. But around 40 percent of millennials preferred brick-and-mortar stores for looking for things; more than 70 percent for trying them, and more than 60 percent for buying them.[27]

Retailers of all sizes, including mall operators, are responding to the three disruptions caused by turbocharged multisided platforms by integrating physical and online methods of serving their customers. They call this "omnichannel" retailing to reflect the fact that they are selling through the mobile, computer, and physical store channels. In the future, we suspect they will go back to just calling this "retailing," as the distinctions between the online and physical worlds continue to blur.

Macy's, for example, has aggressively integrated its physical and online methods of sales in the last several years. This 150-year-old department store chain, which was the fifteenth-largest US retailer in 2014, shows its in-store inventory on its website.[28] According to a Macy's executive, a shopper can see that the Macy's store five blocks away has eight sweaters, in the size and color she's looking for, in stock.[29] While she could click and buy online, she could also stop at the store, try on the sweater, and if she likes it, buy it and take it home.

Macy's has made organizational changes to help tear down the walls between its physical and online efforts. It used to have separate silos for physical and online sales. In early 2015, Terry Lundgren, Macy's CEO, announced that "Going forward, one unified merchandising and marketing organization—a hybrid of store and online buying—will support the entire Macy's business to encourage both store and digital growth."[30]

Burberry, a venerated British brand that has long provided overcoats for movie stars, adventurers, and soldiers in the trenches, backed into the convergence of physical and virtual from necessity. Cash strapped, the company decided in 2006 to focus on millennial consumers in their twenties, especially in emerging economies where the wealthier people tend to be younger. It would use digital media to reach them.[31] According to Angela Ahrendts, Burberry CEO from 2006 through 2014, "[t]hat's when the digital transformation started for Burberry."[32]

Over the next few years, Burberry made its physical stores resemble its online shopping environment and made its online platforms more like its physical stores. According to Ahrendts, it began by asking "how can we use digital innovation to engage our customers more effectively in our physical real estate as well as online?" The sales associates began carrying iPads, which gave them access to "the full global collection." It also streamed its runway shows to the stores and brought more of what it was doing online onto giant screens in the stores. "In this way," said Ahrendts, "we have developed our stores to showcase our digital innovations."

Westfield Group, which is one of the largest mall operators in the world, is reinventing how it persuades shoppers to come to its malls and how it connects shoppers and retailers. It created an innovation center, Westfield Labs, located in San Francisco, to drive reinvention. The lab is focused on "innovating the retail ecosystem by leveraging the social, mobile, and digital market opportunities that converge the digital shopper and the physical world."[33] To counter the decline in foot traffic, Westfield is turning its malls into major consumer destinations for entertainment, leisure, and food as well as for shopping.[34] To integrate online and offline shopping they are experimenting with centers at the malls where consumers can pick up merchandise they bought online.[35]

There's no guarantee that traditional retailers that were successful operating brick-and-mortar stores in the physical world will be successful operating omnichannel stores in the new world. Some of the key innovations in operating physical stores have come from Apple, which operates a highly successful, generally packed chain of physical stores. Early on, it dispensed with cash registers and clunky point-of-sale terminals. Customers can pay one of Apple's sales associates, who are always walking around the store, by swiping a payment card on an iPhone. An app, running on the iOS operating system, does the rest.

In fact, competition in traditional retail may come from entrepreneurs without brick-and-mortar experience who have mastered online commerce. Just as traditional brick-and-mortar retailers have integrated into online selling, some online retailers are moving into physical stores, and they are introducing innovations along the way.

Warby Parker, which started as an online prescription eyeglass company in 2010, had twenty physical stores in major US cities in late November 2015 as well as five showrooms at other stores.[36] "Our retail spaces combine the snappy ease of online ordering with the fun and serendipity of real-shopping," it says. Bonobos, an online men's retailer, had seventeen "guideshops" in 2015, places where customers can look at merchandise and try things on. They then place an order online, in the store or later at home or on their smartphones, and have it shipped. The theory is that this combines the benefit of physical stores, where people can try merchandise, and the efficiency of online, since the store doesn't need to keep a large inventory.[37]

The transformation of retail is happening slowly. That's not surprising. History teaches us that fundamental transformations do not take place in what has been called "Internet time" but over the course of years and, more likely, decades.[38] It also teaches that even the turbocharged multisided platforms we've seen to date aren't the last. Few, if anyone, imagined eBay in 1990, Google in 1995, Facebook in 2000, or Uber in 2005, WeChat in 2009, or the many other matchmakers that have changed the world in the last quarter century. It is impossible to conceive what this ancient but increasingly powerful business model will do in the next quarter century, turbocharged by the technologies we have identified and sitting on the foundational platforms we have described.

Chapter 13

Slower and Faster Than You Think

What History Teaches Us about the Future of Matchmakers

MORE THAN THIRTY THOUSAND PEOPLE WILL RUN THE Boston Marathon on April 18, 2016. Many runners will come from out of town and will bring their families along for support. They will need places to stay. Getting a hotel room in the city isn't easy when the town is packed. Not to mention that hotel rooms are particularly expensive then.

That was a problem in the past for people who didn't plan far ahead. They'd have to resort to putting ads on Craigslist to find somebody's spare room or to stay at a hotel far away from the starting and finish lines. As one runner put it in 2014, "I'm ready to roll; I'm in shape; I just don't know where I'm going to sleep."[1]

In 2016, however, thousands of people in the Boston area will make rooms available to runners. They'll list those rooms and their prices on Airbnb, and runners can search for a place that fits their needs and their budgets. As of November 30, 2015, more than a thousand places were already listed for the 2016 marathon. With Airbnb, runners will have more choices for more convenient places to stay than ever before, and many people in Boston will have some extra income.

Airbnb is one of the leaders in what's known as the "sharing economy." That's one of the most popular business buzzwords of 2015. A Google search of that phrase yields more than 30 million hits. According to Google trends, there weren't any news headlines with "sharing economy" in them before February 2010. There were a hundred in November 2015, more than twice as many as in September 2014. What's novel and what isn't here though?

Airbnb and other companies that are part of the "sharing economy" are multisided platforms. What they have in common is that they are matching up people who have spare capacity—an extra room, a car, or a lawnmower, for example—with people who would benefit from that spare capacity. That's not a recent invention. OpenTable started helping match up restaurants with spare capacity—empty tables—with people looking to go out for dinner in 1999. Before then, people advertised their spare rooms in the classified sections of physical newspapers before there was Airbnb and before there was Craigslist.

Matchmakers aren't new, and those that enable people to share excess capacity aren't novel either. Turbocharged matchmakers *are* a recent development, however. And we've just seen the beginnings of them wiping out frictions.

In these final pages, we will try to give you some perspective on the excitement surrounding new matchmakers. Our five messages might sound contradictory, but they aren't. Trust us.

1. Matchmakers have been around for millennia. Some of them were even part of the sharing economy of years past.

2. A lot of what the new market darlings do is old stuff. They just use technology to improve on things that other matchmakers have done for many years.

3. What *is* pioneering is that modern information and communications technologies have turbocharged the multisided platform business model.

4. The history of matchmakers suggests that today's sharing-economy matchmakers won't be the last to make waves.

5. Turbocharged matchmakers will transform industries. That will happen gradually over the space of decades, but in fast spurts, as innovative new matchmakers rapidly emerge and displace incumbents. Things will be both slower, and faster, than you might think.

Matchmakers Over Three Millennia

No one knows when the first multisided platform started. Most likely, several millennia ago, after people started engaging in bartering—my chicken for your grain—someone came up with the bright idea of having a place where people could agree to come to find trading partners. Organized marketplaces emerged and spread.

More than two thousand years ago, there was a multisided platform in Athens that helped support trading among people around the Mediterranean. It was operated by the city-state itself rather than a private party. By 300 BCE, there was a designated place near the docks in Athens called an emporion where merchants, shipowners, and lenders could connect with each other to do business.[2] Traders could exchange merchandise with each other. They could enter into deals with shipowners to carry them or their goods on their next voyage. And creditors could lend money and provide insurance to shipowners and traders for their next voyage.

The emporion by the docks was a matchmaker between lenders and traders. Traders faced a couple of problems back then. It was expensive to finance voyages. The availability of credit limited the volume of trade. Voyages were also risky. Traders could lose their cargo, or it could be damaged in a storm or in another sort of misadventure on the high seas.[3]

To address both problems, wealthy individuals were willing to lend money that a trader would repay with interest on his successful return, but which they would forgive in the event of disaster.[4]

The trader could therefore get both a loan and insurance from these individuals. The emporion provided a place where wealthy individuals and intrepid voyagers could find each other and do deals.[5]

The Athenian emporion was also a matchmaker between traders and shipowners. It helped an early version of the sharing economy. Shipowners could take several traders at the same time.[6] The emporion helped make more efficient use of ships' capacity by making it easier for shipowners and merchants to find one another and do deals.[7]

Let's move from Athens in 300 BCE to Renaissance Europe in the early 1400s CE. City-states sponsored mini-versions of Alibaba's 1688 matchmaker for businesses. Fairs, at which merchants gathered together and exchanged goods for a given period of time each year, were lively and profitable. There were 102 transactions, for example, at a fair held in Salerno for seven days in the mid-1400s. At that fair, two Frenchmen who lived in Naples sold five thousand hair combs to a German merchant.[8]

Sponsoring city-states offered tax concessions and suspended bans on imports to attract participants. They also had mechanisms for settling disputes between merchants. Merchants, meanwhile, often developed sufficient trust in each other, through repeated dealing, that they were willing to extend credit. One merchant, for example, sold four pieces of cloth to two other merchants who agreed to pay their debt, on demand, at any one of sixteen fairs held during a particular month in the next year.[9]

Now let's move forward another several centuries. The invention of the printing press with movable type by Gutenberg around 1440 led to the explosive growth of the media business, including newspapers. Before 1800, print newspapers had begun to publish classified ads. These ran the gamut from ads for people looking for marriage, to ads for people looking to rent a room, to ads for medical wares or even haberdashery or drapery.[10] According to a history of advertising by the industry publication *Advertising Age*, "[b]y 1800 most English and American newspapers were not only supported by advertising but were the primary medium carrying it."[11]

At first, newspapers didn't impose any structure on the classifieds, so it was hard to find things. Later, they organized the ads into categories to make it easier for interested readers and advertisers to connect. Many of the newspapers during the eighteenth and nineteenth centuries even had classifieds on their front pages.[12]

Of course, these eighteenth-century classifieds helped the sharing economy of the day. If someone had a spare room or several spare rooms to rent, they could run a classified ad in the local newspaper to find someone interested in being a boarder.

Déjà Vu

In 2015, billions of people worldwide are using messaging apps to communicate instead of making phone calls or sending e-mails or text messages. WeChat and WhatsApp are two of the largest messaging apps. These two-sided platforms rely on smartphones to connect senders and receivers of messages. People can also use them to send and receive money. They are very convenient. But they seem like small advances and not that novel, when you look at some older two-sided platforms.

In 1832, with the invention of the telegraph, it became possible to send messages over long distances very quickly. For thousands of years, it had taken about a day to transmit a message or carry money a hundred miles. That's how far one could go in a day on horseback.[13] The telegraph wasn't as quick as a phone call or e-mail because people had to get to telegraph stations and attendants had to code and decode their messages. But it did reduce the time to communicate over long distances to a miniscule fraction of what it had been.

Using the telegraph, the United States became very connected over the course of the nineteenth century. By 1880, Western Union, which had consolidated the telegraph industry by the mid-1860s, had 9,077 telegraph offices in the United States, handling 29.2 million messages over 234,000 miles of cable.[14] Other countries also developed extensive telegraph networks, and cables were laid under oceans and across borders to connect them.

By the late nineteenth century, the telegraph made communication possible around the world. This led to a massive explosion in the amount of information transmitted globally, which transformed markets and industries, while also making it easier for people to communicate with loved ones. For department stores, which began appearing in the 1860s in the United States, "[t]he telegraph was the key to effective inventory control, which gave them a competitive edge" over smaller rivals.[15]

The success of the telegraph soon led to the development of apps built on it. Money transfer was an early one. The telegraph offices became CICO agents. A sender could deposit money with one agent and the recipient could pick it up at another agent, with coded telegraph messages used to make the transactions secure. Western Union became the leading money-transfer operator. It established CICO agents—many of which were third parties—in most countries worldwide. In most ways, except for the use of mobile phones, its business model since 1871 is similar to M-PESA's.

In short, many of the multisided platforms that are transforming industries today are turbocharged versions of matchmakers that did more or less the same things decades or centuries ago with more primitive methods.

Turbocharging

People looking for lodging and people with rooms to spare were connecting over Craigslist more than a decade before they could use Airbnb. They were connecting through classified ads in physical newspapers several hundred years before that.

Online marketplaces such as eBay are similar to shopping malls and to Renaissance fairs held centuries ago. Online marketplaces don't curate the collection of stores as shopping malls do, but they provide ratings and feedback from consumers to control seller quality.

Online media enterprises like YouTube are similar to traditional media such as the major television networks in the United States. Both use content to attract viewers and then sell access to those viewers to advertisers. YouTube figured out a way to get content for free. CBS has to pay for it.

Like the village matchmaker and unlike most nightclubs, online matchmakers such as eHarmony try to make sure that the men and women they connect are right for each other.

Indirect network effects power all multisided platforms. Advances in technology from computer chips, the Internet, and the web, to fixed and mobile broadband, smartphones, programming languages, and the Cloud, have resulted in a huge increase in the power and reach of these effects. That's why turbocharged matchmakers are behind the gales of creative destruction that are transforming industries worldwide.

The End of History (?)

Could this, then, be the golden age of matchmakers? It is remarkable that in the space of only about five years, companies like Airbnb and Uber have become global players in lodging and transportation. Similar sharing-economy matchmakers are popping up all over. With the turbocharged sharing economy, have matchmakers achieved their final destiny?

Several millennia of experience strongly suggest otherwise. We expect that better, or at least different, matchmakers will come along and have their turn at disruption. With all due respect to the brilliant entrepreneurs behind today's unicorns and yesterday's huge IPOs, the telegraph was a far more important multisided platform in terms of its impact on the global economy than anything the Internet has yet spawned. The ancient Athenian emporion probably was, too, at least in its part of the world.

So, when you look at the turbocharged matchmakers of today, whether sharing ones or others, don't fall into the end-of-history illusion that all the good stuff has already happened. It almost certainly hasn't.

Shortly after the credit card became popular in the late 1950s, pundits started predicting the death of cash. The *Economist* wrote about "The Cashless Society" on July 9, 1966. A half century later, Americans use cash for about 26 percent of transactions. Many of these are small, so cash accounts for only 10 percent of the money people spend on the sorts of things they could pay for with a card.[16] Yet, while cash use has indeed declined over time, even in developed countries, it accounts for a large fraction of transactions.[17]

Pundits also predicted that e-commerce would kill brick-and-mortar stores. Some did die. But twenty years after the birth of the commercial Internet, physical retail still accounts for the vast majority of purchases. Happenings in the online world are transforming physical retail, as we saw, but this process will probably continue for decades. We can only guess where it will end, if it ever does.

Many other industries are following similar paths. Newspapers are going into death spirals, and many have closed. Two decades after Yahoo was founded in 1994, however, and after a flood of online media has occurred, over 40 million newspapers were printed daily in the United States.[18]

So far, the "Internet Revolution," which is behind the surge in matchmakers, doesn't look that different from previous technological revolutions. Edison invented the light bulb in 1879, and the first central generating station went online in 1881. By 1900, electricity was widely used for streetlights and trolleys. Only 8 percent of US households in urban areas had electric lights in 1900, however, and electric motors powered only about 5 percent of US factories.[19]

After another twenty years, with the development and growth of electric utilities, about half of urban homes had electric lighting and electricity was used for about half of US factory mechanical drive. By the end of the 1920s, fifty years after Edison, half of US factories were designed to use distributed electric motors, rather than just having a central electric motor replacing a steam engine.[20]

The phenomenal spread of smartphones in the last five years may result in some acceleration in the pace of creative destruction. Nevertheless, the history of matchmakers and the pace of the last twenty years strongly suggest that turbocharged multisided platforms will transform industries over decades rather than years.

That's not to say some things won't happen quickly. Just look at the impact of M-PESA's leapfrogging of traditional banking on Kenya. BlaBlaCar may be poised for similar growth in a number of developing countries in which poor infrastructure means that ride sharing has little competition from other modes of long-distance travel.[21] Or consider how quickly the video rental stores were killed. When a turbocharged multisided platform ignites, it can grow explosively and provide rapidly increasing value for people around the world. Those in the path of such a platform can take little solace in the fact that economywide change takes place slowly and often, as with electricity, in waves.

The Matchmaker: The Newly Discovered Species

There is no doubt, though, that multisided platforms play an extraordinarily important role in today's economy, and their influence is going to increase as existing turbocharged platforms grow and new ones ignite. Anyone who interacts with these matchmakers—as entrepreneur, investor, consumer, or partner—will want to understand how this complex business model works.

As we've noted, economists couldn't provide much help on that before 2000. Neither could anyone else. No one had identified matchmakers as a distinct species. Or unraveled how they worked. Now we have a lot of insights, many of which we've shared in the preceding pages.

To see how important this is, just consider the kinds of questions you'd need to ask to really understand how a multisided platform works. Who's participating in the platform, and how does the platform create value for them? How is the platform designed to promote interactions among those participants? How does the platform use prices to balance participation? Does it have a subsidy side? Does the platform have rules and standards, and how do these affect the ability of the platform to create value? How does the platform encourage all parts of the broader ecosystem that affect its ability to deliver value?

And, of course, how did, or will, it solve the chicken-and-egg puzzle and ignite?

You wouldn't ask these sorts of questions for a traditional business. But you sure wouldn't want to invest money in a multisided platform without knowing the answers to them or at least being confident that good answers to them will emerge, because those answers are central to determining whether the platform is viable and can make money. We also want to suggest that an entrepreneur shouldn't start a matchmaker without having plausible answers for all these questions. She probably won't have enough information to come up with the best answers until she starts and gets a feel for how potential participants respond. But she better have the right answers early in her matchmaker adventure.

Twenty-five years ago, multisided platforms were important players in the economy. But they weren't central. Anyone studying or playing in the business world could get by without a deep knowledge of this peculiar business model. No longer. Matchmakers are vital participants in most developed economies and are helping to drive progress in many less fortunate ones. And they are behind gales of creative destruction that, like the ones driven by electricity and the telegraph, will sweep industries for decades to come—at least.

Glossary

Guide to the Vocabulary of the New Economics of Multisided Platforms

Note: This glossary contains terms that are used outside of multisided platforms. We have focused on their meanings as they apply to multisided platforms.

Access fee: The price that customers are charged for obtaining access to the platform. For example, credit card issuers sometimes charge people an annual fee for using the card, thereby obtaining access to the merchants that accept these cards for payment.

Anchor tenant: A significant customer that helps attract other customers to the platform where the customers could be the same type as the anchor tenant, or the customers could be a different type of customer that is attracted to the anchor tenant. For example, department stores and big-box retailers are anchor tenants at shopping malls; they attract shoppers and they also persuade smaller retailers to take space at the mall in anticipation that these anchor stores will attract traffic.

Behavioral externality: Actions taken by platform participants that directly affect other participants positively or negatively. They are different from network externalities because they don't involve the number of participants but rather the behavior of those participants. For example, an app developer imposes costs on end users when it inserts malware into its app.

Critical mass: The minimum sets of participants for the platform sides that are necessary for the platform to ignite—that is, have self-sustaining growth. For a two-sided platform, critical mass isn't typically a single pair of numbers for each type of participant, but rather there is a range of numbers that could provide critical mass. For example, a B2B exchange has to have enough buyers and enough sellers to interest either side; once it has enough, more will join, while if it doesn't, it will lose the ones it has attracted.

Death spiral: The reinforcing loss of participants on either side of a platform that results when a platform loses a critical mass of customers and eventually collapses. For example, dead malls result from a death spiral in which the mall loses shopper traffic, which results in a loss of retailers, which results in a further loss of traffic, until eventually no retailers want to locate at the mall and no shoppers want to come.

Direct network effect: The impact of the addition of another participant to a network on other participants in the same group. A positive network effect occurs when an additional participant makes other participants of the same sort better off because they can reach and interact with more participants. For example, suppose people both make and receive phone calls to roughly the same degree. An additional person increases the size of the network and increases the number of people all other members can connect with. A negative direct network effect occurs when additional participants make other participants in the same group worse off, perhaps because of congestion or competition; for example, when an additional man goes to a singles bar, it increases competition for other men and may also make it too crowded to easily mingle.

Ecosystem: The businesses, institutions, and other environmental factors that affect the value, positively or negatively, that a platform can generate for the participants on the platform. For example, the value of a shopping mall to retailers is greater if there is easy road access to it and if it is located farther away from competing shopping malls, single-standing department stores, and shopping streets.

Edge provider: An online business that provides services or content by connecting to end users through an Internet Service Provider (ISP). For example, Pandora provides music over the Internet by connecting to people who listen to it over a fixed ISP such as a cable television system that provides broadband or a mobile ISP such as mobile network operator.

Externality: A benefit or cost that one participant imposes on another participant without direct monetary compensation. An externality could arise from a network effect or from a behavioral externality. See the examples for behavioral externality, direct network effects, and indirect network effects.

Foundational platform: A multisided platform that provides core services to other multisided platforms and is therefore a "platform for platforms." These include Internet Service Providers (ISPs), which connect edge providers and end users. For example, Comcast makes it possible for end users to connect over the Internet to Google's search engine. Foundational platforms also include computer operating systems, or invisible engines, which provide a standard platform for app developers and end users; for example, Android provides an operating system that enables app developers to provide apps to end users and for end users to use those apps.

Friction: Costs or other impediments that impede mutually advantageous interactions and exchanges. For example, before there were online reservation services, people who wanted to make dinner reservations had to identify restaurants, get their phone numbers, call them, see if they had a table, possibly leave a message, and try other restaurants if their first choice wasn't available; meanwhile, restaurants had to have someone answering the phone and recording reservations in a notebook.

Governance system: Rules that prohibit bad behavior (that is, negative *behavioral externalities*) by platform participants and mechanisms for enforcing those rules, including methods of detection and punishment. Marketplaces such as eBay, for example, have rules that prohibit sellers from engaging in various activities, such as posting misleading content, that can harm buyers and that prohibit buyers from engaging in various activities, such as not paying for items they have agreed to buy, that can harm sellers.

Ignition: When a multisided platform achieves critical mass and starts a process of self-sustaining growth. For example, once M-PESA had enough people with accounts who wanted to send or receive, and enough cash-in/cash-out agents who sold e-money to senders or who redeemed e-money from receivers, it started to grow very quickly.

Implosion: When a multisided platform can't achieve or maintain critical mass, it starts losing customers and eventually goes into a death spiral. For example, many mobile-money platforms have been unable to get enough subscribers or agents to ignite and have instead withered away.

Indirect network effect: The impact of the addition of one type of participant to a network on another type of participant. A positive indirect network effect arises when an additional participant of one type increases the value that participants of another type get. For example, an additional restaurant on OpenTable increases the value to diners, who now have an additional place to consider and at which to make reservations. A negative indirect network effect arises when an additional participant of one type decreases the value to participants of the other type. For example, more radio ads reduce the value that radio listeners get.

Internet service provider (ISP): An entity the enables end users and edge providers to connect to each other through the Internet. Fixed ISPs have physical wires or cables into households, apartment buildings, and businesses to make connections; people or businesses may then operate wireless networks at those physical locations. Mobile ISPs connect to people with mobile devices over the wireless spectrum using cell towers. For example, Comcast is a fixed ISP operating through a cable system, while T-Mobile is a wireless ISP.

Invisible engine: A computer operating system that provides services through "application programming interfaces" (APIs) that apps can use and that end users can use to run those apps. Invisible engines generally operate computer hardware, including the central processing chip, and make that functionality available to apps and users. Microsoft Windows is an example of an invisible engine for personal computers. Facebook is also an invisible engine because it provides APIs for app developers who write apps that people can use on Facebook. Invisible engines are sometimes called "software platforms."

Marquee customer: See "Anchor tenant."

Matchmaker: A business that helps two or more different kinds of customers find each other and engage in mutually beneficial interactions. Matchmaking does not involve literally finding perfect matches for people—like the old village matchmaker would try to do for a potential marriage—but rather finding good trading parties. A payment card network, for example, helps retailers and consumers get together and transact by using the same, agreed-on payment method. Also see "Multisided platform," which is another name for matchmakers.

Money side: For two-sided platforms, a group of customers that provides all or virtually all of the profits earned by the platform. For multisided platforms, one or more groups could not contribute any profits (see "Subsidy Side"), while two or more groups together could provide all or virtually all of the profits. For example, most newspapers make all of their profit from advertising and subsidize readers by providing them with content.

Multihoming: When platform participants use two or more similar platforms or could easily do so. For example, many consumers carry several different payment cards and select one of them to pay when they go to the store.

Multisided platform: A business that operates a physical or virtual place (a platform) to help two or more different groups find each other and interact. The different groups are called "sides" of the platform. For example, Facebook operates a virtual place where friends can send and receive messages, where advertisers can reach users, and where people can use apps and app developers can provide those apps.

Operating system: See "Invisible engine."

Pioneering platform: A multisided platform that is the first, or one of the first, to identify a friction and create a matchmaker to attempt to solve that friction. A pioneering platform, unlike later attempts to solve the same friction, usually has to be one of the first to solve the pricing, chicken-and-egg, and design issues necessary to solve the friction and ignite a platform. For example, OpenTable was one of the first online restaurant-reservation matchmakers and had to solve the key business issues itself with no guidance from the experience of other firms.

Pricing level: The level of prices that a multisided platform charges to both sides. When the prices to the two sides are fees for transactions, the total price level is the total amount paid by both sides for a transaction. For example, exchanges have set fees for liquidity providers (usually negative) and liquidity takers (usually positive), and the total price level is the total fees to the exchange for a trade, the sum of the fee received by the liquidity provider, and the fee paid by the liquidity taker.

Pricing structure: The distribution of the price or revenue contributed by the different sides of a multisided platform. For example, for fleet cards for paying truck stops on behalf of truck fleets, fleets pay about 25 percent of the total price and the truck stops pay about 75 percent. One side can pay more than 100 percent when there are negative prices to the other side or sides. Restaurants pay more than 100 percent of fees for OpenTable since diners pay no fees and are paid reward points.

Screening device: A method for limiting participation on the platform to participants on each side that are attractive to participants on the other side. Common screening devices are "exclusionary vibes," which provide signals that only certain kinds of participants (such as lower-income people for a mall, or Jewish people for a dating site) should join the platform; and "exclusionary amenities," which provide value only to the type of participants that the platform seeks to attract (such as articles on fly fishing for a magazine that wants to attract purchasers of fly-fishing–related goods and services).

Self-supply: For platforms that connect consumers with providers of goods and services, the platform supplies some of those goods and services itself. It may do this as a tactic during its start-up to help secure ignition, and it may do this longer term simply because it has some expertise in doing so and can make money that way.

Signaling device: An indicator that participants belong to the same platform and could therefore profitably interact. Payment card systems, for example, use logos on cards and at merchant terminals to inform cardholders that they can use their card at that terminal and for merchants to inform cardholders of this fact.

Single-homing: When platform participants standardize on and use only a single platform. For example, most people have a single wired broadband provider at home.

Subsidy side: A group of customers who do not cover their costs of participating on a platform. A multisided platform could have more than one group of subsidized customers, so long as there is one group that functions as the money side. Most consumers of ad-supported media, for example, pay little if anything and are provided content of significant value.

Transaction cost: The economists' term for frictions; see "Friction."

Turbocharged matchmaker: A matchmaker, or multisided platform, that benefits from a significant combination of powerful computer chips, the

Internet, the web, broadband communications, programming languages and operating systems, and the Cloud. Airbnb, for example, benefits from all of these technologies.

Two-sided market: The original name used to refer to industries that had "two-sided platforms." Two-sidedness is a characteristic of businesses, not always of industries, however.

Two-step strategy: An ignition strategy in which the platform secures significant participation by one group and then secures participation by the other group by offering them access to the first group. Advertising-supported media typically do this by securing eyeballs first and then selling access to them to advertisers.

Usage externality: The benefit that one party receives as a result of engaging in an exchange with another party. Two people benefit from being able to use a matchmaker to engage in a transaction, even if they can't connect with any other people. All multisided platforms have indirect network externalities as well as usage externalities.

Usage fee: A fee paid by one or more participants on a multisided platform for interacting with another participant. For example, OpenTable charges restaurants a $1 per person reservation fee.

Zigzag strategy: An ignition strategy in which the platform adopts tactics to increase participation of the different sides simultaneously. It is called zigzag because it imagines that the platform tries to push one group's participation up, then works on another group, and continues this process to secure positive feedbacks. In practice, it may push on all groups at the same time but vary the relative efforts devoted to them.

Notes

Introduction

1. None of these companies necessarily agrees with anything we say in this book, and they have not reviewed this book, much less endorsed it.

Chapter 1

1. The history of OpenTable here draws on a number of sources, including Chuck Templeton (founder of OpenTable), in discussions with the authors, 2015; "OpenTable Founder Chuck Templeton on Starting Up," interview by Katie Morell, *OpenForum* (June 23, 2015), https://www.americanexpress.com/us/small-business/openforum/articles/opentable-founder-chuck-templeton-on-starting-up/?utm_source=web&utm_medium=twitter; "Video: OpenTable Founder Chuck Templeton at Chicago Founders' Stories @ 1871," interview by Pat Ryan (April 25, 2013), http://www.1871.com/video-open-table-founder-chuck-templeton-at-chicago-founders-stories-1871/; Andrew Rachleff and Sara Rosenthal, "OpenTable," Case E418 (Palo Alto, CA: Stanford Graduate School of Business, November 18, 2011); Benjamin Edelman and Karen L. Webster, "Optimization and Expansion at OpenTable," Case 9-915-003 (Boston: Harvard Business School, March 9, 2015); and Maha Atal, "OpenTable—The Hottest Spot in Town," *Fortune*, August 14, 2009, http://fortune.com/2009/08/14/opentable-the-hottest-spot-in-town/.

2. They are also called two-sided markets, intermediaries, and brokers. A few years ago, we tried calling them "catalysts," since, like chemical catalysts, they encourage reactions, but the name has not caught on. See David S. Evans and Richard Schmalensee, *Catalyst Code* (Boston: Harvard Business School Press, 2007).

3. A potential source of confusion is the fact that the word "platform" has two different meanings in the broad business strategy literature: something that can be built on and something that facilitates interactions. To call Microsoft's Windows operating system a software platform, for instance, as we have done elsewhere, is to point to its *technical* role of making it easier to develop many different software apps. (See David S. Evans, Andrei Hagiu,

and Richard Schmalensee, *Invisible Engines: How Software Platforms Drive Innovation and Create Value* [Cambridge, MA: MIT Press, 2006]). To call Windows a multisided platform business, on the other hand, is to emphasize its *business* role in facilitating interactions between app developers and end users. This book focuses exclusively on this second meaning of "platform." A useful discussion of these two meanings is provided by Annabelle Gawer, "Bridging Differing Perspectives on Technological Platforms: Toward an Integrative Framework," *Research Policy* 43, no. 7 (2014): 1239–1249.

4. PricewaterhouseCoopers, "Global Top 100 Companies by Market Capitalization," March 31, 2015, http://www.pwc.com/gx/en/audit-services/capital-market/publications/assets/document/pwc-global-top-100-march-update.pdf.

5. CB Insights, "The Unicorn List: Current Private Companies Valued at $1 Billion and Above," https://www.cbinsights.com/research-unicorn-companies. The following ten companies were the largest in order of valuation; companies in [brackets] are not multisided platforms. Uber, [Xiaomi], Airbnb, [Palantir Technologies], Snapchat, Flipkart, Didi Kuaidi, [SpaceX], Pinterest, and Dropbox.

6. The company was initially called easyeats.com but changed its name early on.

7. The company also signed up restaurants in Chicago at first.

8. Unless otherwise noted, all monetary values we report are not adjusted for inflation.

9. "USA: OpenTable.com Names James Jeffrey Edwards CEO," just-food, May 18, 2000, http://www.just-food.com/news/opentablecom-names-jeffrey-edwards-ceo_id90312.aspx.

10. Chuck Templeton (founder of OpenTable), in discussion with the authors, September 19, 2015.

11. Ibid. OpenTable started this strategy systematically in New York and then used it in other cities later.

12. Erick Schonfeld, "OpenTable Has a Healthy IPO. Shares Shoot Up 59 Percent, Market Cap Passes $600 Million," *TechCrunch*, May 21, 2009, http://techcrunch.com/2009/05/21/opentable-has-a-healthy-ipo-shares-shoot-up-40-percent-market-cap-hits-600-million/.

13. OpenTable, "Press Room," http://press.opentable.com/.

14. David S. Evans and Richard Schmalensee, *Paying with Plastic,* 2nd ed. (Cambridge, MA: MIT Press, 2005), 54.

15. Technically, it was a "charge card" where the consumer had to pay his or her bill in full at the end of the month.

16. Within its first year, Diners Club introduced an annual fee. The card was still a good deal since consumers got free float for a couple of weeks and didn't have to pay for making transactions.

17. "OpenTable Terms of Use," http://www.opentable.com/info/agreement.aspx.

18. See Jean-Charles Rochet and Jean Tirole, "Platform Competition in Two-Sided Markets," *Journal of the European Economic Association* 1,

no. 4 (2003). As is increasingly common in academic economics, their paper was widely circulated several years before it appeared in print. The term "two-sided market" has fallen out of favor, as it has become clear that two- or multisidedness is an attribute of individual businesses, not necessarily of all businesses in a market. A nontechnical discussion of this paper and other early economic papers on multisided platforms is given by Richard Schmalensee, "An Instant Classic: Rochet & Tirole, Platform Competition in Two-Sided Markets," *Competition Policy International* 10, no. 2 (2014).

19. In suburban America, they even give people free parking and, often, entertainment. Single-sided businesses don't provide value to large groups of customers for free on a permanent basis. A perceptive reader might point out that single-sided stores let people in for free and sometimes even provide free parking and even entertainment. The difference is that the single-sided store directly earns money from those consumers when they buy things in the store. No one thinks of the regular store as serving the shopper for free. The shopping mall developer doesn't earn anything directly from the consumer.

20. "The truly personal computer," *The Economist*, February 28, 2015, http://www.economist.com/news/briefing/21645131-smartphone-defining-technology-age-truly-personal-computer.

Chapter 2

1. Andrew Rachleff and Sara Rosenthal, "OpenTable," Case E418 (Palo Alto, CA: Stanford Graduate School of Business, November 18, 2011).

2. A focus on grabbing eyeballs makes more sense for new businesses that hope to be advertiser supported like *Business Insider* or the *Huffington Post*. Even then, of course, not all eyeballs are equally attractive to all advertisers, so a more sophisticated strategy is likely to be required.

3. One of the better early books on network effects addressed to a business audience was Carl Shapiro and Hal R. Varian, *Information Rules* (Boston: Harvard Business School Press, 1998).

4. For a nontechnical discussion of the literature discussed in this paragraph and the next two, see Richard Schmalensee, "Jeffrey Rohlfs' 1974 Model of Facebook: An Introduction," *Competition Policy International* 7, no. 1 (2011).

5. Marvin B. Lieberman and David B. Montgomery, "First Mover Advantage," *Strategic Management Journal* 9, Special Issue: Strategy Content Research (1988).

6. "Google Ngram Viewer," https://books.google.com/ngrams.

7. Jean-Charles Rochet and Jean Tirole, "Platform Competition in Two-Sided Markets," *Journal of the European Economic Association* 1, no. 4 (2003).

8. This discussion is based largely on Andrei Hagiu, "The Last DVD Format War?" Case 9-710-443 (Boston: Harvard Business School, September 15, 2011).

9. At considerable expense, Sony included Blu-ray players in its PlayStation 3 game consoles. More of these consoles were sold than stand-alone HD-DVD players, but console owners were much less likely to rent movies than owners of stand-alone players.

10. Don Lindich, "Blu-ray Wins in Format War, But at What Cost?" *Pittsburgh Post-Gazette*, January 12, 2008, http://www.post-gazette.com/business/tech-news/2008/01/12/Sound-Advice-Blu-ray-wins-in-format-war-but-at-what-cost/stories/200801120153.

11. For a general discussion with some applications to platforms, see Hanna Halaburda and Felix Oberholzer-Gee, "The Limits of Scale," *Harvard Business Review*, April 2014.

12. Informally, a market is thin if it doesn't have enough participants for most of them to find many valuable exchanges most of the time. A market is thick if it does have enough participants for most of them to find valuable exchanges most of the time.

13. For another brief discussion of these decisions, which we will examine in more detail in later chapters, see Andrei Hagiu, "Strategic Decisions for Multisided Platforms," *MIT Sloan Management Review* 55, no. 2 (2014).

Chapter 3

1. A September 24, 2015, Belgian court decision forced Uber to close down its operations. See EurActiv.com with AFP, "Uber Ordered to Shut Brussels Service Within 21 Days," EurActiv.com, September 24, 2015, http://www.euractiv.com/sections/infosociety/uber-ordered-shut-brussels-service-within-21-days-317952

2. Until the mid-2000s, MasterCard and Visa operated as not-for-profit membership associations, not publicly traded companies. According to PricewaterhouseCoopers, as of March 31, 2015, Visa was the thirty-ninth most valuable company in the world, and MasterCard was the seventy-eighth most valuable. PricewaterhouseCoopers, "Global Top 100 Companies by Market Capitalization," March 31, 2015, http://www.pwc.com/gx/en/audit-services/capital-market/publications/assets/document/pwc-global-top-100-march-update.pdf.

3. According to Bloomberg, market capitalization for Apple and Google was $665 billion and $527 billion, respectively, as of November 20, 2015. See Ibid. for the rankings as of March 2015.

4. As of November 25, 2015. CBInsight, "The Unicorn List: Current Private Companies Valued at $1B and Above," https://www.cbinsights.com/research-unicorn-companies.

5. Ibid. These include Uber, Airbnb, Snapchat, Flipkart, Didi Kuaidi, Pinterest and Dropbox.

6. For an interesting history of much of this digital revolution, see Walter Isaacson, *The Innovators: How a Group of Hackers, Geniuses, and Geeks Created the Digital Revolution* (New York: Simon and Schuster, 2014).

7. The iPhone 6 has a speed of 1.4 GHz, compared to 4.77 MHz for the 1981 IBM PC. Clock speed is a somewhat imprecise measure of overall speed, due to the many other factors that affect overall performance. But in the absence of a benchmark suite that can be run on both chips, it is a reasonable way to get a sense of the vastness of the gap between the two machines. "IBM Personal Computing, a Six-Year History," *PC Magazine*, May 26, 1987, 46; Geekbench, "iPhone, iPad, and iPod Benchmarks," https://browser.primatelabs.com/ios-benchmarks.

8. "Worldwide Smart Phone Market Q2 2015 with Country Level Detail," Canalys, August 2015; "Worldwide Tablet Price Band Forecasts," Canalys, April 2015.

9. J. Christopher Westland and Theodore H. K. Clark, *Global Electronic Commerce: Theory and Case Studies* (Cambridge, MA: MIT Press, 1999), 275; CERN, "The Birth of Web," http://home.web.cern.ch/topics/birth-web.

10. Internet Live Stats, "Internet Users in the World," http://www.internetlivestats.com/.

11. Netcraft, "November 2015 Web Server Survey," November 16, 2015, http://news.netcraft.com/archives/2015/11/16/november-2015-web-server-survey.html.

12. ITU, "Fixed broadband subscriptions" (2014).

13. Content delivery networks (CDNs) store content at various locations to reduce the distance the content must travel to its final destination. Akamai, "Akamai's State of the Internet: Q4 2014 Report," March 25, 2015, https://www.stateoftheinternet.com/resources-connectivity-2014-q4-state-of-the-internet-report.html.

14. These figures may overstate the percentage of the population with broadband subscriptions since some people have multiple subscriptions. Broadband Commission, "The State of Broadband 2014," 21.

15. For an interesting history of programming, see Sebastian Anthony, "The Evolution of Computer Languages (infographic)," *ExtremeTech*, August 1, 2011, http://www.extremetech.com/computing/91572-the-evolution-of-computer-languages-infographic.

16. Al Hilwa, "2014 Worldwide Software Developer and ICT-Skilled Worker Estimates," IDC, December 2013, http://www.idc.com/research/viewtoc.jsp?containerId=244709.

17. Netcraft, "November 2015 Web Server Survey," November 16, 2015, http://news.netcraft.com/archives/2015/11/16/november-2015-web-server-survey.html.

18. Some have charged or are trying to charge edge providers either for access or for faster or better service. The net neutrality debate in many parts of the world concerns whether public policy should limit their ability to do so.

19. Netflix tries to store most of its content at or near ISPs so that a viewer's ISP does not have to go over much of the Internet to retrieve the content the viewer wants to stream.

20. Internet Live Stats, "Internet Users in the World," http://www
.internetlivestats.com/; Worldometers, "World Population Clock," http://
www.worldometers.info/world-population/. Just to mention a few examples of
decreases in the cost from 2012 to 2014, in Copenhagen, the provider DLG
increased its prices only six cents and tripled the speeds it offered; in Dublin,
Vodafone decreased its package price 8 percent while increasing the speed by
a factor of twelve; AT&T maintained the price of its package while doubling
the speed. Nick Russo, Robert Morgus, Sarah Morris, and Danielle Kehl,
"The Cost of Connectivity 2014," Open Technology Institute, October 2014,
https://static.newamerica.org/attachments/229-the-cost-of-connectivity-2014/
OTI_The_Cost_of_Connectivity_2014.pdf.

21. Liraz Margalit, "Tinder and the Evolutionary Psychology," *TechCrunch*,
September 27, 2014, http://techcrunch.com/2014/09/27/tinder-and-evolutionary
-psychology/.

22. For an extensive discussion of the role of software platforms in transforming industries prior to 2005, see our earlier book, David S. Evans, Andrei
Hagiu, and Richard Schmalensee, *Invisible Engines* (Cambridge, MA: MIT
Press, 2006). As we noted in chapter 1, note 3, operating systems are often
"platforms" in both senses in which that word is commonly used.

23. The Unix operating system, first released by Bell Laboratories in 1971,
was widely distributed and had a major influence in the design of later systems. In 1991, Linus Torvalds released the first version of the Linux operating system. It is an open source system: anyone can propose changes to the
core system or modify the system and use it for free. It has become a leading
operating system for workhouse computers and powers the core of the Android
operating system for smartphones. The Android operating system for mobile
phones relies on the core portion of Linux known as the kernel.

24. Leena Rao, "Ubercab takes the hassle out of booking a car service,"
TechCrunch, July 5, 2010, http://techcrunch.com/2010/07/05/ubercab-takes-
the-hassle-out-of-booking-a-car-service/.

25. Uber Newsroom, "Our Commitment to Safety," December 17, 2014,
http://newsroom.uber.com/2014/12/our-commitment-to-safety/; Uber, "60
Countries: Available Locally, Expanding Globally," https://www.uber.com/
cities.

26. Google Inc., "Form 10-K for the Period Ending December 31, 2014,"
http://investor.google.com/pdf/20141231_google_10K.pdf; Greg Sterling,
"Report: Google had $12 billion in Mobile Search Revenue, 75 Percent
from iOS," *Marketing Land*, May 28, 2015, http://marketingland
.com/report-google-had-12-billion-in-mobile-search-revenue-75-percent-
from-ios-130248; Facebook Inc., "Form 10-Q for the Period Ending
March 31, 2015," http://investor.fb.com/common/download/sec
.cfm?companyid=AMDA-NJ5DZ&fid=1326801-15-15&cik=1326801.

27. A Google Ngram search of Google Books shows that the word "online"
started being used in the 1950s shortly after it was introduced in a book by
W. Stifler, *High-Speed Computing Devices* (New York: McGraw-Hill, 1950),

http://www.textfiles.com/bitsavers/pdf/era/High_Speed_Computing_
Devices_1950.pdf. The use of the phrase grew rapidly starting in the early
1990s, as did the use of the phrase "offline world."

28. Joseph A. Schumpeter, *Capitalism, Socialism and Democracy* (1942,
repr. London: Routledge, 2010), 83–84.

29. Newspaper Association of America, "Newspaper Revenue," April 18,
2014, http://www.naa.org/Trends-and-Numbers/Newspaper-Revenue/
Newspaper-Media-Industry-Revenue-Profile-2013.aspx; Newspaper Association of America, "Archived Advertising and Circulation Revenue Data," April
2013, http://www.naa.org/~/media/NAACorp/Public%20Files/TrendsAnd-
Numbers/Newspaper-Revenue/Annual-Newspaper-Ad-Revenue.ashx.

30. Newspaper Association of America, "Newspaper Circulation Volume,"
March 30, 2015, http://www.naa.org/~/media/NAACorp/Public%20Files/
TrendsAndNumbers/Circulation/Total-Paid-Circulation.ashx.

31. Newspaper Association of America, "Newspaper Circulation Volume,"
http://www.naa.org/Trends-and-Numbers/Circulation-Volume/Newspaper
-Circulation-Volume.aspx.

32. Ken Doctor, "Newsonomics: The Halving of America's Daily News-
rooms," Nieman Lab, July 28, 2015, http://www.niemanlab.org/2015/07/
newsonomics-the-halving-of-americas-daily-newsrooms/.

33. US Bureau of Labor Statistics, "Occupational Employment Statistics:
41-3041—Travel Agents," http://www.bls.gov/oes/tables.htm; US Census Bureau Population Division, "Table 1. Intercensal Estimates of Population by
Sex and Age for the United States: April 1, 2000 to July 1, 2010," http://www
.census.gov/popest/data/intercensal/national/tables/US-EST00INT-01.xls;
US Census Bureau Population Division, "Annual Estimates of the Resident
Population: April 1, 2010 to July 1, 2014," http://factfinder.census.gov/faces/
tableservices/jsf/pages/productview.xhtml?src=bkmk.

34. Chris Isidore, "New York City's Yellow Cab Crisis," CNN, July 21, 2015,
http://money.cnn.com/2015/07/21/news/companies/nyc-yellow-taxi-
uber/.

35. The price in 2013 was $1.05 million. In January 2015, it was $810,000,
a decrease of 23 percent. Josh Barro, "New York City Taxi Medallion Prices
Keep Falling, Now Down About 25 Percent," *New York Times*, January 7,
2015, http://www.nytimes.com/2015/01/08/upshot/new-york-city-taxi-
medallion-prices-keep-falling-now-down-about-25-percent.html.

Chapter 4

1. "Mr. Zhang Wei" is not a real person but a fictitious, but representative
entrepreneur, we have created based on interviews we have conducted with
small business owners in China, discussions with knowledgeable Chinese colleagues, and our research on the start of Alibaba, including inspections of its
early websites. We then verified with knowledgeable Chinese colleagues that
this example reflected real business circumstances at the time.

Any similarity between Zhang Wei and any real entrepreneur in China is purely coincidental.

2. Deng Xiaoping, meeting with a senior US business delegation organized by US Time Inc., October 23, 1985, http://cpc.people.com.cn/GB/34136/2569304.html.

3. World Bank, "GDP per Capita (Current US$)," http://data.worldbank.org/indicator/NY.GDP.PCAP.CD?page=3 (data for 1998). China's GDP per capita was 2.5 percent of the level in the United States.

4. World Bank, "Fixed Telephone Subscriptions (Per 100 People)," http://data.worldbank.org/indicator/IT.MLT.MAIN.P2?page=3 (data for 1998).

5. World Bank, "Mobile Cellular Subscriptions (Per 100 People)," http://data.worldbank.org/indicator/IT.CEL.SETS.P2?page=3 (data for 1998).

6. World Bank, "Rail Lines (Total Route-km)," http://data.worldbank.org/indicator/IS.RRS.TOTL.KM?page=3 (data for 1998).

7. Xue-Feng He and Li Yuan, "Information Asymmetry, Signaling Game, and Small and Medium-Sized Enterprises (SMEs) Financing in West China," Eighth West Lake International Conference SMB, November 2006, http://www.seiofbluemountain.com/en/search/detail.php?id=3139.

8. World Bank, "GDP (Constant 2005 US$)," http://data.worldbank.org/indicator/NY.GDP.MKTP.KD?page=3.

9. Board of Governors of the Federal Reserve System, "Consumers and Mobile Financial Services 2015," March 2015, http://www.federalreserve.gov/econresdata/consumers-and-mobile-financial-services-report-201503.pdf; Karen Webster, "The Incredible Mobile Payments Myth," PYMNTS.com, September 28, 2015, http://www.pymnts.com/news/2015/the-incredible-mobile-payments-myth/.

10. This discussion is based largely on Porter Erisman, *Alibaba's World: How a Remarkable Chinese Company Is Changing the Face of Global Business* (New York: Palgrave Macmillan, 2015); *Crocodile in the Yangtze: The Alibaba Story*, directed by Porter Erisman (2012; New York: Purple Reel Productions and Taluswood Films).

11. Liu and Avery, *alibaba,* Alibaba Group, "Alibaba.co Brings Trust to Online B2B Commerce for SMEs."

12. Erisman, *Alibaba's World*; *Crocodile in the Yangtze.*

13. Donny Kwok, "Alibaba.com Says Asia Needs E-Business," Reuters News, October 7, 1999.

14. Winter Nie, "A Leap of Faith with Alibaba," June 2014, http://www.imd.org/research/challenges/TC046-14-leap-of-faith-with-alibaba-winter-nie.cfm.

15. Kwok, "Alibaba.com Says Asia Needs E-Business"

16. Alibaba.com's home page (archived February 8, 2000), *Internet Archive Wayback Machine*, https://web.archive.org/web/20000208125348/http://www.alibaba.com/.

17. Alibaba Group, "Alibaba.com Celebrates 1,000,000th Member," December 27, 2001, http://www.alibabagroup.com/en/news/press_pdf/p011227.pdf.

18. Shiying Liu and Martha Avery, *alibaba* (New York: HarperCollins e-books, 2009), 69.

19. Alibaba Group, "Alibaba.com Brings Trust to Online B2B Commerce for SMEs," September 10, 2001, http://www.alibabagroup.com/en/news/press_pdf/p010910.pdf.

20. Liu and Avery, *alibaba*, 70.

21. Alibaba Group, "Alibaba.co Brings Trust to Online B2B Commerce for SMEs."

22. Alibaba.com Limited, "Global Offering," October 23, 2007, http://globaldocuments.morningstar.com/documentlibrary/document/45dda2cbefcb49dc.msdoc/original, 1.

23. Ibid.

24. Ibid., 74.

25. World Bank, "GDP (Constant 2005 US$)," http://data.worldbank.org/indicator/NY.GDP.MKTP.KD?page=2.

26. At the time, many Chinese households did not have bank accounts. Over the next decade, the percentage of Chinese adults (age 15+) with bank accounts increased dramatically. Over just the last few years (2011–2014), the share of Chinese adults (age 15+) with bank accounts increased from 64 percent to 79 percent, which has helped the growth of Alibaba's retail business. World Bank, "Massive Drop in the Number of Unbanked, Says New Report," April 15, 2015, http://www.worldbank.org/en/news/press-release/2015/04/15/massive-drop-in-number-of-unbanked-says-new-report.

27. Confidential interview with a retailer who sold dresses online, August 19, 2015.

28. Domaincom, "阿里巴巴和域名的那些事 (On Alibaba and Its Domain Names)," September 21, 2014, http://www.admin5.com/article/20140921/562982.shtml.

29. Alibaba Group, "Financials and Metrics," http://www.alibabagroup.com/en/ir/financial (data for twelve months ended June 30, 2015); Alibaba Group Holding Limited, "Form 20-F for the Period Ending March 31, 2015," 6, http://hsprod.investis.com/ir/alibaba/Alibaba_as_filed_20-F.pdf.

30. Alibaba Group, "Form 20-F for the Period Ending March 31, 2015," 60, http://hsprod.investis.com/ir/alibaba/Alibaba_as_filed_20-F.pdf.

31. The value of transactions is presented as the gross merchandise value, which is related to the gross merchandise sold, but excludes fees charged. Alibaba Group, "Form 20-F for the Period Ending March 31, 2015," 6, http://hsprod.investis.com/ir/alibaba/Alibaba_as_filed_20-F.pdf.

32. Jack Nickelson and Hideo Owen, "A Theory of B2B Exchanges Formation," June 5, 2002, http://papers.ssrn.com/sol3/papers.cfm?abstract_id=315121.

33. William A. Woods and Arthur B. Sculley, *B2B Exchanges: The Killer Application in the Business-to-Business Internet Revolution* (Hong Kong: ISI Publications, 2000).

34. For the Jupiter and Goldman Sachs estimates see David Lucking-Reilty and Daniel F. Spulber, "Business-to-Business Electronic Commerce," *Journal of Economic Perspectives* 15, no. 1 (2001), http://pubs.aeaweb.org/doi/pdfplus /10.1257/jep.15.1.55. As a sign of the euphoria, one article even claimed that the market cap of the online B2B exchanges would reach $200 trillion by 2010. Mark Vernon, "B2B Business Is Booming," ComputerWeekly.com, December 2000, http://www.computerweekly.com/feature/B2B-business -is-booming. Perhaps it was just a typo.

35. Jack Nickelson and Hideo Owen, "A Theory of B2B Exchanges Formation," June 5, 2002, http://papers.ssrn.com/sol3/papers.cfm?abstract_id=315121.

36. In addition to Ariba, which we discuss next, some specialized vertical B2B exchanges eventually did make a go of it, but in 2015 in the United States, they account for a tiny fraction of the activity that was once predicted for them. Examples include GXS and Sterling (Electronic Data Interchanges), Medidata (clinical trials), Dealertrack (B2B for auto retailing), Concur (travel), GHX and Emdeon (health care), and Fieldglass (contingent labor).

37. Marc H. Meyer and Frederick G. Crane, *Entrepreneurship: An Innovator's Guide to Startups and Corporate Ventures* (Thousand Oaks, CA: Sage Publications, 2011).

38. Bob Solomon, discussion with authors, July 16, 2015.

Chapter 5

1. The importance of the development of enabling technologies is stressed by Jawed Karim, "YouTube: From Concept to Hypergrowth," University of Illinois seminar, October 21, 2006, https://www.youtube.com/watch?v=XA-JEXUNmP5M. This talk provides an interesting and entertaining look at the early history of YouTube.

2. And maybe find a date. Right underneath the sign-in, users were prompted for "I'm a [blank] seeking [a blank] between [the age of blank] and [the age of blank]." YouTube home page (archived April 28, 2005), *Internet Archive Wayback Machine*, https://web.archive.org/web/20050428014715/http://www.youtube.com/.

3. This chapter focuses on situations like that faced by YouTube, in which more participation on any one side attracts more participation on the other side(s). This is true for many but not all multisided platforms. As we noted in chapter 2, for instance, radio advertisers are attracted by listeners, but listeners are not generally attracted by advertisers. Getting enough listeners to be attractive to advertisers and to attain viable scale is necessary for survival, but there is no reason to expect explosive growth to follow. We return to these situations briefly later.

4. Hamdi Ulukaya, "Chobani: The Unlikely King of Yogurt," interview by Sheridan Prasso, *Fortune*, November 30, 2011, http://archive.fortune.com/2011/11/29/smallbusiness/chobani_yogurt_hamdi_ulukaya.fortune/index.htm.

5. This point is more nuanced for advertising-supported media. Advertisers won't show up if there are no users. Users may be more than happy to show up even if there is no advertising. Advertising-media properties can ignite by providing content to attract viewers (which is a subsidy to the viewers) and then sell access to those viewers to the advertisers. We discuss this more later.

6. Federation of American Scientists, "Nuclear Weapon Design," October 21, 1998, http://fas.org/nuke/intro/nuke/design.htm.

7. E-mail from Karim Jawed, quoted in Randall Stross, *Planet Google: One Company's Audacious Plan to Organize Everything We Know* (New York: Free Press, 2009), 116.

8. As of April 28, 2005. This does not appear in Wayback Machine screenshots after this date. YouTube home page (archived April 28, 2005), *Internet Archive Wayback Machine*, https://web.archive.org/web/20050428014715/http://www.youtube.com/.

9. Karim, "YouTube: From Concept to Hypergrowth."

10. Stross, *Planet Google*, 116.

11. YouTube home page (archived September 1, 2005), *Internet Archive Wayback Machine*.

12. Under US copyright law, a site is supposed to take down copyrighted material when it is notified. YouTube was eventually sued over whether it complied. It ultimately prevailed in lower courts, and the case was settled. Jonathan Stempel, "Google, Viacom Settle Landmark YouTube Lawsuit," Reuters, March 28, 2014, http://www.reuters.com/article/2014/03/18/us-google-viacom-lawsuit-idUSBREA2H11220140318.

13. Extracted from Karim, "YouTube: From Concept to Hypergrowth," 7:37. Since the figures were extracted from a screenshot from a YouTube video, the data points are not exact. However, they are likely close, and the shape of the curve is virtually the same as shown in Karim's presentation.

14. Steve Chen, quoted in Stross, *Planet Google*, 116; YouTube home page (archived September 1, 2005), *Internet Archive Wayback Machine*; "YouTube Services Up 100 Million Videos a Day Online," *USA Today*, July 16, 2006, http://usatoday30.usatoday.com/tech/news/2006-07-16-youtube-views_x.htm.

15. "Google Buys YouTube for $1.65 Billion," NBC News, October 10, 2006, http://www.nbcnews.com/id/15196982/ns/business-us_business/t/google-buys-youtube-billion/#.VcDbAz1Viko; "50 Best Websites 2006," *Time*, http://content.time.com/time/specials/packages/0,28757,1949762,00.html.

16. This development is a much simplified description of the results in David S. Evans and Richard Schmalensee, "Failure to Launch: Critical Mass in Platform Businesses," *Review of Network Economics* 9, no. 4 (2010).

17. Frontiers like that shown in figure 5-2 arise when dissatisfied participants leave more quickly than information spreads among those who have not tried the platform. In that case the only practical way to achieve ignition is to get substantial numbers of both uploaders and viewers on board, which YouTube did. For further discussion see "Failure to Launch," cited above.

18. This is related to what have been called "divide and conquer" strategies that can be used by entrants competing with an established platform. The idea is to attract enough members of one customer group, by subsidies if necessary, that enough of the other group will be attracted to join without the need for subsidies. See Bruno Jullien, "Competition in Multi-Sided Markets: Divide-and-Conquer," *American Economic Journal: Microeconomics* 3, no. 4 (2011).

19. Chuck Templeton (founder of OpenTable), in discussion with the authors, September 19, 2015.

20. Mark Sweeney, "First Ads Appear on YouTube Clips," *The Guardian*, August 22, 2007, http://www.theguardian.com/media/2007/aug/22/advertising .digitalmedia; Anna Bennett, "It's Official! Pinterest Is Going To Begin Selling Ads Right Now," *Business 2 Community*, May 14, 2014, http://www .business2community.com/pinterest/ official-pinterest-going-begin-selling-ads-right-now-0883458.

21. Andrei Hagiu, "Multi-Sided Platforms: Foundations and Strategy," No. 714-436 (Boston: Harvard Business School, 2013), http://www.hbs.edu/ faculty/Pages/item.aspx?num=44940.

22. Eric M. Jackson, *The PayPal Wars* (Los Angeles: World Ahead Publishing, 2004), 49.

23. eBay Inc., "Q2 2015 Financial Highlights," 13.

24. eBay acquired PayPal in 2002 for $1.5 billion. Margaret Kane, "eBay Picks up PayPal for $1.5 Billion," CNET, August 18, 2002, http://www .cnet.com/news/ebay-picks-up-paypal-for-1-5-billion/. It was spun off in mid-2015. Leena Rao, "PayPal Makes Big Splash on First Day of Trading After eBay Spinoff," *Fortune*, July 20, 2015, http://fortune.com/2015/07/20/ paypal-ebay-split-valuation/. Its market cap as of October 9, 2015, is $39.07 billion. "PayPal Key Statistics," Yahoo Finance, http://finance.yahoo.com/q/ ks?s=PYPL+Key+Statistics.

25. Greg Jarboe, *YouTube and Video Marketing: An Hour a Day* (Indianapolis: John Wiley & Sons, 2009), 17.

26. Sarah Perez, "Google Shutdowns Continue: iGoogle, Google Video, Google Mini & Others Are Killed," *TechCrunch*, July 3, 2012, http://techcrunch .com/2012/07/03/google-shutdowns-continue-igoogle-google-video-google-mini -others-are-killed/.

27. This discussion relies heavily on Andrei Hagiu and David B. Yoffie, "Brightcove, Inc. in 2007," No. 9-712-424 (Boston: Harvard Business School, 2011).

28. Brightcove did an IPO in February 2012. As of October 2, 2015, its market cap was $169 million.

Chapter 6

1. Considering the value of goods shipped, trucking has a much larger share than air or rail for all lengths of shipment. See US Department of

Transportation, "Freight Facts and Figures 2013," http://www.ops.fhwa
.dot.gov/freight/freight_analysis/nat_freight_stats/docs/13factsfigures/pdfs/
fff2013_highres.pdf.

2. Long-haul—also known as over-the-road—trucking involves long trips,
often overnight, and across multiple states. Short-haul trucking involves day
trips. Our discussion of pricing in this chapter applies to both.

3. Even if he wanted to power through the trip and could carry enough
fuel to do so, he's not supposed to. Federal regulation prohibits driving more
than eleven hours after the previous off-duty period and requires regular
breaks.

4. American Trucker, "Truck Stops," http://trucker.com/truck/stops.

5. Love's has 303 truck stops as part of its chain. See Love's Travel Stops
and Country Stores, "Location Search," http://www.loves.com/LocateUs/
LocationSearchResults.aspx?locationtype=TravelStop. The largest chain,
Pilot Flying J, operated 650 truck stops. Shailesh Kumar, "Stock Review:
$TA—Travel Centers of America—The Ownership Structure Hampers Value
Creation," *Value Stock Guide*, December 15, 2013, http://valuestockguide.com/
smallcapvalue/stock-review-tatravel-centers-of-americathe-ownership-
structure-hampers-value-creation/.

6. This consumption figure is based on 2013. That year year 37,330
of on-highway diesel fuel was consumed, or about 102.3 million gallons a
day. See https://www.eia.gov/petroleum/fueloilkerosene/pdf/foks.pdf . The
average price of on-highway diesel fuel was $3.922 yielding an average daily
expenditure of $401 million. See https://www.eia.gov/dnav/pet/hist/LeafHandler
.ashx?n=PET&s=EMD_EPD2D_PTE_NUS_DPG&f=M. As of November 23,
2015, the price of diesel fuel is lower, at $2.445. Consumption is likely higher
but current data is not available.

7. Comdata was sold to FleetCor, a large transportation payment company,
in 2014 for $3.45 billion. It continues to operate its own brand. FleetCor,
"FleetCor Completes Acquisition of Comdata," November 17, 2014, http://investor
.fleetcor.com/phoenix.zhtml?c=236217&p=irol-newsArticle&ID=1990153.

8. Both companies operate fleet cards for long-haul and short-haul trucking and do so in a number of countries. We focus on the US market in this
chapter. FleetCor Technologies Inc., "Form 10-K for the Period Ending
December 31, 2014," 4–7, http://services.corporate-ir.net/SEC/Document
.Service?id=P3VybD1hSFIwY0RvdkwyRndhUzUwWlc1cmQybDZZWEprTG1O
dmJTOWtiM2R1Ykc5aFpDNXdhSEEvWVdOMGFXOXVQVkJFUmlacGNHR
m5aVDB4TURFeE56UXddOU1p6ZFdKemFFXUTlOVGM9JnR5cGU9MiZmbj1
GTEVFVENPUlRlY2hub2xvZ2llc0luY18xMEtfMjAxNTAzMDIucGRm;
WEX Inc., "Form 10-K for the Period Ending December 31, 2014," 1–2, http://
ir.wexinc.com/phoenix.zhtml?c=186699&p=irol-sec.

9. Love's Travel Stops and Country Stores, "Location Search."

10. The fuel station at truck stops is usually equipped with special point-
of-sale technology that works with fleet cards and is capable of transmitting
data to the fleet card network.

11. Some WEX fleet cards are co-branded with MasterCard. For places that don't accept WEX, the driver could use the card, and the transaction would go over the MasterCard network rather than the proprietary WEX network.

12. WEX Inc., "Form 10-K for the Period Ending December 31, 2014," 6, http://ir.wexinc.com/phoenix.zhtml?c=186699&p=irol-sec.

13. That is likely true if the driver is with a small fleet. Today, however, large truck fleets negotiate deals directly with the large truck stop chains.

14. WEX's fleet card revenues are reported under its Fleet Payment Solutions segment. For Fleet Payment Solutions in 2014, its payment processing revenue (from truck stops) was $357.1 million; its transaction processing revenue (from fleets) was $18.4 million; its account servicing revenue (from fleets) was $81.2 million; and its finance fees (from fleets) was $75.7 million. WEX Inc., "Form 10-K for the Period Ending December 31, 2014," 33. The payment processing fees paid by truck stops were therefore 67 percent of revenues from (payment processing + transaction processing + account servicing + finance). To the extent that account servicing fees include revenues for services other than those related to payment transaction, the 67 percent would understate the share paid by truck stops. If we exclude account servicing fees, then the fees paid by truck stops would account for 78 percent of revenues. We use 75 percent as a rough estimate for the purposes of our discussion.

15. FleetCor Technologies Inc., "Form 10-K for the Period Ending December 31, 2014," 5–8, 45; WEX Inc., "Form 10-K for the Period Ending December 31, 2014," 2–328.

16. Suppose price is P and sales at that price are Q, and suppose a small increase in price, ΔP, causes sales to decline by ΔQ. Then the usual measure of price sensitivity is the demand elasticity, $E = -(\Delta Q/Q)/(\Delta P/P)$, the ratio of the percentage decline in sales to the percentage increase in price. Suppose C is the marginal cost per unit of the product. Then the simple formula for optimal one-sided pricing is that the percentage markup over cost, $(P–C)/P$ must equal $1/E$. N. Gregory Mankiw, *Principles of Microeconomics,* 4th ed. (Mason, OH: Thomson-South Western, 2007), chapter 5.

17. The original Rochet-Tirole paper proves a clear example. If a single-sided firm sells two products with the same cost, basic theory says it should charge a lower price for the product with the more price-sensitive demand. In the particular model presented by Rochet and Tirole, however, it is optimal for a two-sided platform to charge a lower price to the side with the *less* price-sensitive demand in order to build participation on that side. We hasten to point out that this is *not* a general prescription. Jean-Charles Rochet and Jean Tirole, "Platform Competition in Two-Sided Markets," *Journal of the European Economic Association* 1, no. 4 (2003).

18. We are ignoring costs for now to keep things simple. More generally, pricing structure refers to the portion of incremental profit coming from each side.

19. WEX, like other fleet card companies, offers several products. The example here applies to a particular product like its FleetOne card for long-haul trucking. Even here, like many companies, it may set different prices for different customers; the example can be thought of as an average of these prices.

20. We can add the prices charged to each to get a total price when the two sides are both paying only for transactions, as is the case for WEX. For other pricing systems, which we discuss later, defining and calculating the total price is more complicated. But the basic concept remains useful.

21. An ordinary single-sided firm should clearly never set a per-unit price below the cost of supplying an additional unit, since it would lose more money, the more it sold. In the long run, of course, any firm has to charge a price that at least covers all its costs in order to stay in business.

22. Yahoo! Finance, "Google Inc.: Key Statistics," http://finance.yahoo .com/q/ks?s=GOOG+Key+Statistics.

23. Platforms with more than two sides can have multiple money and subsidy sides.

24. Credit cards are a bit more complicated than we are letting on here. Credit card issuers also make money from charging finance fees for cardholders who revolve their balances, and when someone charges something to their card, there's a chance that the cardholder will end up financing that charge and the issuer will earn profits from that loan.

25. YouTube has, however, introduced a premium service for viewers. See Ben Skipper, "YouTube Ad-Free Premium Service to Launch in October," *International Business Times*, September 29, 2015, http://www.ibtimes.co.uk/ youtube-ad-free-premium-service-launch-october-1521650.

26. OpenTable, "How OpenTable Works for Restaurants," http://blog.opent-able.com/2010/how-opentable-works-for-restaurants/.

27. "Earn credits searching the Web with Bing—similar to a frequent flier program. Redeem credits for popular gift cards or even donate them to a charity of your choice. All you have to do is stay signed-in as you search with Bing." "Bing Rewards," http://www.bing.com/explore/rewards-offers?ct= sweeps. In effect, Bing offers a negative access fee in the sense that consumers are rewarded for staying signed into Bing.

28. Comdata gave each fleet a code, and the fleet gave the code to each of its drivers. When a driver gave a valid code to a truck stop, the truck stop wrote a check drawn on Comdata and then cashed it.

29. Comdata Network Inc., "Form 10-K for the Period Ending December 31, 1980," 2–3.

30. Comdata Network Inc., "Form 10-K for the Period Ending December 31, 1985," 3.

31. The data in this paragraph is from Pew Research Center, "State of the Media 2015, Newspapers: Fact Sheet," April 29, 2015, http://www.journalism .org/2015/04/29/newspapers-fact-sheet/.

Chapter 7

1. Based on the number of unique mobile subscribers worldwide during the fourth quarter of 2005, as reported by GSMA Intelligence, "Global Data," https://gsmaintelligence.com/.

2. According to Google's CEO, in 2004, "we had a closet full of more than 100 phones and were building our software pretty much device by device. It was nearly impossible for us to make truly great mobile experiences." Larry Page, "Update from the CEO," Google Official Blog, March 13, 2013, https://googleblog.blogspot.com/2013/03/update-from-ceo.html.

3. Fred Vogelstein, *Dogfight: How Apple and Google Went to War and Started a Revolution* (New York: Sarah Crichton Books, 2013), 49.

4. The discussions in this section and the next have been influenced by the work of Andrei Hagiu. See Andrei Hagiu and Julian Wright, "Do You Really Want to Be an eBay," *Harvard Business Review*, March 2013, https://hbr.org/2013/03/do-you-really-want-to-be-an-ebay; Andrei Hagiu, "Strategic Decisions for Multisided Platforms, *MIT Sloan Management Review*, Winter 2014, http://sloanreview.mit.edu/article/strategic-decisions-for-multisided-platforms/; Andrei Hagiu and Julian Wright, "Enabling versus Controlling," working paper 16-002, Harvard Business School, Boston, 2015, http://www.hbs.edu/faculty/Pages/item.aspx?num=49375.

5. David S. Evans, Andrei Hagiu, and Richard Schmalensee, *Invisible Engines: How Software Platforms Drive Innovation and Transform Industries* (Cambridge, MA: MIT Press, 2006), chapter 6.

6. As our colleague Andrei Hagiu has pointed out to us, however, there may be other benefits from having control over a side. A firm might be able to earn more profits by purchasing goods and assuming the risk of selling them at a profit than by operating a marketplace. Producers of goods would likely get less on average by selling to a single-sided reseller than if they used a marketplace, but they would benefit from the reduced uncertainty of when, if ever, and for how much, a buyer would pay for their goods.

7. In addition, of course, a system in which fares varied from driver to driver would complicate riders' decision making and would likely alienate many for that reason.

8. Amazon, "Form S-1, Amendment 5," May 14, 1997, 4, http://phx.corporate-ir.net/phoenix.zhtml?c=97664&p=irol-sec.

9. Paul Thurrott, "Build 2015: Microsoft Will Allow Desktop Applications in Windows Store," April 29, 2015, https://www.thurrott.com/windows/windows-10/3210/build-2015-microsoft-will-allow-desktop-applications-in-windows-store.

10. Most of the antitrust problems Microsoft has faced over the years have come from its providing apps, or features with its operating system, that compete with the many developers who write apps for Windows.

11. In FY 2013, Microsoft's Windows Division had $19.2 billion in revenue and $9.5 billion in operating income, while its Business Division (Office) had

$24.7 billion in revenue and $16.2 billion in operating income. Microsoft, "10-K for Period Ending June 30, 2013," http://www.microsoft.com/investor/ SEC/default.aspx?year=2013&filing=annual. In subsequent fiscal years, Microsoft reorganized its segments, making the comparison between Windows and Office less clear. Microsoft also develops and markets a version of Office for Apple computers.

12. Thad Rueter, "Amazon Marketplace Sales Double in 2014," *Internet Retailer*, January 6, 2014, https://www.internetretailer.com/2015/01/06/ amazon-marketplace-sales-double-2014.

13. Facebook, "10-K for the Period Ending December 31, 2014," http:// investor.fb.com/sec.cfm?DocType=Annual&Year=2015&FormatFilter=; Lisa Toner, "The History of Facebook Advertising," Hubspot Blogs, September 26, 2013, http://blog.hubspot.com/marketing/history-facebook-adtips -slideshare.

14. Evans et al., *Invisible Engines*, chapter 5.

15. They absorbed Psion, a London-based maker of apps for PDAs. The Psion shareholders were bought out in 2004.

16. Joel West and David Wood, "Tradeoffs of Open Innovation Platform Leadership: The Rise and Fall of Symbian Ltd.," Stanford Social Science and Technology Seminar, March 30, 2011, 7, http://siepr.stanford.edu/ system/files/shared/documents/2011-03_WestWood_SIEPR.pdf. Microsoft had launched its Windows CE operating system for handheld computers in 1996, and beginning in 2000, successor systems were used in smartphones.

17. Except where otherwise noted, the smartphone figures reported in this chapter are based on August 2015 IDC data.

18. Data provided by IDC.

19. West and Wood, "Tradeoffs of Open Innovation Platform Leadership," 29.

20. Ibid., 44. As of 2006, Symbian was owned by Nokia, Ericsson, Sony, Matsushita, Samsung, and Siemens. Nokia had the largest share at 47.9 percent.

21. Ibid., 12.

22. Ibid., 12.

23. Ibid., 23. According to one source, they wanted weak handset suppliers and rarely bought phones from Nokia.

24. Jo Best, "Android Before Android: The Long, Strange History of Symbian and Why It Matters for Nokia's Future," ZDNet, April 4, 2013, http:// www.zdnet.com/article/android-before-android-the-long-strange-history-of -symbian-and-why-it-matters-for-nokias-future/.

25. Richard Miner, "Android: Building a Mobile Platform to Change the Industry," November 28, 2007, 17:53, https://www.youtube.com/watch?v= WUrMI9ZGxQ8.

26. Walter Isaacson, *Steve Jobs* (New York: Simon & Schuster, 2013), 465.

27. In its review of the ROKR, *PC Magazine* said, "[T]he sad truth is that music transfers and the phone's interface both feel clumsy." "Motorola ROKR

E1," *PC Magazine*, September 9, 2005, http://www.pcmag.com/article2/0,2817, 1857265,00.asp.

28. Frank Rose, "Battle for the Soul of the MP3 Phone," *Wired*, November 13, 2005, 2, http://archive.wired.com/wired/archive/13.11/phone. html?tw=wn_tophead_.

29. Isaacson, *Steve Jobs*, 466.

30. "Steve Jobs iPhone 2007 Presentation," January 9, 2007, https://www .youtube.com/watch?v=vN4U5FqrOdQ.

31. Isaacson, *Steve Jobs*, 501.

32. GSMA Intelligence, "Connections Excluding Cellular M2M: *Q2 2007.*"

33. Much of this section is based on Daniel Roth, "Google's Open Source Android OS Will Free the Wireless Web," *Wired*, June 23, 2008, http://archive .wired.com/techbiz/media/magazine/16-07/ff_android?currentPage=all.

34. Larry Page and Sergey Brin had met Andy Rubin and heard about his mobile vision when Rubin gave a talk to an engineering class at Stanford in 2002. John Markoff, "I Robot: The Man Behind the Google Phone," *New York Times*, November 4, 2007, http://www.nytimes.com/2007/11/04/technology/ 04google.html?pagewanted=all.

35. Vogelstein, *Dogfight*, 46–48.

36. Symbian was based on legacy PDA code. West and Wood, "Tradeoffs of Open Innovation Platform Leadership." The Microsoft Mobility story is apparently more complicated. See Brian X. Chen, "The Microsoft Blew It with Windows Mobile," *Wired*, November 17, 2009, http://www.wired.com/2009/11/ microsoft-windows-mobile/.

37. Google used an Apache 2.0 license, which is a particularly permissive version of an open-source license.

38. Vogelstein, *Dogfight*, 61.

39. Ibid., 61.

40. Ibid., 119–121.

41. Google gave the carriers about 25 percent of the app revenue, retaining only about 5 percent for paying payment card processing fees. See Jay Yarow, "Google Is Reportedly Trying to Get a Bigger Slice of Android App Revenue," *Business Insider*, June 28, 2013, http://www.businessinsider.com/ google-play-store-revenue-2013-6; Vogelstein, *Dogfight*, 121.

42. Isaacson, *Steve Jobs*, 500–502.

43. Arnold Kim, "Steve Jobs Announces Third Party SDK for iPhone for February 2008," *MacRumors*, October 17, 2007, http://www.macrumors .com/2007/10/17/steve-jobs-announces-3rd-party-sdk-for-iphone-for-february-2008/; Apple Hot News (archived October 18, 2007), "Third Party Applications on the iPhone," *Internet Archive Wayback Machine*, https://web.archive .org/web/20071018221832/http://www.apple.com/hotnews/.

44. Nielsen Informate, "International Smartphone Mobility Report," March 2015, http://informatemi.com/final_download_report.php?p=240. Application time usage is estimated as total smartphone time usage, less time spent on calls, messaging, chat, VoIP, and web browsing.

45. Android developers still have some problems because, as a result of Google's looser control, a smaller proportion of subscribers upgrade to the latest version of the operating system, compared to Apple.

46. Canalys, "Worldwide Smartphone/Mobile Phone Installed Base Forecasts (Consolidated)," November 2015. These numbers are forecasts for year-end 2015, published as of November 2015.

47. Of the time US consumers spent using apps and browsing on their smartphones in April 2015, iPhones accounted for 55 percent and Android phones, 45 percent. Of the time US consumers spent using apps and browsing on their smartphones and tablets, iOS devices accounted for 62 percent and Android devices accounted for 38 percent. In the EU5 (France, Germany, Italy, Spain, and the United Kingdom), the comparable numbers were 41 percent for iPhones versus 59 percent for Android phones, and 56 percent for iOS devices and 44 percent for Android devices. comScore, MediaMetrix, April 2015, https://www.comscore.com/Products/Audience-Analytics/Media-Metrix. The revenues received by developers for apps were twice as high for the iPhone App Store as the Google Play Store. The iPhone accounts for so much more activity in part because the iPhone users tend to have higher incomes. Developers tend to prioritize writing apps for the iOS because it is easier to make money from iPhone users than from Android users.

48. Canalys, "Smart Phone Analysis Worldwide, 2015 Q2"; John Callaham, "Windows Store Hits 200,000 App Mark, with 385,000 Apps in Windows Phone Store," *Windows Central*, March 3, 2015, http://www.windowscentral.com/windows-store-hits-200000-app-mark-385000-apps-windows-phone-store.

Chapter 8

1. Trip Advisor, "Aventura Mall," http://www.tripadvisor.com/Attraction_Review-g29180-d147218-Reviews-Aventura_Mall-Aventura_Florida.html (comment by Rbenson03 from Central Florida). The mall had 4.5 out of 5 stars from TripAdvisor based on 2,227 reviews.

2. Aventura Mall home page, http://www.aventuramall.com/.

3. For background, see Erik Bojnansky, "Family and Fortune," *Biscayne Times*, January 2012, http://www.biscaynetimes.com/index.php?option=com_content&id=1051:family-a-fortune.

4. Malcom Gladwell, "The Terrazzo Jungle," *New Yorker*, March 15, 2004, http://www.newyorker.com/magazine/2004/03/15/the-terrazzo-jungle; M. Jeffery Hardwick, *Mall Maker* (Philadelphia: University of Pennsylvania Press, 2010).

5. Market makers are sometimes known as liquidity providers, and buyers and sellers are sometimes known as liquidity takers. See Larry Harris, *Trading & Exchanges: Market Microstructure for Practitioners* (Oxford, UK: Oxford University Press, 2002).

6. In the United States, regulation drove the shift to decimalization (tick sizes of one cent). See US Securities and Exchange Commission, "Report to

Congress on Decimalization," July 2012, 4–6, https://www.sec.gov/news/studies/2012/decimalization-072012.pdf.

7. For a very clear discussion of the economics of tick size rules and for details omitted here in the interest of simplicity, see James J. Angel, "Tick Size Regulation: Costs, Benefits, and Risks," UK Government Office of Science, 2012, https://www.gov.uk/government/uploads/system/uploads/attachment_data/file/289037/12-1068-eia7-tick-size-regulation-costs-benefits.pdf.

8. For a general discussion with some applications to platforms, see Hanna Halaburda and Felix Oberholzer-Gee, "The Limits of Scale," *Harvard Business Review*, April 2014, https://hbr.org/2014/04/the-limits-of-scale.

9. The screening device encourages the right people to join and discourages the wrong people from joining by having some combination of *exclusionary amenity* that appeals to the right people but not the wrong people and an *exclusionary vibe* that attracts the right people and discourages the wrong people. For further discussion, see David S. Evans, "Governing Bad Behavior by Users of Multi-Sided Platforms," *Berkeley Technology Law Journal* 27, no. 2 (2012), http://scholarship.law.berkeley.edu/btlj/vol27/iss2/7/.

10. David S. Evans, "Governing Bad Behavior by Users of Multi-Sided Platforms," *Berkeley Technology Law Journal* 2, no. 27 (2012), http://scholarship.law.berkeley.edu/btlj/vol27/iss2/7/.

11. Platforms can also create thicker markets by directly limiting the participants on one side through *entry restrictions*. In "The Limits of Scale," Halaburda and Oberholzer-Gee argue that this explains decisions by app-oriented platforms, such as those involving games, to limit the number of apps. Another plausible explanation, however, is that these platforms restrict entry in order to raise the level of quality and prevent a lemons problem.

12. In economist-speak, this is a negative direct network effect.

13. These are positive *direct* network effects.

14. For a discussion of the role of congestion and the speed of making transactions, see Alvin Roth, *Who Gets What and Why* (New York: Houghton Mifflin Harcourt, 2015).

15. Eye-tracking studies of how consumers use search engines reveal that both the quality of the consumer experience and the attention paid to advertising varies substantially with the layout and organization of the search results page. Erick Schonfeld, "Study Suggests People Prefer Bing's Design to Google's, But Still Won't Switch," *TechCrunch*, June 25, 2009, http://techcrunch.com/2009/06/25/study-suggests-people-prefer-bings-design-to-googles-but-still-wont-switch/.

16. An SMS message is limited to 160 characters. Twitter reserved 20 for the user name, leaving 140 for the message. It could have increased the limit on characters, but this would have resulted in the receiver getting more than a single message.

17. Visa, "International Operating Regulations," April 15, 2015, 125–127 (Use of Marks on Cards), 129 (Display of Marks at the Point of Sale), http://usa.visa.com/download/about_visa/15-April-2015-Visa-Rules-Public.pdf.

18. For a general discussion of the use of search and matching algorithms to facilitate transactions in online markets, see Liran Einav, Chiara Farronato, and Jonathan Levin, "Peer-to-Peer Markets," NBER working paper 21496, August 2015, http://www.nber.org/papers/w21496.

19. Andrei Hagiu and Bruno Jullien, "Why Do Intermediaries Divert Search?" *RAND Journal of Economics* 42, no. 2 (2011). We reserve "search diversion" for design decisions that increase the cost of search for a participant. Hagiu and Jullien also apply the term to any situation in which a participant does not directly benefit from a connection to a participant on the other side and therefore must be compensated for this.

20. For a discussion of the economics of shopping malls, see Eric Gould, Peter Pashigian, and Canice Prendergast, "Contracts, Externalities, and Incentives in Shopping Malls," *Review of Economics and Statistics* 87, no. 3 (2005); Peter Pashigian and Eric Gould, "Internalizing Externalities: The Pricing of Space in Shopping Malls," *Journal of Law and Economics* 41, no. 1 (1998). For a summary of older, but still relevant, literature on shopping malls, see Mark Eppli and John Benjamin, "The Evolution of Shopping Center Research: A Review and Analysis," *Journal of Real Estate Research* 9, no. 1 (1994).

21. MiamiOnTheCheap, "Aventura Mall Free Holiday Lights, Other Events," November 21, 2013, http://miamionthecheap.com/aventura-mall-illumination-holiday-season/.

22. See Mark Eppli and John Benjamin, "The Evolution of Shopping Center Research," for a summary of studies from the 1980s and early 1990s that find that the assortment of retail stores is an important determinant of the consumer's decision to go to a mall, that anchor stores tend to increase sales for non-anchor stores (that is, generate positive direct network externalities), and that the mix of stores is an important determinant of mall success.

23. TripAdvisor, "Aventura Mall," http://www.tripadvisor.com/Attraction_Review-g29180-d147218-Reviews-Aventura_Mall-Aventura_Florida.html (comment by Angela Q.).

24. TripAdvisor, "Aventura Mall," http://www.tripadvisor.com/Attraction_Review-g29180-d147218-Reviews-Aventura_Mall-Aventura_Florida.html (comment by Orlando M.).

25. TripAdvisor, "Aventura Mall," http://www.tripadvisor.com/Attraction_Review-g29180-d147218-Reviews-Aventura_Mall-Aventura_Florida.html (comment by Ligia K.).

Chapter 9

1. For readers who do not follow the misadventures of American B-list celebrities, or in the event Ms. Lohan's fame declines more rapidly than our readership, she starred between the ages of eleven and eighteen in popular

movies such as *The Parent Trap* and *Mean Girls*. Her run-ins with the law began around 2007, when she turned twenty-one. *People* magazine provides a detailed biography. "Lindsay Lohan, Biography," *People*, http://www.people .com/people/lindsay_lohan/biography/0,,20006693,00.html.

2. Duncan Riley, "Lindsay Lohan Banned by Facebook," *Inquisitr*, December 2, 2008, http://www.inquisitr.com/10537/lindsay-lohan-banned-by -facebook/.

3. Felix Gillette, "The Rise and Inglorious Fall of MySpace," *Bloomberg Businessweek*, June 27, 2011, http://www.bloomberg.com/bw/magazine/content/ 11_27/b4235053917570.htm.

4. Nick Summers, "Facebook's 'Pop Cops' Are Key to its Growth," *Newsweek*, April 30, 2009, http://www.newsweek.com/facebooks-porn-cops-are-key -its-growth-77055.

5. Ibid.

6. *United States v. Lori Drew*, 259 F.R.D. 449 (C.D. Cal. 2009).

7. Associated Press, "Mom: MySpace Hoax Led to Daughter's Suicide," Fox News, November 16, 2007, http://www.foxnews.com/story/2007/11/16/ mom-myspace-hoax-led-to-daughter-suicide.html.

8. Marni Battista, "5 Common Lies on His Online Dating Profile," ayi .com, October 24, 2013, http://www.ayi.com/dating-blog/ayi-top-online -dating-profile-lies/.

9. "Amazon struggling to keep counterfeits off market, retailer says," CBS News, May 14, 2014, http://www.cbsnews.com/news/amazon- struggling-to-keep-counterfeits-off-market-retailer-says/; Jeff Reifman, "Amazon Marketplace Fraud Made Easy," March 25, 2014, http://jeffreifman .com/2014/03/25/amazon-makes-fraud-easy-in-marketplace/.

10. UK Office of Fair Trading, "Payment Surcharges—Response to the Which? Super-Complaint," July 2012, http://webarchive.nationalarchives.gov .uk/20140402142426/http://www.oft.gov.uk/shared_oft/super-complaints/ OFT1349resp.pdf.

11. Abby Goodnough, "Medical Student Is Indicted in Craigslist Killing," *New York Times*, June 21, 2009, http://www.nytimes.com/2009/06/22/us/ 22indict.html.

12. BlaBlaCar, "Ladies Only," https://www.blablacar.co.uk/blog/ladies-only.

13. She was prosecuted, but the judge ultimately acquitted her since her actions did not violate the law at the time. The state of Missouri and other states have since passed antibullying laws to cover some of this sort of behavior. "Prosecutor: No Criminal Charges in MySpace Suicide," FOX News, December 3, 2007, http://www.foxnews.com/story/2007/12/03/prosecutor -no-criminal-charges-in-myspace-suicide.html.

14. The classic option contracts are calls, which give the holder the *right* to purchase the stock at a specified price at a specified future date, and puts, which give the holder the *right* to sell the stock at specified price at a specified future date. Futures contracts *require* the holder to buy or sell shares at a specified price at a specified future date.

15. The history in this section is based on Ranald Michie, *The London Stock Exchange: A History* (Oxford, UK: Oxford University Press, 2001); Edward Stringham, "The Emergence of the London Stock Exchange as a Self-Policing Club," *Journal of Private Enterprise* 17, no. 2 (2002): 1–19; Paul Harrison, "What Can We Learn for Today from 300-Year-Old Writings About Stock Markets?" *History of Political Economy* 36, no. 4 (2004): 667–688.

16. Michie, *The London Stock Exchange*, 31.

17. Ibid., 15.

18. Ibid. Fines were levied for minor infractions, but refusal to pay could result in expulsion.

19. Rudolph Eyre Melsheimer and Walter Laurence, *The Law and Customs of the London Stock Exchange* (1879; repr. Charleston, SC: Nabu Press, 2010), 1.

20. David S. Evans, "Governing Bad Behavior by Users of Multi-Sided Platforms," *Berkeley Technology Law Journal* 27, no. 2 (2012), http://scholarship.law.berkeley.edu/btlj/vol27/iss2/7/.

21. BlaBlaCar, "Terms and Conditions," https://www.blablacar.co.uk/blog/terms-and-conditions.

22. eBay, "Rules & Policy," http://pages.ebay.com/help/policies/overview.html.

23. Apple Developer, "App Store Review Guidelines," https://developer.apple.com/app-store/review/guidelines/.

24. Tomer Sarid, "7 Reasons Your App Could Get Rejected by Apple (And How to Avoid It)," como blog, April 29, 2015, http://blog.como.com/2015/04/7-reasons-app-rejected-by-apple/.

25. For general discussions, see Jason Tanz, "How Airbnb and Lyft Finally Got Americans to Trust Each Other," *Wired*, April 23, 2014, http://www.wired.com/2014/04/trust-in-the-share-economy/; Liran Einav, Chiara Farronato, and Jonathan Levin, "Peer-to-Peer Markets," NBER working paper 21496, 2015, section 2.3, http://www.nber.org/papers/w21496.

26. OpenTable, "OpenTable Terms of Use," http://www.opentable.com/info/agreement.aspx.

27. Matt Rosoff, "Google Has Stopped Punishing JC Penney," *Business Insider*, May 25, 2011, http://www.businessinsider.com/google-has-stopped-punishing-jc-penney-2011-5.

28. David Segal, "A Bully Finds a Pulpit on the Web," *New York Times*, November 26, 2010, http://www.nytimes.com/2010/11/28/business/28borker.html.

29. Google's policy of taking websites that have violated its policy far down in the rankings is sometimes referred to as "Google Jail." Dave Johnson, "SEO Dirty Tricks That Can Land Your Company's Website in Google Jail," CBS News, February 28, 2011, http://www.cbsnews.com/8301-505143_162-28650615/seo-dirty-tricks-that-can-land-your-companys-website-in-google-jail.

30. Danah Boyd, "None of this is Real," in *Structures of Participation in Digital Culture,* ed. Joe Karaganis (New York: SSRC, 2007), 133; "A Cautionary Tale," *Fast Company*, May 1, 2007, http://www.fastcompany.com/59447/cautionary-tale

31. "Finding Love Online, Version 2.0," *Bloomberg Businessweek*, June 10, 2003, http://www.bloomberg.com/bw/stories/2003-06-09/finding-love-online-version-2-dot-0.

32. Julia Angwin, *Stealing MySpace: The Battle to Control the Most Popular Website in America* (New York: Random House, 2009), 50.

33. Alexandra Wall, "He Didn't Create a Site to Meet Chicks, But Founder Says a 'Sugar Mama Would Be Cool,'" Jweekly.com, October 31, 2003, http://www.jweekly.com/article/full/20919/he-didn-t-create-a-site-to-meet-chicks-but-founder-says-a-sugar-mama-would-/.

34. Angwin, *Stealing MySpace*, 50.

35. Boyd, "None of this is Real," 148.

36. Ibid., 148–154.

37. Ibid., 151.

38. "Company Overview of MySpace, Inc.: Snapshot," *Bloomberg Business-Week*, http://investing.businessweek.com/research/stocks/private/snapshot.asp?privcapId=120412.

39. Danah Boyd, "Friends, Friendsters, and Top 8: Writing Community into Being on Social Network Sites," *First Monday* 11, no. 12 (2006), http://firstmonday.org/htbin/cgiwrap/bin/ojs/index.php/fm/article/view/1418/1336.

40. Lev Grossman, "Tila Tequila," *Time*, December 16, 2006, http://www.time.com/time/magazine/article/0,9171,1570728,00.html.

41. It was one of comScore's top-fifty web properties in the United States by April 2005. See Angwin, *Stealing MySpace*, 126.

42. Ibid., 181.

43. Gillette, "The Rise and Inglorious Fall of MySpace."

44. MySpace, "Is MySpace Free?" (archived August 22, 2008), *Internet Archive Wayback Machine*, http://web.archive.org/web/20080822094142/http://www.myspace.com/Modules/Help/Pages/HelpCenter.aspx?Category=1&Question=33.

45. Janet Kornblum, "Facebook Will Soon be Available to Everyone," *USA Today*, September 11, 2006, http://www.usatoday.com/tech/news/2006-09-11-facebook-everyone_x.htm.

46. Niall Kennedy, "Facebook Cleanses Pages of Supposed Fakesters," Niall Kennedy's blog, December 1, 2007, http://www.niallkennedy.com/blog/2007/12/facebook-pages-deletions.html. Note, however, that Tila Tequila has a fan page (perhaps the name is no longer viewed as fake) but with less provocative pictures than some she has on MySpace. See "Tila Tequila's Albums," https://www.facebook.com/IamMissTila/photos_stream.

47. FaceBook, "Statement of Rights and Responsibilities," January 30, 2015, http://www.facebook.com/terms.php.

48. Summers, "Facebook's 'Porn Cops' Are Key to its Growth."

49. Statista, "Number of Monthly Active Facebook Users Worldwide as of 3rd Quarter 2015 (In Millions)," http://www.statista.com/statistics/264810/number-of-monthly-active-facebook-users-worldwide/.

Chapter 10

1. "Apple Special Event," September 9, 2014, http://www.apple.com/live/2014-sept-event/.

2. The United States is one of the few major countries still using mag-stripe cards. Elsewhere, payment systems have migrated to "chip-and-pin" cards that rely on the EMV standard. As of mid-2015, businesses in the United States were in the process of replacing mag-stripe cards with cards with chips, though a signature will still be used for authentication rather than a pin number, the standard in most other countries.

3. Apple Pay isn't necessarily a two-sided platform. If merchants all had terminals that automatically accepted it, just as part of what they ordinarily do, then Apple would only have to get consumers to use its payment service. It would be a single-sided firm. In the United Kingdom, many merchants already have terminals that can accept Apple Pay. In the United States, however, as discussed later, most merchants are not equipped to accept Apple Pay, and therefore Apple Pay has to get merchants on board.

4. Karen Webster, "The Google Wallet News That Wasn't," PYMNTS.com, June 10, 2013, http://www.pymnts.com/commentary/2013/the-google-wallet-news-that-wasn-t/#.Vg967WQrIkg; Karen Webster, "The Incredible Shrinking Google Wallet," PYMNTS.com, March 25, 2013, http://www.pymnts.com/uncategorized/2013/the-incredible-shrinking-google-wallet/#.Vg97XWQrIkg; "Softcard Shuts Down After Google Buy," PYMNTS.com, February 27, 2015, http://www.pymnts.com/news/2015/softcard-shuts-down-after-google-buy/#.Vg97pWQrIkg; "Google Buys Softcard Technology and Buries the Brand," PYMNTS.com, February 24, 2015, http://www.pymnts.com/news/2015/google-buys-softcard-technology-and-buries-the-brand/.

5. Dean Takahashi, *Opening the Xbox: Inside Microsoft's Plan to Unleash an Entertainment Revolution* (Roseville, CA: Prima Lifestyles, 2002).

6. We do not consider "store cards" that retailers issue for use only in their own stores in this discussion. The numbers presented later include charge cards—which account holders are supposed to pay off at the end of the month—as well as credit cards. In our discussion of networks, we ignore debit card networks, which are relatively small. Federal Reserve System, "The 2013 Federal Reserve Payments Study," July 2014, 22–23, https://www.frbservices.org/files/communications/pdf/general/2013_fed_res_paymt_study_detailed_rpt.pdf.

7. The precise number of physical point-of-sale locations is not easy to pin down. One source indicates there are around 9.4 million locations that accept American Express, MasterCard, and Visa. See United States of America v. American Express Company, 10-CV-4496 (E.D. of New York, 2015), 93, which reports 6.4 million locations that accept American Express (virtually all of which also accept MasterCard and Visa) and 3 million locations that accept MasterCard and Visa but do not accept American Express. It is unclear whether this figure includes unattended retail locations such as vending machines.

8. "Apple Special Event," September 9, 2014.

9. Juli Clover, "Apple Pay Details: Apple Gets 0.15% Cut of Purchases, Higher Rates for Bluetooth Payments," *MacRumors*, September 12, 2014, http://www.macrumors.com/2014/09/12/more-apple-pay-details/.

10. Bjorn Cumps, "Do Banks Like Apple Pie?" Vlerick Business School, October 21, 2014, http://www.vlerick.com/en/about-vlerick/news/do-banks-like-apple-pie; Sam Frizzel, "Apple Pay: Who Won and Who Lost?" *Time*, October 22, 2014, http://time.com/3532199/apple-pay-winners-losers/.

11. Canalys, "Worldwide Smart Phone Market Q3 2015 with Country Level Detail," November 2015. This calculation is based on the sales reported by Canalys for US iOS smartphones sold at the US price points for the iPhone 6 and iPhone 6 Plus.

12. To get a rough idea of what fraction of people had iPhones, we assumed the iPhone users were all between the ages of eighteen and sixty-five.

13. According to a survey made by the Federal Reserve Bank of Boston, as of 2012, 72.1 percent of consumers had at least one credit card. Scott Schuh and Joanna Stavins, "The 2011 and 2012 Surveys of Consumer Payment Choice," Federal Reserve Bank of Boston, September 29, 2014, 28, http://www.bostonfed.org/economic/rdr/2014/rdr1401.pdf.

14. National Retail Federation, "Top 100 Retailers Chart 2015," https://nrf.com/2015/top100-table; US Census Bureau, "Monthly & Annual Retail Trade," 2014, http://www.census.gov/retail/index.html; Apple, "Apple Pay Set to Transform Mobile Payments Starting October 20," October 16, 2014, http://www.apple.com/pr/library/2014/10/16Apple-Pay-Set-to-Transform-Mobile-Payments-Starting-October-20.html.

15. One confidential source estimates that in 2014, there were about 12,363,000 physical point-of-sale terminals, excluding unattended retail and mobile point of sale. Of these, about 416,000 had NFC. Despite the precise number, these are rough estimates pulled together from various sources. If these figures are correct, then 3.3 percent of merchant terminals could accept Apple Pay in 2014.

16. Daisuke Wakabayashi and Greg Bensinger, "Will Stores Warm Up to Apple Pay?" *Wall Street Journal*, September 10, 2014, http://www.wsj.com/articles/will-stores-warm-up-to-apple-pay-1410392952, quoting Chris Ciabarra, the chief technology officer of Revel Systems. He pointed out than only two customers had NFC.

17. Troy Wolverton, "Apple Pay Is Great, at Stores That Accept It," *San Jose Mercury News*, October 20, 2014, http://www.mercurynews.com/troy-wolverton/ci_26765594/wolverton-apple-pay-great-at-stores-that-accept.

18. The statistics in the next few paragraphs are based on an unpublished survey by InfoScout working with PYMNTS.com. InfoScout uses a large panel of mobile phone users who take pictures of their receipts at stores; it then uses the information on the receipts to identify their purchases; it sells this data to brand owners. It also conducts surveys with these people. It is able to detect what type of phone and operating system people have and can

therefore identify iPhone 6 users, and it can determine whether the terminal they used to shop can accept NFC.

19. These statements are based on a survey of consumers who shopped on November 28, 2014, and were in the InfoScout sample.

20. Out of 100 users, about 17 (16.6 percent) had ever tried Apple Pay and out of the 17 about 5 (30.7 percent of 16.6 percent) used it when they could.

21. In these calculations we assume that all the people who had ever tried Apple Pay still had it on their phones. They therefore likely overstate the number of people who have Apple Pay installed on their phones since of those people some may have deleted it.

22. By October 2015, a survey by PYMNTS and InfoScout reported that 5.1 percent of people who could use Apple Pay at eligible stores, actually purchased using Apple Pay. By the same time, 34.8 percent of American adults had iPhone 6s, which are necessary to pay using Apple Pay. For a typical store that accepts Apple Pay, 1.8 percent (0.348x0.051) of its transactions are going to be performed using the platform. PYMNTS and InfoScout, "Apple Pay Adoption," http://www.pymnts.com/apple-pay-adoption/, US Census Bureau, "Monthly & Annual Retail Trade," 2014, http://www.census.gov/retail/index.html; Canalys, "Worldwide Smart Phone Market Q3 2015 with Country Level Detail," November 2015.

23. US Census Bureau, "Monthly & Annual Retail Trade," 2014, http://www.census.gov/retail/index.html; National Retail Federation, "Top 100 Retailers Chart 2015," https://nrf.com/2015/top100-table; Apple, "Where to Use Apple Pay," http://www.apple.com/apple-pay/where-to-use-apple-pay/. For the count of merchants accepting Apple Pay, we used those listed on Apple's website plus other merchants not listed there, but included in several other sources on the web as accepting Apple Pay.

24. The United States is switching over to chip cards, and increasingly people will dip their cards into a terminal rather than swipe them through it.

25. Calculation based on Canalys, "Worldwide Smart Phone Market Q2 2015 with Country Level Detail," August 2015; US Census Bureau, "State and County Quick Facts," September 30, 2015, http://quickfacts.census.gov/qfd/states/00000.html. For this calculation, we divided a conservative estimate of US iPhone 6 and 6 Plus sales through the second quarter of 2015 by the number of people ages eighteen to sixty-five to get the fraction of US adults with an iPhone 6 or 6 Plus. Note that this calculation is conservative, because it assumes that 100 percent of US iPhone 6 and 6 Plus sales were to consumers between the ages of eighteen and sixty-five, and because it uses a (reasonably tight) upper-bound estimate for US iPhone 6 and 6 Plus sales.

26. Nandita Bose, "In 'Year of Apple Pay,' Many Top Retailers Remain Skeptical," Reuters, June 5, 2015, http://www.reuters.com/article/2015/06/06/us-apple-pay-idUSKBN0OL0CM20150606.

27. The cost for a merchant to implement QR code technologies is lower than for implementing NFC technologies. Cynthia Merrit, "QR Codes versus NFC: Cheaper, but Worth the Risk?" Federal Reserve Bank of Atlanta,

February 27, 2012, http://takeonpayments.frbatlanta.org/2012/02/qr-codes
-versus-nfc-cheaper-but-worth-risk.html.

28. Luke Dormehl, "Starbucks Mobile App Payments Now Represent 16% of
All Starbucks Transactions," *Fast Company*, January 23, 2015, http://www
.fastcompany.com/3041353/fast-feed/starbucks-mobile-app-payments-now
-represent-16-of-all-starbucks-transactions.

Chapter 11

1. World Bank, "GDP per Capita, PPP (Current International $)," http://
data.worldbank.org/indicator/NY.GDP.PCAP.PP.CD?page=1 (data for 2006).
This is GDP converted to US dollars using purchasing power parity exchange
rates.

2. Kenya ranked 120 of 121 countries based on paved roads as percent
of total roads and 145 of 165 countries based on gasoline consumption per
capita. World Bank, "Roads Paved (% of Total Roads)," http://data.worldbank
.org/indicator/IS.ROD.PAVE.ZS (data for 2011); World Bank, "Gasoline Fuel
Consumption per Capita (Kg of Oil Equivalent)," http://data.worldbank.org/
indicator/IS.ROD.SGAS.PC (data for 2011).

3. World Bank, "Commercial Bank Branches (per 100,000 Adults)" http://
data.worldbank.org/indicator/FB.CBK.BRCH.P5 (data for 2006).

4. Sarit Markovich and Charlotte Snyder, "M-Pesa and Mobile Money in
Kenya: Pricing for Success," no. 5-213-250 (Evanston, IL: Northwestern
University, December 3, 2013).

5. No data is available for 2006; however, in 2012, remittances accounted
for 25 percent of the income of the median rural household, according to
research from the Kenya Financial Diaries. Julie Zollmann, "Shilingi Kwa
Shilingi—The Financial Lives of the Poor," August 2014, http://fsdkenya.org/
wp-content/uploads/2015/08/14-08-08_Financial_Diaries_report.pdf.

6. William Jack and Tavneet Suri, "Risk Sharing and Transaction Costs:
Evidence from Kenya's Mobile Money Revolution," *American Economic
Review* 104, no. 1 (2014).

7. Brian Muthiora, "New Infographic: Mobile Money and the Digitization
of Kenya's Retail Payments Systems," GSMA, September 29, 2014, http://
www.gsma.com/mobilefordevelopment/new-infographic-mobile-money-
and-the-digitisation-of-kenyas-retail-payments-systems. Not all of these registered users had activity on the service. In fact, 37 percent of Kenyan
mobile phone users were registered and had activity in the thirty days of
March 2014.

8. Central Bank of Kenya, "Payments System Statistics: Mobile Payments," https://www.centralbank.go.ke/index.php/nps-modernization/mobile-
payments?yr=2015 (data for 2014); World Bank, "GDP (Current US$)," http://
data.worldbank.org/indicator/NY.GDP.MKTP.CD (data for 2014). Mobile
money transfers are not part of GDP; we are using GDP to scale the numbers
and compare across countries.

9. World Bank, "Mobile Cellular Subscriptions," http://data.worldbank.org/indicator/IT.CEL.SETS?page=1; GSMA Intelligence, "Kenya, Connections, excluding cellular M2M: Q4 2006," https://gsmaintelligence.com/.

10. Olga Morawczynski, "Examining the Adoption, Usage and Outcomes of Mobile Money Services: The Case of M-Pesa in Kenya," May 2011, 61, https://www.era.lib.ed.ac.uk/bitstream/handle/1842/5558/Morawczynski2011.pdf;jsessionid=8C18972CF709DB8AA70C004302F5CFA6?sequence=2.

11. Central Bank of Kenya, "Mobile Payments," https://www.centralbank.go.ke/index.php/nps-modernization/mobile-payments.

12. Ignacio Mas and Amolo Ng'weno, "Three Keys to M-Pesa's Success: Branding, Channel Management and Pricing," *Journal of Payments Strategy and Systems* 4, no. 4 (2010). Dollar figures shown in this chapter were converted from the KShs figures obtained from the Central Bank of Kenya to US$ using monthly average market exchange rates obtained from Oanda Corporation. During the 2007–2014 period covered by this chapter, the value of a Kenyan shilling averaged just over US$0.01. Central Bank of Kenya, "Mobile Payments," https://www.centralbank.go.ke/index.php/nps-modernization/mobile-payments; Oanda Corp., "Historical Exchange Rates," http://www.oanda.com/currency/historical-rates/.

13. Mas and Ng'weno, "Three Keys to M-Pesa's Success."

14. YouTube, "M-Pesa Documentary," January 26, 2009, https://www.youtube.com/watch?v=nEZ30K5dBWU.

15. The data on M-PESA reported here was taken directly from the website of the Central Bank of Kenya. Central Bank of Kenya, "Mobile Payments," https://www.centralbank.go.ke/index.php/nps-modernization/mobile-payments.

16. As noted before, money transfers aren't part of GDP, and we show this calculation just to give the reader sense of scale.

17. After 2010, a few other mobile money platforms entered Kenya, although M-PESA still accounted for the preponderance of transactions. The data in figures 11-4–11-6 includes these other schemes. Therefore, it accurately reflects the overall growth in Kenya but overstates the growth of M-PESA somewhat.

18. Central Bank of Kenya, "Mobile Payments," https://www.centralbank.go.ke/index.php/nps-modernization/mobile-payments.

19. GSMA Staff, personal communication with the authors, October 1, 2015.

20. Safaricom, "Lipa Na M-PESA," http://www.safaricom.co.ke/business/m-pesa/lipa-na-m-pesa.

21. GSMA, "2014 State of the Industry: Mobile Financial Services for the Unbanked," 2014, http://www.gsma.com/mobilefordevelopment/wp-content/uploads/2015/03/SOTIR_2014.pdf.

22. David S. Evans and Alexis Pirchio, "An Empirical Examination of Why Mobile Money Schemes Ignite in Some Developing Countries but Flounder in Most," Coase Sandor Working Paper Series in Law and Economics,

no. 723, March 14, 2015, http://chicagounbound.uchicago.edu/cgi/viewcontent
.cgi?article=2413&context=law_and_economics.

23. Jack and Suri, "Risk Sharing and Transaction Costs."

Chapter 12

1. About a year later, on Black Friday, the *Wall Street Journal* reported
"throngs on Friday at malls and shopping districts from Charlotte, N.C., to
Los Angeles were noticeable thinner than in previous years." "Black Friday
Shopping—with Thinner Crowds," November 28, 2015.

2. RetailNext reports that for its sample of more than 65,000 sensors in
retail stores, foot traffic for the holiday months of November and December
declined by 6.5 percent from 2012 to 2013 and 8 percent from 2013 to 2014.
Comparing March 2015 and March 2014, RetailNext finds that traffic declined by 7 percent to 10 percent. Chitra Balasubramanian, "Full 2013
Holiday Performance Data: Brick and Mortar Traffic Down 6.5% YOY,"
RetailNext, January 14, 2014, http://retailnext.net/blog/full-2013-holiday
-performance-data-brick-mortar-traffic-down-6-5-yoy/; Nandita Bose, "Holiday Season U.S. Store Sales Down 8 percent in 2014: RetailNext," Reuters,
January 7, 2015, http://www.reuters.com/article/2015/01/08/us-usa-
holidaysales-idUSKBN0KH01P20150108; "Why a Decline in Foot Traffic has
Retailers Looking Up," PYMNTS.com, June 11, 2015, http://www.pymnts.
com/in-depth/2015/why-a-decline-in-foot-traffic-has-retailers-looking-up/.
Additionally, we obtained more recent data from RetailNext that shows that
traffic continued to decline in 2015, with average monthly traffic 10.4 percent
lower between January and August 2015 than it was between January and
August 2014. The RetailNext data is based on specialty and large-format
retail stores that use the company's analytics platform, which tracks store
visits; it is exclusive of gasoline, automobiles, and warehouse clubs. Retail-
Next, personal communication with the authors, October 8, 2015. This data
is broadly consistent with anecdotal data from retailers and analysts. See
Shelly Banjo and Drew Fitzgerald, "Stores Confront New World of Reduced
Shopper Traffic," *Wall Street Journal*, January 16, 2014, http://www.wsj.com/
articles/SB10001424052702304419104579325100372435802. The decline in
foot traffic is also not just a US phenomenon. The British Retail Consortium
has also found declines in foot traffic, including on high streets in the UK.
See Dominic Sacco, "Why Are There More Shops But Fewer Shoppers on the
UK High Street?" PCR, August 17, 2015, http://www.pcr-online.biz/news/
read/why-are-there-more-shops-but-fewer-shoppers-on-the-uk-high-street/
036751.

3. US Census Bureau, "Quarterly Retail E-Commerce Sales, 1st Quarter
2015," May 15, 2015, http://www.census.gov/retail/ecommerce/historic_
releases.html, Table 1: Estimated Quarterly US Retail Sales: Total and
E-Commerce (Not Adjusted); US Census Bureau, "County Business Patterns
(CBP)," April 2015, http://www.census.gov/econ/cbp/.

4. Barbara Farfan, "All 2014 Store Closings—US Retail Industry Chains to Close Stores," About Money, http://retailindustry.about.com/od/USRetailStore ClosingInfoFAQs/fl/All-2014-Store-Closings-US-Retail-Industry-Chains-to-Close-Stores.htm.

5. Ibid.

6. "Teen Clothing Retailer Delia's Will Close Stores, Shut Down," *Oregonian*, December 8, 2014, http://www.oregonlive.com/window-shop/index.ssf/2014/12/delias_will_shut_down.html.

7. Emily Gera, "RadioShack Will Close Over 1,700 Stores Following Bankruptcy Filing," *Polygon*, February 9, 2015, http://www.polygon.com/2015/2/9/8003733/radioshack-bankrupt-closing.

8. Nelson D. Schwartz, "The Economics (and Nostalgia) of Dead Malls," *New York Times*, January 3, 2015, http://www.nytimes.com/2015/01/04/business/the-economics-and-nostalgia-of-dead-malls.html?_r=0.

9. Melanie Hicken, "This Is Why Big Box Retailers Are Making Smaller Stores," *Business Insider*, January 26, 2012, http://www.businessinsider.com/this-is-why-big-box-retailers-are-making-smaller-stores-2012-1.

10. Shelley E. Kohan, "Top Retail Trends of 2014-15," August 26, 2014, http://retailnext.net/blog/top-retail-trends-2014/. Kohan goes on to say that stores are also considering "pop-up shops, vending machines and brand boutiques within their larger stores."

11. Shan Li, "Best Buy Will Shrink Its Big-Box Stores by Sharing Space," *Seattle Times*, July 9, 2011, http://www.seattletimes.com/business/best-buy-will-shrink-its-big-box-stores-by-sharing-space/.

12. From U.S. Bureau of the Census, Latest Quarterly E-commerce Report, http://www.census.gov/retail/mrts/www/data/excel/tsnotadjustedsales.xls. In using the Census e-commerce data, it is important to note that according to Census procedures, sales of all firms with distinct online operations, regardless of the firm's main line of business, are to be reported under NAICS industry 454, Non-Store Retailers. Thus the Census reports e-commerce sales of only $88 million for General Merchandise Stores (industry 452), even though Walmart and several other large general merchandise retailers report online sales in the billion of dollors to the capital markets. For Euromonitor data on ecommerce penetration and growth in several nations, see Bart J. Bronnenberg and Paul B. Ellickson, "Adolescence and the Path to Maturity in Global Retail," *Journal of Economic Perspectives* 29, no. 4, (Fall 2015): 113–134.

13. Shelly Banjo and Drew Fitzgerald, "Stores Confront New World of Reduced Shopper Traffic," *Wall Street Journal*, January 16, 2014, http://www.wsj.com/articles/SB10001424052702304419104579325100372435802.

14. Pew Research Center, "Device Ownership Over Time," http://www.pewinternet.org/data-trend/mobile/device-ownership/; Deloitte Digital, "Navigating the New Digital Divide: Capitalization on Digital Influence in Retail," May 13, 2015, 6, http://www2.deloitte.com/content/dam/Deloitte/us/Documents/consumer-business/us-cb-navigating-the-new-digital-divide-051315.pdf.

15. Ed Zimmer, "The Death of Retail," *Entrepreneur Network*, 1999, http://tenonline.org/art/9909.html.

16. Ali Hortaçsu and Chad Syverson, "The Ongoing Evolution of US Retail: A Format Tug-of-War," *Journal of Economic Perspectives* 29, no. 4 (Fall 2015): 89–112.

17. Netflix Inc., "Form 10-K for the Period Ending December 31, 2005," 2, http://files.shareholder.com/downloads/NFLX/702012556x0xS1193125-06-56663/1065280/filing.pdf.

18. Greg Sandoval, "Blockbuster laughed at Netflix Partnership Offer," CNET, December 9, 2010, http://www.cnet.com/news/blockbuster-laughed-at-netflix-partnership-offer/.

19. Gina Keating, *Netflixed: The Epic Battle for America's Eyeballs* (New York: Portfolio, 2013), 68.

20. Netflix Inc., "Form 10-K for the Period Ending December 31, 2013," 1, http://files.shareholder.com/downloads/NFLX/782912702x0xS1065280-14-6/1065280/filing.pdf.

21. Clay Christensen, *The Innovator's Dilemma* (Boston: Harvard Business School Press, 1997).

22. Gary Moskowitz, "Comedy Nights and Party Supplies: How Local Video Stores Are Scrambling to Survive," *Time*, November 15, 2013, http://entertainment.time.com/2013/11/15/film-camp-and-party-supplies-how-local-video-stores-are-scrambling-to-survive/.

23. Ibid.

24. Schwartz, "The Economics (and Nostalgia) of Dead Malls."

25. "A Dying Breed, the American Shopping Mall," CBS News, March 23, 2014, http://www.cbsnews.com/news/a-dying-breed-the-american-shopping-mall/.

26. Schwartz, "The Economics (and Nostalgia) of Dead Malls."

27. The A.T. Kearney study was funded by mall operators and real-estate developers who obviously have a financial interest in the continued success of physical retail. Michael Brown, Mike Moriarty, and Andres Mendoza-Pena, "On Solid Ground: Brick and Mortar Is the Foundation of Omnichannel Retailing," A.T. Kearney, 2014, 7, https://www.atkearney.com/consumer-products-retail/on-solid-ground.

28. National Retail Federation, "Top 100 Retailers Chart 2015," https://nrf.com/2015/top100-table.

29. Jennifer Kasper, "Macy's Goes Omni-Channel," interview by ThinkWithGoogle, October 2014, https://www.thinkwithgoogle.com/interviews/macys-goes-omni-channel.html.

30. "Macy's Inc. Evolves with Changing Customer Landscape, Invests for Continued Sales Growth," *BusinessWire*, January 8, 2015, http://www.businesswire.com/news/home/20150108006314/en/Macy%E2%80%99s-Evolves-Changing-Customer-Landscape-Invests-Continued#.Vd9S4NNVhBd.

31. Angela Ahrendts, "Burberry's Digital Transformation," interview by Capgemini Consulting, 2012, https://www.capgemini.com/resource-file-access/resource/pdf/DIGITAL_LEADERSHIP__An_interview_with_Angela_Ahrendts.pdf.

32. Ibid.

33. Westfield Labs, "Homepage," http://www.westfieldlabs.com/.

34. Kate Abnett, "Kevin McKenzie on Reinventing the Shopping Mall," Business of Fashion, January 7, 2015, http://www.businessoffashion.com/ articles/long-view/kevin-mckenzie-reinventing-shopping-mall.

35. Ibid.

36. Warby Parker, "Homepage," https://www.warbyparker.com/.

37. Dennis Green, "Bonobos Is Opening Retail Stores—But You Can't Actually Take Any of the Clothes Home," *Business Insider*, July 16, 2015, http://www.businessinsider.com/bonobos-opened-a-store-where-you-cant -physically-buy-anything-2015-7.

38. Michael Cusumano and David B. Yoffie, *Competing on Internet Time* (New York: Free Press, 2000).

Chapter 13

1. Richard Valdmanis, "For Boston Marathon, Finding Lodgings Could Be the Hard Part," Reuters, March 19, 2014, http://www.reuters.com/ article/2014/03/19/us-usa-boston-marathon-lodging-idUSBREA2I1UN20140319.

2. The emporion had several covered walkways, supported by columns, where people could meet to make business deals or display their wares. It was run by a group of ten elected supervisors. There was also a special court where lenders, merchants, and shipowners could go to settle disputes. In fact, what we know about the emporion comes from the record of those cases. It appears that the traders were the money side. They paid a docking fee to access the emporion, as well as 2 percent of the value of their cargo. See Robert Garland, *The Piraeus: From the Fifth to the First Century B.C.* (Ithaca, NY: Cornell University Press, 1987), 83–95, for a description of this physical space and its internal institutions.

3. For more information on ancient trade, see Pascal Arnaud, "Ancient Sailing-Routes and Trade Patterns: The Impact of Human Factors," in *Maritime Archaeology and Ancient Trade in the Mediterranean*, ed. Damian Robinson and Andrew Wilson (Oxford, UK: Oxford Centre for Maritime Archaeology, 2011), 59–78.

4. One trader, for example, borrowed money in Athens to finance a trip to buy wine in one port, then sailed to others to trade for other things, and then returned to Athens to sell his cargo. To finance the trip, he paid a 22.5 percent interest rate; the rate would increase to 30 percent if he sailed back in the autumn when storms were more frequent. See Demosthenes, *Androcles Against Lacritus* (Orations 35) in *Demosthenes IV: Private Orations XXVII–XL*, ed. A. T. Murray (Cambridge, MA: Harvard University Press, 1965).

5. For a survey of the types of lending transactions that were possible in the emporion, see Edward E. Cohen, *Athenian Economy and Society: A Banking Perspective* (Princeton, NJ: Princeton University Press, 1992), 136–189.

6. This is attested in Athenian forensic speeches and bottomry loan contracts, such as that found in Demosthenes Orations 35 §11, which contained a provision that in the case of a storm, all of the merchants aboard the ship would hold a vote on whether to jettison the cargo, and if they voted to do so, the borrower would not be held liable for a loan secured on this cargo.

7. For a survey of the types of lending transactions that were possible in the emporion, see Cohen, *Athenian Economy and Society*, 136–189.

8. Evelyn Welch, *Shopping in the Renaissance* (New Haven, CT: Yale University Press, 2005), 172. Welch does not provide a precise date for this, although it appears to have been before 1469 when the rights to the fair were revoked.

9. Ibid., 172.

10. John McDonough and Karen Egolf, eds., *The* Advertising Age *Encyclopedia of Advertising* (Chicago: Fitzroy Dearborn Publishers, 2002), 325.

11. Ibid., 326.

12. Ibid., 325.

13. Based on Tom Standage, *The Victorian Internet* (New York: Walker Co., 1998), 2.

14. The miles of cable and number of offices had tripled since 1866 when Western Union had 76,000 miles of cable that connected 2,250 telegraph offices across the United States. US Census Bureau, *Historical Statistics of the United States: Colonial Times to 1970*, vol. 2 (Washington, DC: US Government Printing Office, 1975), 788.

15. William J. Phalen, *How the Telegraph Changed the World* (1942, repr. Jefferson, NC: McFarland & Co., 2014), Kindle edition.

16. Calculation based on US Bureau of Economic Analysis, "Consumer Spending," http://www.bea.gov/national/consumer_spending.htm; US Federal Reserve System, "The 2013 Federal Reserve Payments Study," July 2014, https://www.frbservices.org/files/communications/pdf/general/2013_fed_res_paymt_study_detailed_rpt.pdf; Federal Reserve Bank of Boston, "The 2013 Survey of Consumer Payment Choice," July 27, 2015, http://www.bostonfed.org/economic/cprc/scpc/.

17. David S. Evans, Karen Webster, Gloria Knapp Colgan, and Scott R. Murray, "Payments Innovation and the Use of Cash," June 3, 2013, http://ssrn.com/abstract=2273216. We expect the use of cash would be slightly lower in 2015.

18. Newspaper Association of America, "Newspaper Circulation Volume," http://www.naa.org/Trends-and-Numbers/Circulation-Volume/Newspaper-Circulation-Volume.aspx.

19. Paul David, "The Dynamo and the Computer: An Historical Perspective on the Modern Productivity Paradox," *American Economic Review* 80, no. 2 (1990), 356.

20. Ibid., 356–357.

21. Kirsten Korosec, "Another Ride-Sharing Startup Becomes a Unicorn: BlaBlaCar Valued at $1.6 Billion," *Fortune*, September 16, 2015, http://fortune.com/2015/09/16/blablacar-unicorn-list/.

Index

Acknowledgments

Since around 2000, we have been working on multisided platform businesses not only as economists contributing to the literature and authors of leading surveys of the field, but also as consultants to multisided platforms ranging from global giants to unfunded start-ups. This book reflects the knowledge and insights we have developed over that time. Our debts to fellow economists, entrepreneurs, and executives for shaping and deepening our understanding of these businesses are enormous. We could never possibly mention or even remember everyone who has contributed to this book.

We have to start, though, with our friends and colleagues Jean-Charles Rochet and Jean Tirole, who shared an early draft of their pioneering paper on multisided platforms with us and who have been a source of inspiration and ideas ever since. Since 2000, many other economists have contributed to the literature on multisided platforms. We have learned a tremendous amount from their work. We would especially like to thank Andrei Hagiu and Glen Weyl, both for their brilliant papers on the economic theory of multisided platforms and for numerous enlightening discussions we have had over the years.

Diane Schmalensee, a well-known marketing professional and exceptionally thoughtful critic, read drafts of this book, as well as many of our earlier writings, and made valuable suggestions and edits.

We have worked closely since 2004 with Karen Webster, the CEO of Market Platform Dynamics (MPD), an advisory firm the three of us cofounded. She has made significant contributions to our understanding of matchmaker strategies through discussions and our joint work on advising companies. For this book, in addition to making valuable suggestions on our earlier drafts, she provided important insights for chapters 10 (regarding Apple Pay) and 12 (regarding retail). Working with Karen, we have also learned a lot from advising early-stage multisided platforms and from a couple of platforms she has started and led.

Howard Chang, who has been an invaluable colleague for many years, reviewed the final manuscript and made valuable edits and comments and, as usual, kept us from making mistakes, though neither he nor anyone else can be blamed for any that nonetheless remain. Alexis Pirchio did an admirable job, under tight deadlines and with many other obligations, in coordinating the research for this book. Other contributors to the research effort include Clara Campbell, Madeleine Chen, Maria Eugenia Gonzalez, Federico Haslop, Steve Joyce, Scott Murray, Nick Venable, Juan Pablo Vila Martinez, and Vanessa Zhang. Amanda Depalma did an exceptional job turning our primitive drawings into many of the figures in the preceding pages.

We have benefited enormously from insightful guidance and detailed edits that have improved our exposition provided by Lisa Adams, our literary agent, as well as Jane Gebhart, our copyeditor. Tim Sullivan from Harvard Business Review Press has been incredibly supportive and has worked closely with us in shaping *Matchmakers*.

Last, and of course not least, our wives have provided love and encouragement that has been essential for writing this book as well as for just about everything else in our lives.

About the Authors

David S. Evans and **Richard Schmalensee** have done pioneering research into the new economics of multisided platforms and have contributed widely to the academic and business literature on the topic. They collaborated on a trilogy of major books concerning matchmakers and their impacts: *Paying with Plastic: The Digital Revolution in Buying and Borrowing* (2005); *Invisible Engines: How Software Platforms Drive Innovation and Transform Industries* (2006); and *Catalyst Code: The Strategies Behind the World's Most Dynamic Companies* (2007). Their writing has been informed and enriched by many years of advising new and established matchmakers.

David is an economist, business adviser, and entrepreneur. He cofounded, and helps lead, two consulting organizations: Global Economics Group, which provides economic expertise on antitrust and regulatory matters, and Market Platform Dynamics, which advises companies on multisided platform strategies. He is also Chairman of PYMNTS.com, a multisided media and data analytics platform he cofounded. He has consulted for many of the largest multisided platform businesses in the world and served as an adviser to a number of start-up matchmakers. In addition, David has an active academic career. At the University College London he is Executive Director of the Jevons Institute for Competition Law and Economics as well as a visiting professor. He is also a lecturer at the University of Chicago Law School. David is the author, coauthor, or editor of ten books and has written more than one hundred scholarly articles, many of which address the economics of entrepreneurship, business dynamics, and multisided platforms. He is a graduate of the University of Chicago, from which he earned a BA, an MA, and a PhD, all in economics.

Richard is the Howard W. Johnson Professor of Management and Economics, Emeritus, at the Massachusetts Institute of Technology and served for nine years as dean of the MIT Sloan School of Management. A former member of the President's Council of Economic Advisers, Richard is one of the world's leading scholars on the economics of industrial organization and its application to government policy and business strategy. He is the author or coauthor of twelve books and more than 130 scholarly articles. He was the 2012 Distinguished Fellow of the Industrial Organization Society. Richard is Chairman of Market Platform Dynamics and has served on the boards of several matchmakers, including the International Securities Exchange and the International Data Group. He advises matchmakers worldwide on strategic issues. He holds a PhD as well as an undergraduate degree in economics from MIT.